DARIEN

A JOURNEY IN SEARCH
OF EMPIRE

JOHN McKENDRICK

BIRLINN

For

VLADIMIR ANTONIO

This edition first published in 2018 by
Birlinn Limited
West Newington House
10 Newington Road
Edinburgh
EH9 1QS

First published in hardback in 2016

www.birlinn.co.uk

ISBN 978 1 78027 503 1

British Library Cataloguing-in-Publication Data
A catalogue record for this book is available from the British Library

Typeset by Iolaire Typesetting, Newtonmore
Printed and bound by Gutenberg Press, Malta

CONTENTS

ACKNOWLEDGEMENTS

There are many people to thank who helped me to write this book. I would particuarly like to thank the editorial team at Birlinn: Andrew, Deborah and Helen. I would also like to thank the staff of the National Archives in Panama City for their patience and the staff at the National Archives of Scotland. Jim Malcolm deserves a huge thanks for his encouragement in Panama and since, and particular thanks for the use of his stunning photographs. Thank you also to the staff at the South Carolina Historical Society. I would also like to particularly thank the people on the island of Jamaica, who never failed to smile and the people of the isthmus of Panama, who whilst not always friendly, deserve my gratitude. Thanks also to my mother and father and Vladimir, who all encouraged and inspired me in different ways.

LIST OF THE MAJOR SHIPS

FIRST EXPEDITION

Saint Andrew, captained by Robert Pennecuik
Caledonia, captained by Robert Drummond
Unicorn, captained by Robert Pinkerton
Dolphin, captained by Thomas Fullarton
Endeavour, captained by John Malloch

SECOND EXPEDITION

Rising Sun, captained by James Gibson
Duke of Hamilton, captained by Walter Duncan
Hope of Bo'ness, captained by Richard Dalling
Hope, captained by James Miller

A SELECTION OF THE RELIEF SHIPS

Ann of Caledonia
Dispatch
Olive Branch
Hopeful Binning

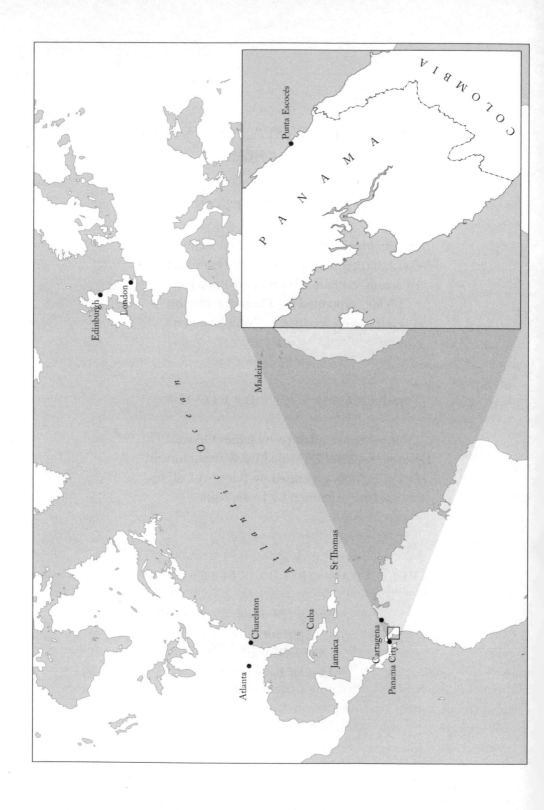

ONE

INTRODUCTION

Much have I travell'd in the realms of gold,
And many goodly states and kingdoms seen;
Round man-y western islands have I been
Which bards in fealty to Apollo hold.
Oft of one wide expanse had I been told
That deep-brow'd Homer ruled as his demesne;
Yet did I never breathe its pure serene
Till I heard Chapman speak out loud and bold:
Then felt I like some watcher of the skies
When a new planet swims into his ken;
Or like stout Cortez when with eagle eyes
He star'd at the Pacific – and all his men
Look'd at each other with a wild surmise –
Silent, upon a peak in Darien.

There has always been confusion about Darien. John Keats made the unforgivable mistake of placing the wrong sharp-eyed conquistador upon a peak in Darien in his poem 'On First Looking into Chapman's Homer'. If Panamanians read romantic English poetry (most don't) they would be horrified: Balboa stood on that slippery peak, not Cortez, and is revered in Panama as the country's founding father, immortalised by having not only the currency named after him, but more importantly a local beer.

Who knows if Keats, writing in 1816, knew much about the Scots clambering around the same hills in Darien, but his sonnet could have been written for them. Keats was staggered by his reading of Homer's *Odyssey* and Odysseus's journey, and so too were the Scots staggered by their own journey around 'western isles' to 'stand upon a peak in Darien' in what they very much hoped would be for them 'the realms of gold'. Darien was home to the shortlived Scottish colony: the Darien project or the 'Darien Disaster' as the late seventeenth-century Scottish colonial venture is often termed. That one-time lonely outpost of Scotland, Caledonia, is no longer in Darien; according to modern Panamanian political geography it is now in the Comarca de Kuna Yala, and there are good grounds to consider it far removed from being a disaster. The failures that befell the Scots in the green jungles of Darien were to push the reluctant Scots down another path, a very different odyssey, that would lead them to greater fame, greater trade and greater riches: the Act of Union. Not all about the Darien Disaster is as it seems.

The story of the Scots and Darien is now well known, if not a stalwart of the history syllabus, and many people have heard of the energetic William Paterson: Caribbean merchant; financier; and author of the Scots' 'disaster' at Darien. His project, on paper at least, was a brilliant one. He planned to establish a trading company in Scotland; to found a colony on the Caribbean side of the isthmus of Panama; to facilitate the exchange of goods between east and west; and create a centre of international trade and commerce and a hub for buying and selling. In the impoverished late seventeenth century, Scots enthusiastically bought into this tropical dream and in doing so heavily mortgaged the nation's future in Paterson's scheme. In the face of English commercial opposition to the project, nationalism stirred the patriotism of Scots to considerable heights and the expectations that sailed with the first fleet were as high as the depths of disappointment and despair the very same people would experience shortly thereafter, when the painfully thin survivors limped home from American and Caribbean staging posts. They were the lucky ones. All but one of the once magnificent ships lost, over 2,000 Scots dead and all hope of financial success left lying, rotting in the hot, steamy jungles of Darien.

The first expedition set sail from Leith in 1698 with four ships and one thousand two hundred men. They founded Caledonia, only to abandon it six months later, in the hope of returning home to Scotland, not victims of Spanish aggression, but of disease, ill-discipline and poor leadership.

The second expedition arrived six weeks later in mid 1699 to find the deserted settlement. Initially bolstered by a small military victory against the Spaniards at Tubuganti, the colony soon faced the same problems and found itself fatally weakened when the Spanish moved in to dislodge them in early 1700. Caledonia was not to be the panacea for Scotland's chronic poverty and the underachievement of several centuries. After the heady excitement, the launch of the great undertaking, it must have been with a humiliating sense of foreboding that Scots anticipated from where they might next find salvation.

After the publication of several (now out-of-print) books in the early twentieth century, Darien was largely forgotten, but a resurgence of interest in the Scots colony gathered pace in the late twentieth century. An expedition to the ruins, led by the Royal Geographical Society, took place in 1978; the republication of John Prebble's book *The Darien Disaster* in 1999; a BBC documentary in 2003;[1] a museum exhibition displayed around Scotland in the 1990s which eventually made it to Panama City in 2005; and the publication of Douglas Watt's excellent economic history, *The Price of Scotland*. Darien was also much discussed by those with a historical and political interest in the 2014 Scottish independence referendum debate. But it has not shed its image of disaster. For many, there can be no other way to see it. Not only did Scotland's major attempt to compete as an equal with her European rivals end in total disaster (why not attempt if other small nations, such as Holland and Portugal, could succeed?), but worse was to come as the nation's leadership stumbled forward, heads hung low, into parliamentary union with England – for many a disaster for Scottish identity and public life. For those involved the experience of Darien was distressing and tragic; it financially ruined Scotland and everyone knew someone – a brother, cousin or neighbour – who lost his (or her) life in Darien, or lost their money backing it.

After Darien, Scotland was weakened, vindictive and sore. There was no greater manifestation of this than the hanging of the crew of the *Worcester* – unfortunates unfairly accused of piracy against the designers of the Darien colonial scheme, the Company of Scotland off the African coast – whose real crime was to be English. The Scots were bitter and blamed English treachery above all for the calamity which befell them.

3

But in the early eighteenth century, these tumultuous years led to reflection in Scotland, and with reflection came realism and with realism, inevitably, Union. When Scotland dissolved its ancient parliament, she had one fifth of the population of her larger neighbour, but only one fortieth of its economy. She was a European weakling. Darien had brutally demonstrated the shortcomings of Scottish society. When Scotland collectively looked in the mirror, there was a deceptive profile: it had more literate people than almost any other in Europe; the Scots produced good doctors and lawyers, and had more than double the number of English universities, but all the hard work and learning did not instil in the Scots the commercial common sense found in abundance in London or Lisbon, Amsterdam or Antwerp. Scottish trade to the Baltics or London was not large-scale colonial trade and the naivety of those involved in the heady years in Edinburgh leading up to 1698 would soon be replaced by harder men whose experience of English colonial trading would utterly transform Scotland over the next 100 years.

It is hard to imagine the changes that took place in Scottish society between 1680 and 1780: from witchcraft trials and persecution to David Hume and the Enlightenment; from the run-rig farms and poverty to the 'wealth of nations' and the riches of the tobacco trade. Scotland was utterly transformed. This was not all due to the Union, and the Union did not come about solely because of the effects of the failure of Darien, but Darien was the defining event during the lives of those who united Scotland with England. These great men had challenged the political order of the times, the English parliament and King William. The English commercial estab-lishment was opposed to the Company of Scotland and reputation and liberty had been risked and political capital lost to support the scheme. Those who determined Scotland's future were only too well aware of the limitations of continuing alone.

This book is not all history. It partly relies upon other people's historical research to tell a story. Every historian or writer of this period must rely on the pioneering work of Dr George Pratt Insh, a Scottish academic at the University of Glasgow in the early to mid twentieth century. He wrote extensively on Scotland and her place in the modern world and personally rescued from obscurity many of the papers of the Company of Scotland. *Historian's Odyssey* is the title of Insh's description of his own adventure to put together the documents and create a history of *The Company of Scotland Trading to Africa and the Indies.* The fruits of his history have largely provided us today with our knowledge of the Company of Scotland. He has been an essential guide for my own mini odyssey. Little did I know as a school boy in Scotland twenty years ago, when I sat in darkened classrooms getting my head around the iambic pentameters of John Keats' verdant poetry, that I, too, would embark upon my own journey to Darien. This book tells the story of the Scots in Darien with the help of these works and unpublished manuscripts found in Edinburgh and Panama City. It has new insights and relies upon previously unused materials, mostly found in the Panamanian National Archives.² It sets out the depth of Spanish opposition to Caledonia and the impossibilities of the scheme ever succeeding. It reveals for the first time that the English helped the Caledonians and defended the colony from a military strike by the Spanish Armada de Barlovento (called 'the Windward fleet').

This book retraces the steps of those Scots involved in the Darien Scheme, whether it was as directors in Edinburgh, sailors on the voyage to the Panamanian coast, gentleman volunteers arriving at Golden Island, Scots living on the Panamanian isthmus, prisoners in Cartagena, survivors in Jamaica, missionaries in South Carolina, lost interpreters in Cuba or even just young Scots keen to embark on a new adventure. The beholding of these places adds something to the sorry tale of the Caledonians; so much of their history was related to their environment, to the weather, the jungle, the sheer distances involved in their venture. The retracing of the steps is a sorry odyssey leading from the pages of old manuscripts, textbooks and desperate journals to the very same wonders of nature and culture that enthralled and defeated the Caledonians.

⁂

I arrived in Panama for the first time in the late summer of 2003. I knew very little about Darien – it was a blurred image of a shady memory of a half-understood history lesson from years before. Ostensibly I had been backpacking around Colombia and Venezuela in the hope of learning some Spanish. In the Venezuelan Andes I led a monastic life in a simple home, spending mornings practising Spanish verbs and afternoons napping and walking. My evenings revolved around inflicting my fledgling Spanish on locals in run-down shops and stuffy cantinas. From the Andes by bus to Caracas and onwards to Ciudad Bolivar (or Angostura as it was known in the days of Bolivar's British irregulars) my summer was a blur of new towns, air-conditioned buses and minor adventures. I kayaked up to the Angel Falls in a *cayuko*, wandered around the mighty tepuis and played chess at what seemed like the end of earth: the claustrophobic Venezuelan–Brazilian border, towns like islands in a sea of swamping jungle, incongruously decorated with plastic flowers. In metropolitan Caracas I enjoyed the fleshpots of the city with a friend: parties; meeting diplomats and journalists, all of whom loathed the dangerous Venezuelan capital; and hearty carbohydrate-heavy criollo food. Everywhere loomed the larger-than-life figure of Chavez, part general, part messiah, part crook, part provocateur, all rolled into one all-dominating political and social force; Venezuela was on the edge.

If Caracas was the barracks, they said in Bolivar's day, Bogotá in Colombia was the university (and Quito in Ecuador the church). The sprawling Colombian capital, airily lodged on the Sabana de Bogotá is cool and cerebral. Ten years ago it was also intense, tumultuous and heavily armed but noted for its progressive policies and fantastic culture. From the capital of Latin America's most beautiful country I ventured forth: visiting churches and museums; horse-riding in Antioquia; working on a coffee farm in Quindio; supporting the local football team in Medellín and ending up in a small hotel in Santa Marta in northern Colombia. On my birthday I called home, and after wishing me a happy birthday my mother launched into an anxiety-filled tirade against the dangers of travelling in Colombia – her next -door neighbour had hidden insights to share with her about Colombian guerrilla movements. As is so often the case, mothers are right and eight foreign tourists were kidnapped by the *Ejercito de Liberacion Nacional* (ELN) only days after the call and only a few miles from where I was staying. My luck had run out and my mother's patience was not to be tried any longer. Unsure where to go, I flew to Panama.

I had not expected to go to Panama. I viewed it as no more than a longish transit, less than three days before heading by bus to Managua, the torpid

Nicaraguan capital, but I was there long enough to understand a return visit was a must. Panama City is derided as the Milton Keynes of Latin America, but the reality is somewhat different. A cosmopolitan atmosphere pervades, providing the backdrop to a green city divided between bland high-rise towers and narrow cobbled streets corralled by once-elegant colonial homes. Panama is much more than the sum of its physical parts, this small isthmian country reeks of international espionage and the murky shiftiness for which it has become too well known. In the city, empty, darkened tower blocks populated by invented tenants paying astronomical, money-laundering rents are everywhere; powerful, well-connected law firms discreetly solve their off-shore clients' problems; expensive restaurants are patronised by Colombians doing deals with Taiwanese businessmen; and floating around the edges of all this, the watchful eyes and ever-listening presence of a large diplomatic community.

Panama is, above all, international. Of course, the Scots know this: it was their idea. William Paterson's pioneer trading post, rotten in its damp, ill-thought-out foundations is alive and well, if somewhat further along the coast. Panama is still the 'door to the seas and the key to the universe' – its canal ensures this, perhaps even more dramatically than the Caledonians could have conceived. Despite the fact that the canal seems to become smaller every day, and eagerly awaits the expansion of its mighty locks, it remains the key shortcut for shipping lanes and the rapid increase in port facilities, banking and other canal and maritime-related services and a large free-trade zone, cast Panama, more or less, as the entrepôt economy the Scots once looked to for national salvation. A strange coincidence then, that Panama celebrated the centenary of its canal in the same year the Scots voted on whether to return to their pre-Darien disaster sovereignty.

My distant history classes probably did not touch upon Darien, but the small panel in the back of my shabby guidebook, which briefly told the tale of Caledonia, whetted my appetite and all around was the development of the idea, touching upon every aspect of Panama's booming economy. As Keats reminds us, for years odysseys have been launched from the new world to the old: conquistadors and Caledonians; canal constructions workers; traders; bankers; even tailors. The pages that follow pay tribute to the brave steps of the original Caledonians and today's much less courageous ones in their pursuit.

TWO

A PLAN IS FORMED

It is with regret that Scots must record the invitation sent to a young English would-be surgeon, Lionel Wafer, inviting him to join his brother, then living in Port Royal, Jamaica, in the spring of 1679. Wafer, who had tasted life overseas in the East Indies, needed little convincing and left as soon as he could put together the cost of his passage, and installed himself in his brother's Port Royal home. On the island he began to develop his limited practice in surgery, or as he might have put it 'administering Physick and Phlebotomy'. Despite the professionalism of his new career and elevated status, the boredom of life on the island and the excitement of the lives of the buccaneers who regularly sailed to and from this English colonial outpost, tempted Wafer to join them on one of their frequent sorties against the Spanish Main.

It was on one such trip that he was injured and forced to remain with the Indians of Darien for some months. Later escaping and returning to England, he published *A New Voyage and Description of the Isthmus of America* in 1699, the early, unprinted edition of which fell into the hands of William Paterson, who found what he wanted to read in this exotic account of a jungle paradise and would use it in time to convince himself, and crucially the directors of the Company of Scotland, of the soundness of locating a trading colony on the isthmus of Panama. At the outset there was no inevitability that Panama would be the destination of the Company of Scotland's trading efforts. Wafer's text persuaded Paterson, and Paterson persuaded the Edinburgh-based directors of the Company. Wafer's text changed the course of British history. Wafer's text was instrumental in creating Great Britain.

❦

The Governor of Jamaica had until recently been the notorious Sir Thomas Moodyford, who had grown rich turning a blind eye to the buccaneers and encouraging privateering against Spanish commercial interests (he would later serve a spell in the Tower of London for his wilful negligence). Spain persisted in its doomed and pointless mercantilist policies outlawing all trade between foreign nations (particularly the heretical English) and its American possessions. Trade was officially limited to a small number of Spanish merchants based in Cadiz and Seville. This stifled competitive pricing and unsurprisingly contraband trade and piracy soon raged across the Caribbean and down the Pacific coast of modern-day Peru and Chile. The English, French and Dutch plundered at will, reaping great rewards with limited risks because of the cumbersome nature of Spanish colonial administration and the poor quality of military defences.

Wafer, having left his island-based medical practice, found himself, in early 1680, on a mission to raid the Spanish Main, with the intention of making off with sacks of Spanish gold and wealthy hostages. A motley crew of buccaneers had appointed him as their doctor. The pirates, some 400 of them, congregated on a little island off the Darien shore and, leaving some men to protect the ships, set off across the isthmus on foot with the intention of attacking the gold-washing station of Santa Maria on the southern Pacific side of modern-day Panama.

Unlike Henry Morgan's adventures on the isthmus ten years earlier, which pirates thereafter sought to emulate, this lot were to meet with little luck: the Spaniards having heard of their approach had fled from Santa Maria with anything of value, and when the plan was altered to sack the newly founded Panama City, the Spaniards there had also been warned and ships sailed from the town to engage the pirates. As usual the treasure-driven corsairs had the best of it against five ships and three barques and succeeded in capturing the Spanish warship *La Santissima Trinidad,* yet they appear not to have landed. The pirates were beset with leadership difficulties and their captain, Coxon, in a fit of pique, set back across the isthmus when rumours

9

of his cowardice in joining the Spaniards in battle off the coast of Panama reached him. His replacement, Captain Sawkins, did not last long: he was killed in an attempt to take Puebla Nueva, and facing so many obstacles the pirates became disorganised and split again, with another group returning across the isthmus whilst another, led by Bartholomew Sharp, sailed south to attack the shipping off the coast of the Vice-Royalties of Lima and Gran Colombia.

Wafer was sorely disappointed. As the surgeon he was kept busy as the body-count mounted, and yet he was no closer to the riches he had dreamed of. He chose to remain in the Pacific to see what else might turn up and was accompanied by another famous pirate, William Dampier, who wrote more extensively of his trips than Wafer.[1] Dampier is the better known of the two, partly thanks to his claim to have discovered Australia around a hundred years before James Cook and partly because of his descriptions of the Galapagos Islands one hundred and fifty years before Charles Darwin arrived to write about evolution. Dampier was the more seasoned pirate and had toughened himself up by spending some time with logwood cutters in the Bay of Campeche logging dye-rich trees. In 1776 a hurricane struck the bay and Dampier, determined to make his fortune, reasoned the hard work was not worth the returns and threw his hat in with the pirates. Wafer and Dampier found themselves together with no real prospects on the Pacific coast and joined the others to return across the isthmus in late April 1681 after the relative failure of their privateering activities. They had fruitlessly sailed down the coast of modern-day Ecuador and Peru, but met with little success and too much attention from the Spaniards. A good pirate in those days took a long view of the profit opportunities and so, with the democracy of decision-making for which they are famed, the pirates returned to the warmer waters of the Caribbean and home. The return involved crossing the isthmus of Panama on foot. They had narrowly missed Panama's dry season and found the going exceptionally tough underfoot, with relentless rain both day and night adding to their discomfort. May is one of the most unpleasant months in Panama as the dry season ends and the rains begin. Dampier, knowing they would be hunted down by the Spaniards, had warned that anyone falling behind would be shot to ensure they did not reveal the direction and strength of the pirates as they hurried back to the Caribbean.

Wafer was aware of this when, during the journey, his knee was badly injured by a fellow pirate's carelessness drying gunpowder by a naked flame: it exploded and burnt Wafer's knee down to the bone. With the aid of slaves carrying his possessions he hobbled on until the pain overcame him and he was left at an Indian settlement with two others too fatigued to continue in the sodden jungle. Dampier's threat was quietly forgotten and as a result Wafer would spend several months in Darien with the Indians, researching the manuscript that would eventually so influence William Paterson. Under the care of the Indians, Wafer's health improved. They masticated a selection of herbs and placed them with a large plantain leaf over his burnt knee and, so he writes, he was better within twenty days, excepting a slight weakness to the knee. He was delighted and impressed by the knowledge of the natives.

Despite his treatment the Indians were cautious. They decided if their compatriots who had left with the other pirates did not return within ten days they would kill Wafer and his colleagues – they would be burned alive. The threat was never carried out and soon afterwards Wafer and the others were purportedly marched across to the Caribbean by Indian guides. However, when supplies ran out the Indians retuned to their settlement and after several days of half-starved attempts to find the Caribbean coast, Wafer, much to his disgust but relief, returned to the Indian village from where he had started. Tired from his incessant travels and weakened from his injury, he was content to remain with the Indians for some time and so he began to fall into the daily routine of hunter-gatherer life on the isthmus.

He had also fallen into favour with their chief, a wise Indian called Lancets. With his medical skill he had cured the chief's wife of fever by drawing blood from her arm and so was granted freedom and privileges. He lived amongst the Indians, taking part in their daily life, eating their food and immersing himself in their customs. He had gone increasingly 'native' and wore only a loin cloth and a large number of skin paintings (although he refused tattoos). However fun this life was, it was bound to come to an end and Wafer was anxious to make his way to the Caribbean to find a ship back to Jamaica. He left, promising to return, and was delighted to arrive at the coast to find Dampier and the ships. Mischievously, he pretended for some hours to be one of the Indians before his friends rumbled his disguise and welcomed him back.

It was these experiences which Wafer drew upon to produce his book: a clear account of the land, fauna and people of Darien. Paterson, however, would draw one-sided conclusions from Wafer's manuscript. Amongst the picture of a tropical Eden, the book amounts to a litany of warnings. Wafer, for example, recounted that when he and his companions set off from the Indian camp to reach the Caribbean coast and reunite themselves with their fellow pirates, they wandered around the isthmus, hopelessly lost and near-drowned for over five days – a considerable achievement given the relatively narrow nature of Panama's geography. Wafer recounted: 'But not long after Sun-set, it fell a Raining as of Heaven and Earth would meet; which Storm was accompanied with horrid Claps of Thunder, and such flashes of Lightning, of a Sulpherous smell, that we were almost stifled in the open Air.'

The rain and the unhealthiness of the climate are a constant feature of his account. 'The Country all about here is Woody and Low, and very unhealthy; the Rivers so Oazy, that the stinking Mud infects the Air.' He describes the new town of Panama as 'very sickly' but 'very healthy in comparison of Portobel' of which he writes 'I have already said that it is an un-healthy Place. The East-side is low and swampy; and the Sea at low Water leaves the Shore within the Harbour bare, a great way from the Houses; which having a black filthy Mud, it stinks very much, and breeds noisome Vapours, thro' the Heat of the Climate.'

Wafer's account of the nature of the Panamanian climate remains accurate today:

The Weather is much the same here as in other places of the Torrid Zone in this Latitude; but inclining rather to the Wet Extreme. The Season of Rain begins in April or May; and during the Months of June, July and August, the Rains are very violent. It is very hot also about this time, where-ever the Sun breaks out of a Cloud: For the Air is then very sultry, because then usually there are no Breezes to fan and cool it, but 'tis all glowing hot ... So that 'tis a very wet Country, and has Rains for Two Thirds, if not Three Quarters of a Year. Their first coming is after the manner of our suddain April Showers, or hasty Thunder Showers, one in a day at first. After this, two or three in a Day; at length, a Shower almost every Hour: and frequently accompanied with violent Thunder and Lightning: During which time, the

Air has often a faint Sulpherous Smell ... [T]here will be several fair Days intermix'd, with only Tornado's or Thunder-Showers; and that some-times for a Week together ... .When the Shower is over, you shall hear for a great way together the Croaking of Frogs and Toads, the humming of Moskitos or Gnats, and the hissing or shrieking of Snakes and other Insects, loud and unpleasant; some like the quacking of Ducks. The Moskitos chiefly infest the low swampy or Mangrove Lands near the River or Seas ...

More warnings are apparent. The manuscript also contained descriptions of the topography of the land: '[t]he Land of this Continent is almost every where of unequal Surface, distinguished with Hills and Valleys, of great variety for height, depth and extent.' Less than ideal for settlement and more importantly it clearly describes the difficulty accessing the Pacific side of the isthmus to advance trading to the Indies. Paterson also overlooked why Wafer, Dampier and the other pirates favoured such a spot: its very isolation and relative distance from settlements in the Caribbean. A paradise for fugitive pirates, but too remote for merchants in search of consumer markets and trade.

It is likely that in a time of maritime discovery and burgeoning maritime trade, Paterson became most animated by Wafer's description of the isthmus as a place of natural harbours. We know that in 1698, when the fleet sailed from Leith with the directors' 'secret' orders, they instructed Robert Pennecuik, who insisted on the title of 'commodore', to sail to the pleasantly sounding Golden Island, off the coast of Darien. Wafer's description was relied upon by the board of directors:

The Eastermost of those three [islands] is Golden Island, a small one, with a fair deep Channel between it and the Main. It is rocky and steep all round to the Sea (and thereby naturally fortified), except only the Landing-place, which is a small Sandy Bay on the South side, towards the Harbour, from whence it gently rises. It is moderately high, and cover'd with small Trees or Shrubs. The Land of the Isthmus opposite to it, to the South East, is excellent fruitful Land, of a black Mold, with sand intermix'd; and is pretty level for 4 or 5 Mile, till you come to the foot of the Hills.

The directors would order the expeditions' commanders to make fortified bases both on Golden Island and on the coast nearby. It would turn out to be less 'fruitful' than Wafer described, but his writing directly led the directors to believe remote Darien was the best place to establish both a trading colony and a populated settlement. The obvious concerns about climate and health were banished by the thoughts of fortified harbours there for the taking.

Wafer's description of Darien is a spellbinding one: a lush strip of land sparsely populated with friendly Indians and overgrown with exotic trees, flowers and fruits. To the people of famine-ravaged Scotland it would have seemed a tropical paradise: a land of opportunity and adventure and of course the Scots were more than used to a little rain. Given the repeated crop failures at this time in Scotland, Wafer's account of the many lush fruits that simply grew on trees allured and deceived the Scots in equal measure. He peppers his account with descriptions of fruits a Scotsman would have been unlikely to have heard of: plantains ('in great abundance'); bonano's ('thick, sweet and mealy'); mammee ('wholesome and declicious'); mammee sappota ('fine beautiful Colour when ripe'); sapadillo's ('small as a Bergamasco Pear, and is coated like a Russet-Pippin'); pine-apples (''tis very juicy'); and prickle pears ('It's a good fruit'). And as a final appeal for the directors, Wafer wrote of Logwood or Campeachy trees, viewed in those times as a valuable find by traders because of their rich dye, extracted from the trunks.

Wafer paints a South Pacific-style portrait of loosely clad native beauties, temptation throughout the ages for all manner of northern Europeans. History has left us surprisingly few accounts of the Caledonians' interactions with flower-garlanded, seductive natives. Perhaps they took on board Wafer's warning of the punishments meted out for debauching a virgin – 'they thrust a fort of Bryer up the passage of his Penis, and turn it round ten or a dozen times: Which is not only a great Torment, but commonly mortifies the part; and the Person dies of it; but he has liberty to cure himself if he can'.

Wafer's guidebook to the Indians even contains a traveller's guide to their language, albeit limited to a few essential basics, but helpful nonetheless and still useful to this very day:

Pa poonah eetah Caupah? – Woman, have you got the Hammock?

Paterson had been in the Caribbean for a few years, but had never ventured as far as Darien and its bryer-wielding natives. With his academic comportment he did not often leave Port Royal. He was, however, drawn to the idea of exploiting international trade and found in Wafer's manuscript the blueprints for the location of his trading posts between the two great oceans. The exoticism of Wafer's manuscript helped make up Paterson's mind. The directors of the Company were also to become so reliant on Wafer's manuscript that they even invited him to Edinburgh to discuss offering him a position with the Company in return for delaying the publication of his book.

Paterson had planned his proposal long before Wafer's unpublished manuscript came into his hands. His critics claim he had trailed the idea around for years trying to find backers and this may well be true, but it does not diminish people's enthusiasm for the project at the time. No one before or since has explained the great idea as well as Paterson himself:

> The time and expense of navigation to China, Japan and the Spice Islands, and the far greatest part of the East Indies will be lessened by more than half, and the consumption of European commodities and manufactories will soon be more than dobled. Trade will increase trade, and money will beget money, and the trading world shall need no more to want work for their hands, but will rather want hands for their work. Thus this door of the seas, and the key of the universe, with anything of a sort of reasonable management, will of course enable its proprietors to give laws to both oceans, without being liable to the fatigues, expenses and dangers, or contracting the guilt and blood of Alexander and Caesar.

Paterson wanted to create a peaceful Scottish trading post on the north coast of Panama with access to the southern coast and the Pacific sea. The colony would use the world's greatest shortcut to create an international focus on trade and create an entrepôt economy on the isthmus, in effect an international trading post in the Americas, trading with both Europe and Asia. He believed, after reading Wafer's manuscript, he would have the evidence he needed, when the time came, to convince people of the soundness of his plan, but first he needed to find a vehicle for it and the financial backers.

William Paterson was born in Skipmyre in rural Dumfriesshire in 1658.[2] As every writer and historian has conceded, little is known of his early childhood, Paterson being a man far too serious to have left behind a nostalgic autobiography. His father sent him to live with family in Bristol and little is known of his life or schooling there, nor the reasons why he was sent there. Probably it was to provide him with a better education and opportunities than would have existed in rural Scotland, especially in the south-west, where Covenanters were resisting the restored Charles II's attempts to reform the Church and, from 1685, James II and VII's attempts at toleration of all creeds. Men had died a generation before over the issue of whether bishops should have the power to interfere in their worship of God, and many Scots fiercely believed in the equality of men before God. In 1666 the Covenanters from the south-west rose up against the government and marched on Edinburgh − they were defeated at Rullion Green and over the years the government used Highland troops to brutally put down Covenant uprisings. This was no place for a young boy intent on making his fortune.

Paterson is likely to have felt more at home in Bristol, an international port open to the world and its influences, yet he tired of the town and left to seek work in Jamaica. Like many a young Scotsman, he was tempted by the allure of foreign places, strange names and graphic tales of faraway places. He spent a reasonable period of time in Jamaica and met some of the leading buccaneers and privateers of the time. What he did out there is a mystery. It is hard to imagine him having become involved, like Wafer, in daring exploits raiding the Spanish Main. Paterson was a red-faced, serious man and teetotal − characteristics unlikely to have tempted him to a buccaneering way of life. He took himself seriously and is said to have lacked a sense of humour. Many contemporaries describe him as a bore and he was obsessive about his projects. He nursed a sense of grievance: coming from a humble background but graced with considerable intellect, he found himself mixing with wealthy and powerful men who failed to give him the position in society he felt he deserved. Most viewed him as bright, but many thought him some sort of charlatan and questioned his judgement.

Paterson's judgement had been questioned before Caledonia. He had suffered an ignominious exit from the Bank of England, which he helped to found in 1694, but his early involvement is clear proof of his abilities. In the late seventeenth century, government finances were stretched to breaking point by William III's wars with Louis XIV. The war, then known as the War of Grand Alliance, endured until 1697 and exacted a considerable toll on the English Treasury, taking place, as it did, both on mainland Europe, at sea and in the North American colonies. Paterson developed an innovative idea to ease the strain on the Treasury and in the process he helped create the Bank of England. It is a strange coincidence that though many point to the Scottish roots of the Bank of England, yet the same man did more to ensure union with England than any other contemporary.

The development of joint stock companies has long been attributed a prominent place in the economic history of Europe and in the development of capitalism in the Netherlands and England particularly. The end of the seventeenth century saw significant investment in such structures. Paterson, under the influence of his continental friends and travels in the Netherlands, was quick to grasp the idea and in 1691, the year of his return to London from travels abroad, he formed, under the joint stock principle of raising capital, the Hampstead Water Company. This was a success and Paterson channelled his energies into the bigger and more rewarding project of creating a financial system to lend money to the beleaguered Treasury. He relied on the principle of the joint stock company: investors, giving money to the company, would receive shares, and this money would be lent to the Treasury at a competitive interest rate, which could then be split and given to the shareholders as an annual dividend. In addition this loan or investment could be traded, given that it was based in a shareholding and the projected bank had an excellent image, given that the State was paying the interest and because one-fifth of the money held by the bank was converted into gold or coin. Financially, it was an excellent scheme, but politically there were doubts. It had to be approved by parliament and when Paterson went before a Committee of Inquiry in 1692, a difficulty soon emerged with the ability of the bank's receipts to be used as legal currency. Parliament dismissed the idea and again raised taxes.

This short-term solution would soon become untenable: the financing scheme and the war were bound up together and as King William and his allies' defeats increased, so would the demand for easier access to funds. Paterson required titled men, influential merchants or other men of standing to back his scheme: credibility was essential in a time when many schemes were ill-thought-out or plain fraudulent. In 1691 Sir William Phipps, a wealthy merchant and colonist, returned from Massachusetts and was convinced by Paterson's scheme and agreed to become a leading backer. He had previously led a large colonial militia force in an unsuccessful attack on French positions in Quebec. He was a man eager to back a system for increased funds to fight war; he had seen his own troops defeated, in part, by a lack of resources and training.

Paterson befriended Charles Montagu, an aristocratic young MP and Treasury minister, who teamed up with him to convince the government of the merits of Paterson's proposal and to find a way to obtain parliamentary approval for the scheme. Parliament again rejected a reformulated plan in which Montagu had discarded giving the receipts of the Company the status of legal tender. This further setback brought out the politician in Montagu, who formulated with Paterson's help a design for a new bank, but instead of pushing a Bill through parliament solely for this purpose, the relevant statutory provisions were contained within the 'Tunnage Bill', which on the face of it was part of the Budget and sought to increase taxes on the weight of ships using English ports. With an increasingly desperate Treasury and losses mounting on the battlefield, despite concerns raised in parliament, the Bill was passed and so it came to be that the Bank of England was founded in 1694 – the development of William Paterson's original idea and, for Scotland, his first and last great achievement.

Paterson went on to become a director of the bank, but with his prickly character he did not enjoy the company of his fellow directors. His request for financial acknowledgment in proposing the scheme which founded the bank was rudely rejected and when the board was invited to answer questions about the success of the scheme before a parliamentary committee, he was not invited. His vanity was unable to accept the insult. The final straw, which severed Paterson's connection with the bank, was his involvement in another joint stock company bank, called the Orphans' Bank (so-named to raise funds to replenish a depleted orphans' account run by the corporation of the City of London) became public. The court of directors of the Bank of England publicly rebuked Paterson – his actions were a breach of trust, detracting from his fiduciary role as a director. Paterson, shocked by this, never returned to a further board meeting. Further ignominy awaited him as the Orphans' Bank crashed after two years and his great friend, James Smith, was imprisoned for involvement in committing a fraud on the Bank of England on behalf of the Orphans' Bank.

Paterson's achievement in helping to create the Bank of England is evidence enough of his brilliance and foresight. It also demonstrated some of the qualities which were to make him a liability for the Scotsmen who supported his scheme in Darien. He could be a poor judge of character (Smith's name was associated with fraud later) and his vanity blinded him to how others might perceive him and at times his judgement was far from sound. Paterson was above all else a man who could see an opportunity and was able to sell it; he was a man of ideas, from a country, at that time, lacking in development and enterprise.

Scotland was not a place for opportunities in the late seventeenth century. It was a poor country, rife with religious division, superstition, famine and endemic poverty. The nation was particularly afflicted by two ills: religious strife and famine. Both had a debilitating effect on efforts to relieve poverty and strengthen the institutions to bring about national modernisation.

In his book on the Scottish Enlightenment, Arthur Herman recounts the chilling case of Thomas Aitkenhead, vividly demonstrating the transformation of Scottish society around this time. In 1696, the same year as the Bank of England was settling into everyday financial life and Paterson was seeking to promote his next great idea, Scotland was transfixed by altogether very different matters.

During an uncommonly cold August, four young men walked down the High Street, past the Tron Church. Amongst them was an eighteen-year-old man called Aitkenhead. He was heard to have said, 'I wish right now I were in the place Ezra called hell, to warm myself there.' His companions, not content to ignore the remark and no doubt unpleasantly ambitious would-be clergymen, promptly told the Kirk authorities and the very next day and upon closer examination it emerged Aitkenhead had previously challenged accepted Church teachings and mocked Christ himself. This foolish eighteen-year-old boy could never have known the trouble his off-the-cuff remarks would get him into. Unfortunately, the Lord Advocate, a devout member of the Kirk, heard of his transgressions and decided here was a case upon which he could take a moral stand against the increasing tide of looser reasoned theology flowing northwards. Religious pressure from the General Assembly of the Kirk had resulted in draconian laws: three offences of blasphemy could result in punishment by death because of the obstinacy of the blaspheming, but only one count of blasphemy, in which the blasphemer 'railed and cursed' against God and offended the Holy Trinity was also sufficient for the death penalty. The Lord Advocate had Aitkenhead arrested in November 1696 and he was imprisoned in the Tolbooth in Edinburgh; after initial denials he quickly sought mercy by admitting his transgressions, confirming his true Christian beliefs and asking for mercy. Scotland, however, was not interested in listening.

The Lord Advocate himself prosecuted the trial and defence counsel was disposed with. In such circumstances, with the incriminatory affidavits from his supposed friends and his repentance, unsurprisingly, the jury found him guilty. The fifteen God-fearing middle-class members of Edinburgh society had been put under enormous pressures by the Kirk and the legal establishment to arrive at a holy verdict. The Lord Advocate zealously demanded the death sentence for Aitkenhead's wickedness. The teenager would hang in January 1697 for the words he had uttered. John Locke, the eminent English jurist and writer, became involved, attempting as he was, at the end of his career, to leave writings on the separation of Church from State. He argued religious belief was a matter of private conscience and public authorities had no right to intervene in such matters. This view was not a popular one in Scotland at the time. Religion was very much a matter for the state and nothing illustrates this more than the Scottish enthusiasm for witchcraft trials in the seventeenth century.

Leading Scottish historian T.C. Smout estimates that between 1560 and 1707 'considerably more than 3,500 people, and perhaps as many as 4,500'[3] were put to death for practising the black arts of witchcraft, four times more than in England. These, mostly elderly women, were strangled, covered in pitch and then burned at the stake. This was not, however, an unsupervised populist practice; as late as 1662 the Privy Council set down basic civil rights for the trial of witches. The establishment was behind the practice and they were, somewhat incredibly, concerned to see fairer procedures for witchcraft trials. Laws were passed to outlaw witch-pricking (the practice of proving communion with the Devil by pricking a sharp pin over the alleged witch's body until a spot is found where no pain is felt); torture to extract confessions; and a law was passed to ensure the sanity of those who voluntary admitted witchcraft was verified. Only fifty years before the birth of Scottish Enlightenment philosopher David Hume, women were burned alive for witchcraft, and the Scottish establishment's response was to insist on safeguards as outlandish as outlawing witch-pricking.

Thomas Aitkenhead had little chance. His appeal was rejected at all levels: by the appellate court, the Privy Council, the Lord Chancellor and even by their majesties William and Mary. He was helped from the Tolbooth on a January day in 1697 and made to walk to Leith, where before him he could see the wooden scaffold: the embodiment of the Scottish Church's obsession with doctrine, a graceless lack of compassion. Aitkenhead himself stood before the crowds, shaking in the cold, yet exuding more dignity than the rabid ranks of Edinburgh's legal and religious elites who had sent this young man to his death, and forgave those involved in the trial against him and declared that; 'it was out of pure love of truth, and my own happiness that I acted … an insatiable inclination to truth'.

It is to the credit of the Caledonians that their own laws in steamy Panama would be very different from this world they sailed away from.

Scotland, at this time, was not only a backward place, but a poor place too. Famines had been common in the seventeenth century but the repeated failure of harvests in the 1690s was particularly devastating for the majority of the population who were peasants. Some parishes saw burial rates increase fivefold in the worse years of the famine. Smout quotes a contemporary writer:

> Everyone may see Death in the face of the poor that abound everywhere; the thinness of the visage, their ghostly looks, their feebleness, their agues and their fluxes threaten them with sudden death if care be not taken of them. And it is not only common wandering beggars that are in this case, but many householders who lived well by their labour and their industry are now by want forced to abandon their dwellings.[4]

Scottish political life was little better. It was moribund, with the parliament in Edinburgh not nearly as effective or as powerful as its Westminster equivalent. Corruption and vested interests were rife, and members of the parliament were commonly bought off by the king's powerful secretaries of state. For this impoverished, repressed, politically corrupt country, Darien represented an ideal: an opportunity to reverse Scotland's fortunes and allow it to modernise and keep pace with other European countries. Scottish civil society was a poor midwife for the birth of the Company of Scotland. The failures of Darien can be traced back to the shortcomings of its Scottish conception.

THREE

THE COMPANY OF SCOTLAND

Paterson was desperate to find a means to make his great idea a reality. In June 1695 a Scottish Act of Parliament, 'An Act in favour of the Scots Company Trading to Africa and the Indies' had been passed by the parliament in Edinburgh and Paterson was determined to take advantage of the opportunities the Act presented. Despite the obvious Scottish foundation of the Company, Paterson, unconcerned by borders, and wary of the commercial competence of his compatriots, had devised a scheme to ensure the stock and the directors would be split between Edinburgh and London.

The oppressive trade practices of the English East India Company resulted in many London merchants being keen to invest in a rival company with similar wide-sweeping powers. The history of the Company in India demonstrated just how far beyond commercial activities its role was permitted to grow. With its power and influence, the East India Company was not about to stand by as a serious, state-backed, commercial rival was born. Shortly after the necessary £300,000 had been raised in the subscription books in London, the English parliament called a halt to the entire proceedings. The powerful East India Company had intervened, lobbying Parliament to crush a potential competitor, strangling the infant company at birth. Parliament declared the directors of the board were guilty of 'high crimes and misdemeanours'. In January 1696 the House of Commons passed a resolution arraigning many of the directors of the Company, charging them with treason. This brought a swift end to the project and Paterson was forced to put together a purely Scottish venture, without the help, wealth and experience of the English. He turned north and headed to Edinburgh.

Arriving in early 1696, he was received with a wave of adulation. He was
seen as a national hero for standing up for Scottish interests, suffering for the
national good at the hands of unfairness and English spite. Paterson enjoyed
the attention. He was respected. Distinguished men acknowledged him and
the great and good sought him out. Ballads were even written about him
and his project. The inelegantly sounding 'Trade Release, being an excellent new ballad to the tune of "Turks are all Confounded"' had this to say:

> Come, rouse up your Heads, Come rouse up anon!
> Think of the Wisdom of old Solomon,
> And heartily Join with our own Paterson,
> To fetch home Indian Treasures:
> Solomon sent afar for Gold,
> Let us do now as he did of old,
> Wait but three Years, for a Hundred-fold
> Of Riches and all Pleasures.

The attention went to Paterson's head and he became more convinced of
the soundness of his project. With Scotland in a miserable condition, many
were eager for salvation and Paterson provided profile for the projected
company, transforming it (against his better judgement) from an Anglo-
Scottish venture to a purely Scottish one. Nationalism created unstoppable
momentum. The Edinburgh merchants lost little time opening a Scottish
subscription book and surprised even themselves by demanding £400,000
in subscriptions, which was a huge sum for those times for a small country,
impoverished more than normal by famine and hunger. Adam Smith in
his *The Wealth of Nations* estimated Scottish capital in 1700 must have been
around £1 million, although T.C. Smout notes that when the coinage
was called in after Union in 1707, just £411,000 was discovered in circula-
tion.[1] The Company would consume nearly one half of all available Scottish
capital.

The subscription book opened on Wednesday, 26 February 1696, at Mrs
Purdie's coffee house by Mercat Cross, a popular meeting place for the
cognoscenti of the day. On the first day there was the predictable rush to
subscribe, helped by a number of aristocratic and high-profile subscribers
committing themselves early. The list of subscribers is, in itself, a fascinating

historical document mapping the nature of Scottish society and its economy shortly before Union. First to sign was the Duchess of Hamilton and Chatelherault. She subscribed £3,000 and committed one of the most aristocratic families in Scotland to the great project. Her lead ensured many others followed to give away their life savings to a flawed project, but they were not to know that; Edinburgh was buoyant with enthusiasm.

Not every subscriber had a title of course; amongst the more surprising subscriptions are Robert Douglas, a soap boiler from Leith (£100); Thomas Gemill, a hammerman from the Gorbals, who gave £100; and Thomas Baxter, a Glaswegian tailor who contributed a hefty £400. Towns and institutions also contributed to allow those who could not afford the £100 minimum investment to subscribe. Perth, a wealthy market town, gave £2,000, whilst the incorporation of tailors in Glasgow gave £200. Paterson was pleased to see his home town of Dumfries support its successful son to the sum of £500. Old rivalries preserved down the centuries; 'the town of Glasgow' contributed £3,000, but was not accorded the same title as Edinburgh, which also gave £3,000, but was inscribed as 'the Good Town of Edinburgh'.

Many subscribers were merchants seeking preferment from the Company to provide goods for the trading missions. Most came from Glasgow and Edinburgh, with a few from Dundee. The legal profession in Edinburgh contributed a significant amount, including four Senators of the College of Justice. The greatest contributors were the landed classes, not surprising given the undeveloped state of the Scottish economy. W. Douglas Jones in his interesting article entitled 'The Bold Adventurers' provides interesting insights into both the class and gender mixes of the list by way of comparison with the list of subscribers to the Bank of Scotland, a contemporary rival.

Thirteen servants and ninety-one women contributed to the Company, an indicator of the broad appeal of the Company, but also the meritocratic approach taken; this was not solely an elite project, but an inclusive, national one. The Bank of Scotland's subscribers by comparison did not include any servants, students, soldiers, tradesmen or clergy. It was dominated instead by landed people, who held 36 per cent of the stock, higher than the 26 per cent of stock held by landed people in the Company of Scotland. This is underlined by the number of institutions who contributed, even small ones, like Cowane Hospital in Stirling, and the number of towns, which gave people across a broad range of social positions the opportunity to be stakeholders in the great undertaking. The Company motivated and involved ordinary Scottish people in a commercial project to an extent that has never been seen before or since. Nationalism created a heady atmosphere to separate Scots from their hard-earned savings.

The sums involved were truly extraordinary. Jones calculates the £400,000 invested would have represented two and a half times Scotland's annual exports, which would result in a modern investment of well over £100 billion today. All the more extraordinary given the demands to subscribe to the Bank of Scotland in a country that had never seen formal lending institutions before 1695. This placed a huge strain on the economy and demonstrates the scale of the crisis when Caledonia failed. It was a colossal achievement for a small country and says much about Paterson's and the others' skill in promoting the idea to the nation. Jones remarks, however: '[t]he subscription books are the first chapter in the financial odyssey that delivered Scotland into one of the most lucrative commercial empires the world has ever known. The Darien experience initiated a financial revolution in Scotland whose innovations informed the development of the modern banking system'. He attributes the development of the Royal Bank of Scotland, founded in 1727, to the Scots' resulting familiarity with banking and stock ventures. Until recently it stood as one of Scotland's major business success stories: one of the largest banks in the world and run from Edinburgh. Today it is a humbled giant, ruined by aggressive expansion and limited regulatory oversight. The collapse of the Royal Bank and the huge state bail-out that followed would have destroyed an independent Scotland's economy. The Union took the strain. The parallels to the effect on Scottish economy of the collapse of Caledonia following the widespread subscription and the resulting need for Union in 1707 are obvious.

With this vast sum of money paid up, the Company began to purchase goods, hire men and organise itself for the challenges ahead. Roderick McKenzie was appointed the Company's first Secretary. He would go on to hate the English for the manner in which the Company was treated in London and how he himself was summoned to appear before Parliament. But in the hopeful early days he knew no bitterness as he began to organise his army of clerks, couriers, tellers and cashiers, who were to be the foot soldiers carrying out the orders which began to emanate from Mylne's

Square. At this rather grand address by the Tron kirk stood a fine grey building which housed the Company's headquarters, found by Paterson himself.

The fact that Paterson had been assigned such a relatively lowly task demonstrates some of the resentment that had begun to build up towards him by some of the wealthier Scottish landowners. Worse still, he was nearly excluded from the Board of Directors by a series of mischievous resolutions passed by a committee set up by the shareholders. In the end he was appointed to the board, but it would not be the last time his position at the centre of events would be challenged. The great men who took over Patterson's scheme were wary of this Dumfriesshire upstart and had difficulty deferring to a man from a lower social class. The building was taken on and the chatter of hiring and buying soon emanated from its thick walls just off the Royal Mile. Secretary McKenzie had taken the liberty of housing himself and his family on the top floor, whilst below, on a daily basis, the Court of Directors would meet and receive reports, debate proposals and, in the early days, illegally turn the Company into a rival bank (contrary to the king's grant of a twenty-one-year monopoly to the Bank of Scotland) to put the Company's money to better use and make the inadequate capital go that little bit further (whilst many had pledged significant sums, not all the money had been paid to the Company, creating a cash shortfall). John Holland, the Bank of Scotland's principal projector, was alarmed by this development, but with so many of Edinburgh's elite, particularly advocates and judges, patriotically subscribing to the Company of Scotland, the Bank took on board the fact it was better to say little, and they were proved right when a premature halt was brought to this project by the Company's dwindling liquidity.

With so many preparations underway, the directors gathered to plan how and where they would invest the record sums of money they were pledged to soon receive. On 28 July 1696 the board of the 'Company of Scotland Trading to Africa and the Indies' met in Mylne's Square to decide upon the destination of their first trading colony. The directors asked Paterson to give them the benefit of his experiences of trade; he had, after all, travelled to the Caribbean and extensively in Europe and England. He enjoyed the opportunity to direct the course of events and put into place his long-cherished plan to increase world trade: he was ready and rose to the challenge.

He arrived, clutching maps, charts, bundles of documents and manuscripts and set about catching the imaginations of the elderly Scottish gentlemen sitting before him. He had fine material to draw on: Lionel Wafer's magical account of the isthmus of Darien, with its friendly Indians, beautiful flora, succulent fruits, abundant fish and safe harbours.

This description mattered to the directors for a reason Paterson did not really advocate: the founding and creation of a substantial settlement was also on the minds of these Scots, anxious for their place in history and mindful of the earlier Scottish failure at settling South Carolina in the mid seventeenth century. They were not content only with trade, they wanted to be the founders of a 'new world' empire. Paterson viewed this meeting as one of the most crucial of his life: he was the man capable of pulling off this great project and of changing the nature of world trade, a change as significant as the creation of the Panamanian isthmus itself, which rose out of the sea, forced up by seismic shifts to create a land barrier, which for evermore changed the flow, currents and tides of the great oceans and utterly transformed the Earth. Paterson was aiming for nothing less dramatic in the world of trade.

The directors who sat on the Committee for Trade were easily persuaded by Paterson's project, they asked to keep his papers and had McKenzie bind them up, seal and sign them. They wanted to ensure they arrived in Darien before anyone else. Paterson, however, never one to relax, became concerned about the low level of capital for such a large project and demanded fresh efforts be made to find further backers. The Company began again to appreciate his value. Compared to the mighty East India Company, which had a capitalisation of more than three times the total capital pledged to the Company of Scotland, the Edinburgh outfit looked distinctly under-funded. Paterson, as always, had a plan – the Company should re-open its books in London and he proposed he should go to Holland and the German states to seek further capital and backers for the Company and at the same time supervise the construction of the Company's fine ships, at that time being built in Amsterdam and Lübeck. The directors of the Company readily agreed.

Paterson was to be accompanied on his trip to Holland by John Haldane of Gleneagles, a respected landowner, and John Erskine, an army officer and Governor of Stirling Castle. Paterson and Erskine travelled by boat, whilst

Haldane rode to London to collect James Smith (Paterson's colleague from earlier projects), who had been sent there earlier to purchase merchandise. The Company had given Paterson £25,000 to fund purchases and he, placing much trust in Smith, had given him £17,000 of this money to honour drafts issued abroad, as Edinburgh in those days did not possess the financial sophistication for such transactions.

Paterson and Erskine arrived in Holland in November 1696 after a particularly awful three-week voyage and immediately began seeking out further investors. It did not take them long to realise their reception would be frosty: a cold winter had descended upon the Continent, bringing shipbuilding to a halt and even the Dutch proved to be risk-averse. Amsterdam was home to the powerful and successful Dutch East and West India Companies. Quietly, the Scots inadvertently set about destroying potential investors' confidence in the scheme with the Company's emphasis on secrecy over the destination of the investment. It is hardly surprising the Dutch did not invest in greater numbers than they did: there were many investment opportunities available in the world's most sophisticated financial market, and so the Dutch snubbed the investment opportunity offered them. With shipbuilding halted and frozen ports, trade was at a low ebb and it was not the time for speculative capital outlays. As T.C. Smout points out, the Dutch East and West India Companies ensured attempts to raise capital for a rival were foiled.[2]

More alarming news would greet the Scotsmen in Amsterdam. John Haldane, suspecting something odd with the accounts, had discovered £8,000 was missing from the monies Paterson had given to Smith, and Smith himself appeared unable to explain the loss. With this whiff of scandal following them, they headed for Hamburg in January.

Paterson's optimism was reflected in his correspondence, and he was right to have hoped for further backing in the Hanseatic ports. The merchants of Hamburg, Lübeck, Danzig and Bremen had been engulfed in many regional rivalries and were far behind their European contemporaries in searching out a place in the sun. Paterson hoped they would eagerly buy into his investment opportunity, and at first they were interested. Paterson met many wealthy merchants and appeared on the verge of securing the backing of the dukes of Brunswick, Zell and Wolfenbüttel. Two factors were to erode and finally destroy the foundations of this early optimism: English diplomatic clout and the suspected fraud in the midst of the Company itself.

John Prebble's account[3] of the English Resident Minister in Hamburg, Sir Paul Rycaut, paints him as a dry man, who took a certain delight undermining the Scots. Prebble appears to suggest he disliked Scots and was particularly content to understand from Whitehall the venture should not prosper. However, Prebble's description of the fervent anti-Scots approach of the English diplomat may not be very balanced. Rycaut's correspondence rather praised William Paterson, saying:

> ... how farre ye Dutch may adventure therein I know not, for Mr Paterson, who is a diligent Projector, lyes hard at them, and representing nothing but riches and a golden age ...[4]

He sent long-winded letters to all the major local towns, hectoring the merchants with King William's displeasure at the Scots' actions. He summoned the Hamburg Senate before him and pointedly lectured them and in a final flourish he sent out a letter, in Latin, threatening the residents against backing the Scottish Company. Despite this, Paterson bounded onto the scene and with a combination of seriousness and enthusiasm made reasonable progress, convincing some of the leading merchants they should back him. Profit was, after all, profit. This early interest was given a considerable fillip by the completion of the Company's ships in early March in Lübeck. The *Caledonia* and the *Instauration*, proudly flew the cross of St Andrew and the Company of Scotland's flag: bold and very real visions of an optimistic venture.

Despite these small successes the tide would once again be turned. James Smith and a strong whiff of financial irregularity arrived just as progress was being made. Rycaut, of course, made it his business to circulate this news as far and wide as he could and may have been behind an anonymous pamphlet which made much of the allegations of fraud amongst the Scots Company promoters in Hamburg. Nonetheless the Company persevered and opened a room in which to receive much-needed subscription monies. Although the infuriated Rycaut tried but failed in his demands of the Burgomaster to have the sign removed from the building, they need not have bothered – in a final flourish Rycaut summoned deputies of the Senate and bluntly told the Germans that involvement in the Scots Company would be an affront to King William. The bullying and the scandal put paid to Paterson's hopes. He opened the subscription books but nobody came.

Paterson returned to Edinburgh, where worse news was to face him. An inquiry into Smith's loss of funds cleared him of wrongdoing, but nonetheless the directors sacked Paterson, and thus at the crucial time of preparations, he was relegated to a peripheral role. Smith headed back to London to attempt to make good the loss and sold shares in the Hampstead Water Company, but this was insufficient and as the Company closed in on him, he packed and fled for the Continent, but was arrested at Dover.

The Company could take some comfort from the Continent. Its fine vessels sailed into harbour in Leith in the autumn of 1697. The directors comfortably ensconced in Mylne's Square felt more at ease in their wood-panelled surrounds and the anxious Scots bustling around Edinburgh felt a swelling of pride as the ships waited to transport men and dreams across the Atlantic. The flagship was German-built and sailed from Hamburg. Initially named the *Instauration,* meaning the start or establishment of something, she was renamed the *Saint Andrew*. She was certainly the start of something, but not anything the Scots could have predicted in 1698. She would be commanded by Captain Robert Pennecuik and abandoned in Port Royal, Jamaica, several years later. She was joined by the *Caledonia*, whose name would be echoed down the pages of history when Darien was finally reached and the same name was used to christen the colonial outpost. She was captained by Robert Drummond and was one of the very few ships to return to port. The fleet was strengthened by a clever purchase by James Gibson in Amsterdam of a vessel named the *Saint Francis*, but one of Catholicism's favourite saints could not be used in Presbyterian Scotland. Gibson renamed her the *Union*, a more accurate harbinger of things to come. She was eventually renamed the *Unicorn* and captained by Robert Pinkerton. She would end up abandoned in New England. Two smaller boats sailed with the first fleet, the *Dolphin* and the *Endeavour,* the first would be captured by the Spanish at Cartagena and the second would end up below the waves of the Caribbean.

Nobody in Edinburgh in 1697 foresaw these miserable endings and merchants strode around the city rubbing their hands together, dreaming of the vast amounts of money to be spent providing the victuals for the sail, and the goods required to stock the colony's trading post. William Arbuckle, a Glasgow merchant, headed up the powerful Committee for

Equipping Ships and unsurprisingly became a well-dined man in early 1697, as merchants curried favour with him in the hope that his committee would place orders with them. Large warehouses in Leith were leased and slowly filled with the goods that would keep the Scots en route to Darien fed, as well as the wares that would be traded from the great entrepôt.

The list of the goods brought to Darien does not make for happy reading. Much criticism has been made of the decision to take hundreds of English bibles, hundreds of periwigs, bob wigs and campaign wigs, and some of this criticism is certainly deserved. Wigs may have been worn by Spaniards on the Spanish main and by English colonists in the Caribbean and in North America, but the decision to bring these good underlines the strategic ill-thinking of the Scots. The Spanish would not trade with them and it made little commercial sense to take goods from Scotland to Darien and then back to South Carolina. And if the plan really had been to trade to the Far East, what use would such goods have been there? The Kirk, a strong backer of the venture, demanded bibles be brought and demanded a Presbytery be set up. There were souls to be saved from the 'popish devils'. Nobody laughed when the Spanish brought the Holy Mother Church (if not bibles) to the Indians and transformed the religious beliefs of an entire continent.

Over £18,500-worth of goods was loaded onto the waiting ships. Many of the goods brought on board were there to build the colony: nails, axes, hammers, tools for blacksmiths and carpenters. And arms to defend the colony: canons, shot, gunpowder, muskets, pistols, cutlasses, swords and spikes. And to provide for everyday life for the Scots: frying pans, jugs and pots. Among the goods that can be identified as trading goods because of their large quantities were cloth, of every imaginable type: tartan (of course), muslin, serge, canvas, linen, hodden-grey and harn; utensils, such as basins and jugs of pewter, glass drinking cups and horn spoons; miscellaneous items such as soap, buttons, combs, needles and balls of twine; and thousands of David Montgomery's white clay pipes (which may still be found by the very fortunate today in the mud at Darien and, when recovered, in the air-conditioned salons of wealthy Panamanians). It is apparent from the list of the goods shipped that the focus of the colony had changed; there was less emphasis on trading through Panama to the East and more emphasis on providing a settlement and Caribbean colony. Paterson's absence from the Court of Directors was already being felt.

The goods brought on board to feed the Scots sounded, on paper at least, to be fairly appetising: salted beef, pork, prunes, biscuits (coarse, middle and fine), suet, flour and wheat. More impressive yet were the quantities of alcohol brought on board: 1,700 gallons of rum, 1,200 of claret, and 5,000 of brandy. These victuals were provided to sustain the 1,200 colonists both during the voyage and during the initial weeks and months when it was hoped New Edinburgh would rise up from the jungle.

As the ships sat ready in Leith, the provisions and trading cargo were slowly brought on board to fill their holds. All that was missing were the crew, officers and planters who would sail from Leith to raise the Company's flag and plant a new chapter in Scottish history in the jungles of Darien. In March 1698 Roderick McKenzie placed a large notice at the entrance to Mylne's Square inviting volunteers to accompany the ships. For those who endured the deprivations of Scotland in the 1690s the offer of 50 acres of plantable land and 50-feet square of land in the chief city or town was a very inviting offer. People flocked to Mylne's Square. Chief amongst those who sought office or passage were the soldiers and officers made redundant by the Treaty of Ryswick, which had temporarily ended King William's war with Louis XIV. After fighting in Flanders thousands of Scots were sent back to their impoverished homeland where, understandably, they clamoured to obtain positions with the Company. Many received commissions, but those who were able to have first refusal were the gentleman volunteers, the sons of Scottish nobility and wealthy merchants who sought to either extend or restore familial pride and wealth by reaping the benefits of colonial opportunities.

It is easy to imagine how older landowners must have impressed upon their sons the need for discipline, hard work and courage in the new colony to provide the path out of poverty at home and the restoration of the family name. Most, however, were former soldiers or sailors, despite the Company often proclaiming the civil and trading nature of the expedition. To emphasise this no ranks were supposed to be used, instead the terms overseer, sub-overseer and planter were to be used, but they were soon replaced by conventional military ranks or social greetings. Sixty officers were listed as overseers or sub-oversees, and amongst them were a large numbers of Highlanders, both in the ranks and as officers. Some estimates claim a third of those who went to Darien spoke only Gaelic. The officers were well rewarded, with £150 of Company stock for every captain, £100 in

33

stock for every lieutenant and a less impressive £5 in stock for each ensign. Along with the large numbers of soldiers, several professionals were also dispatched: doctors, surgeons, apothecaries, clerks, ministers and translators. Correspondence between the Spanish officials, found in the Panamanian archives, reveals that there were many amongst the Company who were not Scots, but from mainland Europe.

It is not clear how the majority of the ordinary men were chosen. The gentleman volunteers would, of course, rely on their name and connections. The officers were subjected to a rigorous interview by a special committee which investigated their feelings and expectations of work and life in the colony. It is less clear how the directors went about organising the command and management structure of the colony. It was the work of men too long members of committees, with little experience of the realities their compatriots would face or the need for decisive leadership in arduous circumstances. The Company was more interested in demonstrating its commitment to liberty, by proposing that a parliament should be created as soon as possible. The inept suggestion in the meantime was that a seven-man council should provide leadership with the yet more unrealistic idea that the leadership of the council would weekly rotate between the council members. The council comprised four land leaders and three sea captains. Here, at almost the very beginning, the directors sowed a bed of indecision, incompetence and weakness, which would fatally undermine Caledonia when difficult decisions were required to be taken and leadership was required to stiffen the resolve of the planters.

The dominant sea captain was Captain Robert Pennecuik. Thirty-two years old, he had served as captain of a bomb ketch in the Royal Navy. He had been out of Scotland for twenty-one years. Robert Jolly, the second sea captain, was really a merchant with experience of trading in Germany and had not commanded a vessel for over twelve years. He was tasked with the command of the *Caledonia*, which he successfully brought to Panama. The third naval officer offered some glimmer of hope: Robert Pinkerton. He was almost universally liked and admired, especially by his crew, and as the colony became increasingly divided, he was even respected by the landsmen. He had few airs and graces, lived aboard his command, the *Unicorn*, in a simple cabin and was careful to look after his crew.

Two soldiers were made land councillors. Major James Cunningham had never left Scotland nor seen military action. He was a 'pillar of the Kirk' but his strengths did not extend as far as courage – he would be the first officer to leave. The other soldier council member was James Montgomerie. He had been an ensign in the Scots Guards, and whilst not lacking courage, he lacked experience and tactical know-how. His appointment was explained by family connections: his grandfather was an earl, his father a major-general and his uncle a privy councillor and a Lord of the Treasury.

A lawyer was sent along too. His name was Daniel Mackay and he made few friends. The fourth man was William Vetch. A former soldier who fought in the Low Countries with the Royal Scots Greys, he had been invalided out of the army six years earlier and suffered from a wound. His fitness to travel to Darien was always in doubt and just days before the fleet sailed he would be replaced, by none other than William Paterson. Paterson's star had continued to sink after the Smith affair and he anxiously waited in the wings, unsure, even, whether he would be allowed to voyage to Darien. Two other characters stand out: the brothers Thomas and Robert Drummond. They played key roles in the history of the Scottish colony. Robert was initially given charge of the *Dolphin* but later took charge of the *Caledonia*, whilst his brother Thomas was appointed an overseer.

With the goods and trading items aboard, the crew ready and the volunteers below decks, Commodore Pennecuik was ready to weigh anchor and lead the fleet out of the Firth of Forth and round Scotland, trailing dreams, hopes and aspirations in her wake. The Company's ambitious flag fluttered above the ships, depicting a rising sun in yellow, red and blue. The late Colombian historian Germán Arciniegas observed this was the first time a yellow, red and blue flag was found in Latin America, colours which persist today in the national flags of Colombia, Venezuela and Ecuador. On 14 July 1698, the commodore weighed anchor and to the cries, shouts, prayers and tears of the crowded well-wishers, relatives, interested merchants and anxious Company directors huddled on the quayside at Leith, the ships departed to claim their part in the history of Scotland. Few on board or on the quayside would have predicted this adventure to strengthen the Scottish nation would fatally undermine her, throwing her exhausted into the arms of the auld enemy.

FOUR

FROM THE OLD WORLD
TO THE NEW

When the fleet finally departed for their odyssey to the new world they did not get very far – they stopped twelve miles later at Kirkcaldy, by no stretch of the imagination an exotic destination. An important cargo was loaded: Paterson, his wife and his clerk. The once mighty Paterson was accepted as a volunteer without rank. Almost as soon as he had settled into his cabin aboard the *Unicorn* he left it, however, and demanded to be rowed across to the *Saint Andrew*, where he collared the astounded Commodore Pennecuik and suggested an inspection of the stores be carried out to permit resupply before sailing. He received short shrift, or as Paterson himself would write when he had returned to Edinburgh, desperate to protect his reputation, Pennecuik had retorted to 'give him leave to think that he knew his business and the instructions he had to follow'. Paterson was correct to have demanded an inventory, as the Caledonians would discover to their cost some time later.

Pennecuik had more important matters on his mind. The destination of the Scots' colony was apparently very much a secret, or so the directors thought. The English Board of Trade had already guessed the likely destination and had met to discuss the matter. They had heard of the possible riches of Darien from the two Englishmen who knew it best, William Dampier and Lionel Wafer, and had formed a view that this was a project worth pursuing. None other than John Locke was assigned to the task and his rushed report, completed in August, urged the English to take possession of Golden Island before the Scots arrived. Unaware of this but revelling in the subterfuge, Pennecuik stood on the bridge of his fine ship with three small packages wrapped tightly in oiled sailcloth: one to be opened upon the fleet's departure from the Firth of Forth, another to be opened upon arrival at the destination contained in the first, and the third to be opened upon arrival at the final destination. As the ships eased out of the Firth, Pennecuik carefully removed the sailcloth from the first package, to reveal instructions to sail for Madeira. This innocuous destination had been chosen by the directors in the hope competitors would assume the fleet would sail from there for Africa.

John Prebble tells us that crowds flocked to the beaches of St Andrews, Anstruther and Elie and cheerfully waved the fleet past. This entire part of the journey was unnecessary. However, as the Company was based in Edinburgh and the capital was the dominant economic, financial and trading city, little thought was given to the point of departure and that honour fell to Leith almost by default.

Glasgow was not yet the major trading city it was soon to become in the wealthy days of Union and empire. However, it was Glasgow's very geographical advantages of being located on the west coast of Scotland that would provide it with a much shorter transatlantic crossing and underpin the city's huge growth and riches under the reign of the tobacco lords some sixty to seventy years later. Paterson was more than aware of this advantage and wrote to the directors later that future fleets should leave from Glasgow. The crossing around the north of Scotland had been very trying. At Aberdeen the fleet was stranded in a windless sea, listlessly bobbing around, but shortly after that more bad fortune descended upon the fleet in two forms: fog and dissension. The fog was the lesser of the two problems. A delayed survey of the stores had produced a shocking and highly dispiriting discovery: the nine months of stores would only last six. Pennecuik gathered the councillors and sea captains to his cabin to discuss the matter during the calm off Aberdeen. This was the first time the councillors were asked to provide leadership and they demonstrated how poorly equipped they were to meet the challenge. They bickered, fell out and grew suspicious of one another without achieving anything, except each others' lasting enmity. Drummond, the captain of the *Caledonia*, in particular, left the *Saint Andrew* thinking dark thoughts about Pennecuik and his capacity to lead.

Pennecuik ordered the ships to sail in close and head for the Orkney islands to pick up further supplies, but the fog continued to trouble the fleet. They could barely stay together, and were reliant upon firing signal guns and muskets to verify their positions. The Company had supplied the captains with sailing orders. They paint an odd picture of micro-management from Mylne's Square:[1]

Signals to be observed in a Fog:
1. If it grow thick and foggy weather the Commodore will continue with the same sail he had set before the fog came on and will fire every half hour a gun, which the other ships are to answer by firing muskets, ringing of bells and beating of drums.
2. When the Commodore would have the fleet to anchor in a fog he will fire two guns, and lest these should not be heard by some of the fleet who may be far astern, he will fire two more half an hour after.
3. If any discovers danger in a fog, which he can avoid by tacking and standing from it, he is to make the signal for tacking in a fog, but if he should chance to strike or stick fast he is to fire gun after gun till he thinks the ships are out of danger.

As the seas rose and the winds picked up the officers realised landing in Orkney would be impossible, moreover, in the fog it became increasingly clear they were unsure of their location and very soon the white blanket of fog severed contact between the ships. In what must have been a tense two or three days, the ships groped their way around the north coast between the Orkneys, always fearful of running aground or hitting the dangerous rocks amongst the islands. No orders from Edinburgh, ringing of bells, or beating of drums could keep the ships together. The morale of the men on board plummeted; not only were their ships aimlessly drifting in an alien white world, but they became aware they had sailed without sufficient victuals. On 31 July the fog eventually cleared but not the uneasy feeling in the pits of stomachs. The crew aboard each ship awoke that day to find themselves in the Atlantic but alone. Less than two weeks from the glorious Leith departure, the fleet was three months short of provisions, seething with bad feeling after one councillors' meeting, demoralised, exhausted from the northern passage and separated. It was by no means a good start.

Despite this the *Unicorn*, some time later, sighted the *Endeavour*, whilst the *Saint Andrew* reunited with the *Caledonia* and the *Dolphin*. In their separate ways the officers hoped for calmer seas as they navigated towards the Portuguese island of Madeira. Whilst the seas were largely tranquil, the tempers of the officers were not. The *Caledonia* frequently lagged behind the *Saint Andrew*, and Pennecuik was forced to wait each dawn for the ship to catch up. He assumed Drummond was deliberately irritating him and tempers frayed as signals passed between the ships.

The *Unicorn* and the *Endeavour* came upon Madeira on 20 August and Captain Pinkerton set out in his pinnace for Santa Cruz, the second city on the island. The Scots had seen a large 50-gun ship riding in the harbour of the capital town, Funchal. In Santa Cruz the governor's representative enquired of the Scots who they were and what the nature of their business was, whilst the Scots asked about the large ship in Funchal Bay. The Portuguese, seemingly unaware of its presence, were alarmed by the presence of a Flemish-built ship armed with fifty guns and sent messengers along the coast to the governor's castle as soon as the Scots left. They in turn found out the other ship was Genoese and contained a valuable cargo: a bishop and a young bride who had married a merchant of the island by proxy in Lisbon and had arrived to confirm her marriage. One eager (anonymous) Scots diarist remarked, 'It is reckoned that the charges of the marriage stood the gentleman £15,000 sterling, and yet the woman was no beauty for all that.'[2]

The Genoese ship turned out to be under Portuguese command and the governor gave orders for it to make ready and confront the Scots. Before a clash ensued, Pinkerton had himself rowed into Funchal and explained the Scots' presence to the governor, who heard him out and was satisfied they were no 'rogues'. Indeed, as the diarist comments, '… all the pinnace crew had the *Unicorn* head richly embroidered and silver on their caps. This startled him [the Governor] a little again for he thought that was not the equipage of merchantmen, besides he was told by the English that our country could never produce such a ship though at the same time (he had been told) who they were and where agoing.' The English were not surprised by the appearance of such well-kitted-out Scots. All across Europe their spies, merchants and intelligence-gathering community had trained watchful eyes on the Company's movements. Upon entering the bay, the *Unicorn* fired twelve guns to salute the Castle of Funchal, where the governor lived. The governor ordered that his soldiers' guns return the welcome to the Scots entering the bay by returning fire. The Scots came ashore, relieved to be on dry land after their exhausting journey from Leith. The sea and land captains headed to the English consul's house and the governor panicked once more at the sight of so many well-dressed soldiers. A sentry was briefly put on the ships before the suspicious governor was again assured all was well.

The commodore on the *Saint Andrew* arrived with the other ships six days later. Pinkerton rowed out to meet them to brief them and explain that he had told the Portuguese their journey was a trading mission down the African coast. Pennecuik, already bad-tempered, called a meeting of the councillors to strip the Drummonds of their ranks and set them ashore. His charge was mutiny. Unsurprisingly the motion was defeated and the effect was to entrench suspicion of the commodore and sow hatred in the minds of the Drummonds. It would not be the last of the quarrels. The wearied Scots were delighted to be on terra firma again, particularly an island as pleasant as Madeira. They sought out fresh food and wine, desperate to obtain nourishment after the stomach-churning parts of the voyage around Scotland and in the Bay of Biscay. There certainly appears to have been plenty of wine, as our anonymous diarist records; despite the hilly, mountainous nature of the island, there was a large stretch of some two or three miles of vineyards along the coast. He describes the Madeirans as no more than Portuguese bandits who retained their thievish manners, but notes, perhaps with a little envy, how well the English lived on the island.

More significantly, and unsurprisingly, whilst at Madeira Paterson was elected to the sixth and empty chair on the council (one of the original seven council members having been prevented by ill health from taking up his post). He was delighted, but found the atmosphere unpleasant, contaminated by too much alcohol-fuelled intrigue, factions and fights. Paterson's own common-sense agenda wisely concerned the structure of the council upon arrival and the hapless scheme to transfer the presidency upon a different councillor every week. Paterson's proposal was to provide each temporary president with one month's tenure and to provide the four 'land councillors' with the first tenures to allow them four months to establish the colony. His proposal was dismissed.

On 2 September the commodore set sail and headed out to the Atlantic Ocean, with noise and smoke filling the air, the *Saint Andrew* fired her guns fifteen times, the *Unicorn* thirteen and the *Caledonia* eleven. Each time the governor replied with two less. Clutching the second of the sailcloth parcels of instructions, Pennecuik stood on the bridge of his ship on the verge of opening them to reveal the long-awaited but badly kept secret. It is worth reproducing the instructions in full:

> By virtue of the power and authority to us given by the Court of Directors of the Indian and African Company of Scotland, you are hereby ordered in pursuance of your voyage to make the Crab Island, and if you find it free to take possession thereof in the name of the Company; and from thence you are to proceed to the Bay of Darien and make the isle called the Golden Island, in and about eight degrees of north latitude; and there make a settlement on the mainland as well as the said island, if proper (as we believe) and un-possessed by an European nation or state in amity with his Majesty; but if otherways, you are to bear to the leeward and view the coast of the mainland towards Bocco de Toros and Bocco de Drago, and there make a settlement on some convenient place of the coast. Tho in your way you are to visit the Island of Providence or Santa Catalina to know the state thereof and to take possession of the same or not as you shall find convenient, for doing whereof this shall be to you a sufficient warrant. Given under our hands at Edinburgh the twelfth day of July 1698.[3]

The Spaniards did not view the Darien as un-possessed, they may not have fully settled it, but they could little afford to lose control over such a vital artery in their empire. Bocas del Toro and Providence Island had long featured as destinations for the Caribbean pirates. It should have been obvious to the Scots these were not places to settle and if they did so, they would be challenged by the Spaniards. With the destination now known, the Scots set out across the Atlantic with a renewed sense of purpose. The trade winds filled their sails, propelling them to another continent and their destiny. Captain Pennecuik's journal noted that he saw flying fish on 5 September 1698. They observed the traditional celebrations on crossing the Tropic of Cancer on 10 September 1698, ducking several crewmen under the waves (three times) for those who could not 'pay their tropick bottle' whilst others handed over bottles of wine and brandy. 'Pretty good sport', commented Hugh Rose, one of the colonists, in his brief journal[4] of the voyage and arrival on the isthmus, which was a deliberately upbeat account to be sent back to the directors in Edinburgh, although most of it was a copy of the commodore's own log.

By 28 September the fleet was firmly in the Caribbean and passed the islands of Antigua, Montserrat and Nevis, 'a very pleasant-like island' commented Rose, and the passing ships and Fort Charles on Nevis acknowledged each other by raising their respective colours. Another diarist from the *Endeavour* commented that the island of Redonda was, 'a small rock about a mile long, inhabited only by Noddies and Boobies'.[5] Shortly afterwards the council met and decided to split the fleet; the *Unicorn* would go to St Thomas, a Danish colony, whilst the rest of the fleet, as per the orders, headed for Crab Island.

The Scots were warmly received by the Danes and the small harbour of St Thomas resounded with the crack of gunshot as the Scots rowed ashore. The governor was Johan Lorentz, who had been in post since 1690 and would remain until he died in 1702. Given his long stint on the island he was happy to converse with fellow Europeans, other than Spaniards. The Scots were entertained and provided with sugarcane and pineapples, a delight to seasick travellers coming from famine-ravaged Scotland. The little town in the wide bay on the island was called Charlotte Amalie and its centre was focused on a small hill in the middle of the bay. The commanding Fort Christian nestled down by the water, and up the hill behind the castle sat Skytsborg, a small fortified tower which overlooked the bay, providing the Danish with advance warning of Spanish or pirate attack. The port attracted a rough mix of traders and privateers who found the port a relatively peaceful place to exchange Caribbean gossip and find work.

In a tavern on the seafront Paterson came across Captain Robert Allison ('one of the eldest Privateers now alive' wrote Rose), who agreed to act as pilot to find Golden Island and safely bring the Scot to harbour there. He was an old sea dog who had raided with the same Sharp who had led the expedition across Darien during which Lionel Wafer had been injured and left behind. Paterson excitedly talked to him of the old days and boasted a little of his future plans on the isthmus.

Meanwhile the others had arrived at Crab Island in early October and landed men, claiming the island as they were entitled to do under the long-winded terms of the Act of Parliament constituting The Company of Scotland, Trading to Africa and the Indies of 1695. However, despite the Company's extensive powers the Scots soon came upon a small tent, fifteen men and a Danish flag. The friendly governor had sent troops to assert the King of Denmark's rights to the island, but according to Rose the Danes, 'wished with all their hearts wee settled there, for then they would have a bulwark between them and those of Portorico (a rich and large Island and very populous very near) who were very troublesome neighbouring'. The Scots, buffeted by much rain, wind, lightning and thunder, decided not to bother pressing for the island and so after unsuccessfully trying to exchange goods with an English sloop they departed Crab Island on 7 October.

From there down through the western Caribbean to Darien the journey was unpleasant, with squalls, thunder and lightning and lots of rain. The Scots were nearing their wits' end and sickness and death had increased. Rose writes the decks were frequently rubbed down with vinegar and the holds were smoked to alleviate the 'sickly' Scots. The tropics were beginning to take their toll and unfortunately for the beleaguered, pale Scots, they were yet to experience the dangers of the tropical climate. In addition, bad water had been taken onboard at Crab Island, which led many to suffer from the flux and increased the mortality rate. Just when it appeared the Scots were unwilling to endure much more of their tormented journey, on 17 October a much-needed cry went up: 'Land Ahoy!' The relieved Scots looked to Allison, who confirmed it was Spanish land and that Golden Island was further along the coast. A frustrating two more weeks of slow sailing followed. With winds against them, the Scots had to laboriously tack in and out against the wind as the ships ploughed their way down to the far corner of the Caribbean. The men on board were entertained by the strange sights and sounds of the lush green coastline, with its large river mouths, plunging cliffs and the odd indigenous canoe filled with waving Indians.

On 30 October the Scots anchored at what they assumed to be three leagues westward of the Gulf of Darien. Two canoes of Indians approached them, and those Scots who had read of these noble savages in Wafer's manuscript saw them for the first time. There is little description of the Scot's reaction to the short, dark, mostly naked men who appeared out of the jungle to stand before them on the decks of their ships. The Scots provided them with alcohol (there being no shortage of it on board) and as Rose writes, 'In their cups wee endeavoured to pump them, who told they had expected us these two years; that wee were very welcome, and that all the countrey was at war with the Spaniard.' This should have alerted the Scots to the fact the land they assumed to be free and 'unclaimed by any European Prince' was part of the Spanish Indies, however poorly administered, but there is little evidence that the Scots recognised this. Pennecuick's log notes that the Indians spoke a few words of English and 'indifferent' Spanish. The Caledonians had travelled with interpreters who spoke French, Italian and Spanish, but not the Indian languages.

Tired, but pleased to have shared a glass with the Indians, and after a 110-day voyage, the Scots sailed into the bay surrounding Golden Island and an air of relief fell upon them as they realised Golden Island existed, stood before them, and above all else that they had arrived. Rose reported:

> In the afternoon wee went in our boats to sound all about Golden Island, which wee did with great exactness, but found it not convenient for our shipes, there being not room enough about the point of the main for ships of our length to swing in. 'Tis true there is room near the Island, but then wee might be attacked by the greatest either from Eastward or Westward, for they can come in both wayes, nor is ther a drop of water within a mile of the point. On the main and all the bay round full of mangrow and swampy ground, which is very unwholesome.[6]

No sooner had they arrived than, as a result of their survey, they abandoned the island and looked to the mainland to establish their settlement.

After the hardships and deaths during the long voyage, the Scots felt relieved to have arrived, even though they were still aboard the ships, and hope rekindled as they gazed upon the green forest of the Darien coast and listened to the call of strange birds and the screams of howler monkeys. The air was hot as they went to sleep that first night, grateful for calmer waters and a safe passage. Paterson, despite the achievement of having arrived, suffered with a heavy heart; his good friend the Reverend Thomas James had died on 23 October. His faithful clerk who had boarded the *Unicorn* with him in a wave of excitement, Thomas Fenner, also died the day they arrived at Golden Island. More tragically for Paterson, his wife Hannah was also gravely ill. Twelve days later she was dead. Public joy mixed with private grief marked Paterson's arrival at his long-dreamed-of project.

FIVE

TIERRA FIRMA

Commodore Pennecuik was determined to continue to play a central leadership role after the fleet's arrival in Darien. This disheartened William Paterson, whose report to the directors upon his return to Edinburgh complained bitterly that, '… our Masters at sea had sufficiently taught us that we fresh-water men knew nothing of their salt-water business, – yet when at land, they were so far from letting us turn the chase, that they took upon them to know everything better than we.' The sea captains were anxious to find a decent harbour for their ships and, as noted, viewed the waters around Golden Island unsuitable for safe anchorage. Lying some four miles east of the island, however, was the narrow mouth of a natural inland harbour. Demonstrating an admirably hands-on approach, Pennecuik set forth with some men in his rowing boat to take a closer look. Hugh Rose's journal picks up the story:

> Novr. 3d, Yesterday in the afternoon, wee went in our boats to sound a bay 4 miles to the eastward of Golden Island, and found a most excellent harbour. The harbour is within a great bay lying to the westward of it, made by Golden Island and a point of land bearing from thence east about a league. From that easternmost point to the opposite one is a random cannon shot, and in the middle of the entry lyes a rock about 3 feet above the water, on which the Sea beats furiously, when the wind is out and blowes hard. This looks terrible (when in the bay) to those who know not the place well, but in both sides of this rock is a very good and wide Channel, that to the southward being about 3 cable-length breadth, with 7 fathom water

closs to the rocks nose, and the other to the northward near 2 cables length. There is a small rock under water, a little within the points bearing off of the southernmost S.S.W. and of the northernmost S.S.E. and of the rock without S.E. & B.E. [*sic*]. From these two outwardmost points the harbour runs away east a good league, and near the middle on the right hand the land sets out, so that its not a musquet shot over, and thus farr there is not less than 6 fathom water with a very good easy ground, and here you ride landlocked every way that no wind can possibly hurt you. Within this to the bottom of the harbour, till within a cable length of the shoare, wee have not less than 3 fathom water, nor can a hurricane make the least sea here. The land on the left hand coming in is a peninsula and about 3 miles long, very high and steep towards the sea, where it will be extremely difficult for any body to land till ye come to the Isthmus, where is a small sandy bay. Small ships may ride, but this by a good ditch and fort may safely be secured. The westernmost point towards the harbour is low and very fit for a battery to command the entry, which would be excellently secured by another on the opposite shoar. The land on the Peninsula is extraordinary good, and full of stately trees fit for all uses, and full of pleasant birds, as is also the opposite shoar, and hath several small springs which wee hope will hold in the driest season. But on the other side are 4 or 5 fine rivers that never do dry. The harbour is capable of containing 1000 of the best ships in the world, and with no great trouble wharfs may be run out to which ships of the greatest burthen may lay their sides and unload.[1]

The more optimistic diarist, the anonymous sailor from the *Endeavour,* paints a picture of abundance:

The Soil is rich, the Air good and temperate, the Water is Sweet, and every-thing contributes to make it healthful and convenient. The Product of the place, I mean in the Harbour and Creeks hereabouts is Turtle, Manatee, and a vast variety of very good small Fish, from the bigness of a Salmon to that of a Perch. The Land afford Monkeys of different Sorts, Wild Deer, Indian Rabbits, Wild Hog, Parrots of many kinds, Parakites, Macwas, Pelicans and a hundred more Birds we have got no name to. There are moreover Land Crabs, Souldiers, Land-Turtle, Lizards. Guanhas, back-Lizards and Scorpions: I had almost forgotten Partridges, Pheasants, and a kind of

Turkey. All the Birds in this Country are beautiful, but none of them that I could observe have any Notes. We have a Monkey aboard that chirms like a Lark; it will never be bigger than a Rat. This place affords legions of monstrous Plants, enough to confound all the Methods of Botany ever hitherto thought upon ...[2]

In many ways Punta Escocés (Scottish Point as it is now known) was the ideal harbour and place of settlement for Caledonia. It is a large bay, some two miles deep, easily defended and with good sources of fresh water. It was as good a place as any the Scots could have chosen but it had one major drawback: the direction of the wind. The wind blew from the south, across the Pacific and over the isthmus, blowing northward, which trapped the ships in the bay, given the angle of the wind against the exit from the bay. Over the coming months the Scots would find considerable difficulty forcing their ships out of the harbour, but despite this there appears to have been no reconsideration of the fact this may have prejudiced the success of a trading empire, which surely must have relied upon the easy access and exit of a large number of trading vessels.

The Scots also found themselves in greater difficulties because they did not possess either a sloop or a brigantine, the most used trading ships in the Caribbean. Given the colony's extreme south-westerly position in the Caribbean, their ships had to sail into the usual north-eastern trade winds. Their shallow-keeled vessels were all but useless in such sailing conditions. Without this they were more or less cut off from trading, which made the selling of their assorted wigs all the more difficult. The lack of practical trading ships would send brave sailors into Spanish captivity in Cartagena quite soon. This defect had been pointed out to the directors by a Scots London merchant, Robert Douglas, but the directors had ignored his advice. Their inexperience of colonial and Caribbean trading was beginning to show.

As Pennecuik reconnoitred the bay he noticed the rustling of trees on the far away shore and on the shoreline appeared a number of curious Indians. They appeared anxious to speak. Despite the language barriers they informed him their leader would come to visit the Scots the following day. Pennecuik was heartened by the friendliness of the natives, which could not be taken for granted, and he was pleased with the diplomatic contacts and efforts that were taking place so soon after their arrival. In fact during the Scots' early months they would spend almost as much time welcoming and feeding various visitors as they would building their colony. Most Scots had never left their native land, and those that had, had left mostly to fight in the Low Countries. Meeting the Indians was a fascinating exchange of cultures. The diarist from the *Endeavour* leaves us his own description:

> Now we come to their people. The men are generally very civil and saga-cious, have all of them good Faces, are of low stature, but very well built; they are of a copper Colour and have black hair; they us'd to go naked, but now are well cloath'd as our selves; they wear a plate of Gold in the Nose, and a great many rows of Beads about their Neck and Wrists … The Women are generally the most pitiful like things that ever man saw; their habit differs from the men, for they ordinarily wear a ring in their Nose: they have Petticoats and a Veil over their Face.[3]

The Indian chief who clambered over the deck the next day was a curious sight, a Kuna Indian, dressed with a 'loose red stuff coat, an old hat, a pair of white drawers, but no shoes nor stockens'. He was short and his name was Andreas and he was accompanied by ten or twelve bodyguards. He was anxious to know why the Scots had arrived in the jungle. White men were not new to them, buccaneers often passed through this part of the world fleeing the Spanish or returning to their ships with looted gold. It is more than likely he assumed the Scots to be English privateers. Despite Pennecuik's attempts to explain they were Scots and that they were there to trade, Andreas embarked upon a long adulation of former privateer friends of his, but the Scots 'received it coldly' and brought the audience to an end by gifting Andreas with a hat 'braded with a broad gold galoo[n]'. The Indians informed the Scots they had been anticipating their arrival: some years ago it had been predicted a white people would come, settle and live amongst them. The Indians, if they knew, did not explain how the prediction ended.

Despite Pennecuik's brusqueness Andreas appears to have been happy with his gift and returned some days later with his 'travelling' wife and Pennecuik, perhaps wistfully, took note of the acceptability of polygamy amongst the Indians. Andreas wanted to reassure himself of the Scots' intentions. The English, he told them, had carried his people away before, after having been initially friendly towards them, which no doubt provided Pennecuik an excuse to extol the virtues of the Scots over their southerly neighbours. Andreas left promising to introduce another chief, Pedro, when it became clearer the Scots meant them no harm.

Aside from their early diplomatic efforts the Scots had to confront the task of landing and constructing their new settlement. This was no small task, as they stared out across the bay at the dense green jungle and its low-lying impenetrable growth. On 3 November 1698 they landed some men and a short religious ceremony was held, offering thanks to God for the safe arrival and no doubt asking him for guidance and help in the coming months. They repeated:

> What should they do but sing his praise,
> Who led them through the watery maze?

The following day the ships, with lowered sails, slipped into the bay which Pennecuik had surveyed the day before. The *Unicorn*'s helmsman clipped a sunken rock and lost much of her sheathing. With limited ships, limited food and a high sickness rate, they could well have avoided the extra repair work and the loss of limited materials. They began to unload some of the men, and the equipment required was brought up from the musty holds to help construct the centre of the world's newest trading empire. Drummond was charged with clearing land and was provided with forty men from each ship to complete the task. The colony experienced, with entitlement, some satisfaction in feeling progress was being achieved. We know from Rose the sun was out, and the heat was tempered with gentle breezes, as the pale Scots sweated and toiled away, attacking the lush green undergrowth with sharpened machetes brought from Scotland. It was a fair scene as the ships sat anchored in the bay, whilst rowing boats ferried back and forward to the coast, where men constructed huts of palm fronds to store goods and protect themselves from the sun, before moving in under the swaying palm trees to chop back the green undergrowth. Hope burned in their hearts.

However, the rain soon started and it became apparent most men were overwhelmed with weakness, hunger and, apparently, overindulgence in the fleet's fine variety of alcohol, to achieve sustained progress. More men became sick and the sea captains obstructed the work, keeping their men from it and finding other uses for their rowing boats. James Samuel Barbour's account of the Darien expedition provides a long, disapproving Edwardian footnote regarding the overindulgence of alcohol, which Paterson complained of himself in his report to the directors. Few were prepared in their bewildering new circumstances to give up their cherished dram, especially as some were very quickly beginning to have doubts about the whole venture. Barbour, writing of the Caledonians in 1906, had this to say:

> According to modern ideas, the Company would appear to have been far too lavish in their supplies of alcohol to the Colony. With every ship carrying provisions, they sent supplies of what they call 'strong liquors' – chiefly rum and brandy – the free use of which, in the hot and pestilential climate of Darien, must have been prejudicial to health.

He then goes on to provide numerous examples of how the directors relied upon it as one of the 'mainstays' of the expedition. Certainly the ministers of the second expedition would be very critical of what they viewed as the immoral behaviour of the Caledonians. God appeared to agree: the last minister the Scots brought with them on the first expedition, Adam Scott, died on 20 November, and the men, left without spiritual guidance, sought even more solace in alcohol as their morale rapidly began to plummet. The councillors, in their December 1698 letter to the directors, pleaded with them to ask the General Assembly to send more ministers 'to supply that great want'. In the meantime, spiritual welfare was abandoned.

The Scots laboured for two months to clear ground and build huts, but it became apparent to Paterson first, and then gradually to everyone else, that the proposed site of the colony was incorrect. According to Paterson it was: 'a mere Morass, neither fit to be fortified nor planted, nor indeed for the men to lie upon.' They conceded defeat, wasted two months' work and moved the settlement from its original sandy promontory further along the coast of the bay to the position where Fort St Andrew and New Edinburgh were finally built. As the last days of the colony's fate were played out, the Scots would come to regret positioning the settlement here too.

During this time of frustrating work the officers were entertained by a full cast of visitors. Many more Indians visited including Andreas again, this time with his 'sedentary' wife and sister, whom Rose took to be typical of the female Indians and described as, 'generally of a small size as well as the men; their features are indifferent (bating their colour), only their eyes are too small. They had a single cloath wrapt around them in form of a petticoat made of cotton, with a sort of linen mantle about their shoulders; a great many beads about their necks and arms, with large gold rings put through the gristle that divides their nostrils ...'. Indian political life was complex and dominated by small groupings which resulted in many rivalries between leaders, or *caciques*. The Scots failed to grasp the complexity of local rivalries and welcomed another Indian chief, Ambrosio, who visited with his son-in-law and sub-chief Pedro, who had been a captive of the Spaniards in Panama City. He spoke good French and was more easily able to communicate with those Scots who shared the language. Ambrosio was keen to enlist the Scots in his battles with the Spanish, and knowing white men well, he talked their language by tempting them with stories of Spanish gold mines, which they would find en route if they joined with him in making war on the Spanish. Victory and many riches were theirs, he assured them. Pennecuik listened, interested in these stories of gold, but dismissed these fanciful ideas and stuck to the yet more fanciful notion that a viable trading settlement could be created in this remote, rain-swept land. Ambrosio left bemused: who were these crazy Presbyterian Scots, who would rather sell pans and wigs than make war and search for gold? He very well knew the Spaniards were bound to, had to, attack the Scots or they would risk compromising the integrity of their entire colonial system, yet the Scots seemed oblivious of the need to prepare at least to defend their position.

Andreas meanwhile made himself increasingly popular with the Scots, despite rumours of his closeness to the Spaniards. During a spell of increasingly bad weather in early December he was invited aboard by the council to receive a written commission to act as the Company's captain amongst the Indians, 'to command the Natives in and about his own territories, and received him and all submitting to him into the protection of their Government, he being thereby obliged with his followers to obey, assist and defend them and all their concerns upon all occasions'. These solemn words were spoken and recorded in writing before a short ceremony took place whereby gifts were swapped. The Scots gave him a fine sword and pair of pistols and in return he presented a bow and arrow. As was increasingly common, a 'hearty glass' was indulged in, accompanied by a few blasts of the cannon. In their choice of ally, the Scots' selection, like so many others, would soon turn out to be the wrong one.

Pennecuik's indulgence of the Indians was not out of any personal regard for them. He was following orders. Enclosed with his sailing orders in the sealed packets given to him by the directors were other instructions, which stated:

Gentlemen: When you are landed where your sailing orders doth direct, you are to take all possible methods to oblige the natives, and to enter into a strict correspondence with them, thereby to procure their right or consent for any settlement that you may make, for which end you are to take special care that no injury or injustice be done to them by any of your men, and if there be, that you make them full satisfaction for the same, by punishing the offenders or otherways as the nature of the offence may happen to require.[4]

The Indians were not the only visitors: a number of Europeans arrived, causing alarm and suspicion. A ship had been seen by the sentry on duty on Point Lookout (a hilltop lookout positioned on a peak, overlooking the bay of Caledonia) but soon disappeared from view. The Scots were anxious to know who had been spying on them. Two days later a small boat rowed into the bay with an English naval officer sitting in the bow, one Captain Richard Long. He had sailed from Dover on the *Rupert Prize* on a commission from the King of England, but deliberately failed to provide more details. Despite the concern amongst the Scots, who suspected him of being an English spy, he was welcomed and provided with fine hospitality at the table of the commodore and of Captain Pinkerton. He enjoyed a drink and gladly returned the hospitality aboard his own vessel when he ran into a party of the Scots near the Isle of Pines. Pennecuik had set out to find a 'grove of Bloodwood not many leagues to the leeward of Golden Island and about two miles from the sea, nearby a river side' which had been expressly ordered of him by the directors, relying on Lionel Wafer. He had found nothing and encountered Long on his return.

Pennecuik did not like the man: 'Whatever the King or Government of

England may have found in Captain Long we know not, but as in all his conversations he appeared a most ridiculous, shallow-pated fellow, laughed at and despised to his face by his own officers and continually drunk.'[5] Curiously, Rose commented, 'What others have found or may think of Lang wee know, but he appears to us to be of no great reach; he has a full and ample commission, his principal design it seems was to find wrecks and fish.'[6] The Scots may not have wanted to commit to writing their fears about his real role amongst them, but they were probably justified. Returning to Jamaica, he wrote a detailed report ('They are in such a crabbed hold, that it may be difficult to beat them out of it ...')[7] for the Jamaican colonial administration which was speedily sent to London.

Later, in early December, a compatriot of the other half of that ancient, but by then very much defunct auld alliance, arrived; a Frenchman called Captain Duvivier Thomas of the *Maurepas*. He was a privateer with letters of commission from King Louis, interested in taking refuge in the Scots' 'crabbed hold' as the Barlovento Fleet (the collection of Spanish ships put together to protect the Caribbean from pirate attack) had massed along the coast. The Scots readily agreed. As ever, ceremonial gunfire was exchanged between the *Maurepas* and the *Saint Andrew* as they sailed into Caledonia bay to anchor. Captain Thomas enjoyed the Scots' hospitality, and provided them with useful information regarding the Spaniards' reaction to their arrival. The President of Panama, he told them over wine and brandy, had written reports to the Governors of Cartagena and Portobello, and the Barlovento fleet had assembled with ships of forty-five, thirty-six and twenty-eight guns. Rose's journal records that the Frenchman told them four ships had sailed from Spain with around fifty guns each. Andreas soon after confirmed the threat: the Spanish had marched from Panama to Portobello and were preparing to attack.

The pressure was increasing on the Scots already and they had little to show for their time on the isthmus. Pennecuik ordered work to complete Fort St Andrew be given priority and the ships formed a defensive line across the entrance to the harbour. Despite the risks of imminent battle and bloodshed, the colonists were pleased: it roused them from the tedious land clearing and hut building, it offered the opportunity for leadership and heroism. Rose exhorted, 'our men are very hearty and seem to long for a visit from Jaque, that they might have a just pretence to their gold mines far off ... wee are now in such a condition as that nothing more is wished than a visit from Jaque', he boasted upon noting the battery was finished and mounted with sixteen 12-pound guns.

The Spanish had of course been expecting the Scots. The Spanish resident in Hamburg had been as interested in Paterson's activities as Sir Paul Rycaut. He had informed his masters in Madrid of what he had heard but as was usual with Spanish colonial administration, decision-making was cumbersome and responses were slow. Despite the advanced warning the Conde de Canillas, the President of the Audencia of Panama was dismayed to learn in November 1698 of the Scots' arrival. His intelligence reports told him they had arrived in solid ships, were large in number and intended to settle on the coast of Darien, at a place the Spanish referred to as Rancho Viejo. The Spanish intelligence network appears to have been quite sophisticated, with reports being sent to Panama from both Cartagena in New Granada and from the viceroy of New Spain, the Conde de Moctezuma, based in modern-day Mexico. Sailors from Cuba had learned of the passage and intent of the Scots as they sailed through the Caribbean and they had relayed the reports to their masters.

The Spanish were appalled. They were determined to dislodge the Scots and, unhappily remembering the sacking of Panama by Henry Morgan and a few hundred pirates in 1681, understandably had serious fears the Scots would repeat such an affront to his Most Catholic Majesty. The viceroy of New Spain ordered recently arrived troops from Spain to sail to Cuba to collect more troops and then to sail to Darien to deal with the Scots. At the same time, the Barlovento fleet was making for Portobello and the Conde de Canillas, President of Panama, began to draw up his own plans for a land invasion of Caledonia.

Whilst the Scots were keen to fight, their energies would have been better directed against poor leadership, illness and bad organisation: these were the real threats to the first expedition. As 1698 drew to a close there would be little cause for cheer amongst the colonists. There would be, however, a little shortlived excitement as the year drew to a close. In keeping with the, by then, established custom of the Company, the Scots were celebrating Christmas early. Their French friends aboard the *Maurepas* remained in the bay and were happily indulging in Scottish hospitality. By all accounts a particularly indulgent night was enjoyed on 22 December 1698, when with little else to do but stare out to the horizon they had begun drinking early and heavily. Early the next morning, with a thick head, Captain Thomas called the order to weigh anchor and proceeded to head out of the bay with the early morning mist. His timing was spectacularly bad, however, and his helmsman was clumsy navigating the ship out of the mouth of the bay. Riding several strong waves which pounded in from the open sea, the ship careered to the side and dashed itself on the half-submerged rocks. Pennecuik, up on deck early, watched all this with amazement and set out for the stricken ship in his longboat. Under the direction of his orders, the ship was hauled off the rock with the aid of more boats, as Thomas watched on helpless. He was lucky: the ship was not particularly badly damaged. Acting on Pennecuik's advice, he lowered both his anchors and waited for calmer seas. His ship vulnerably rode up and down on the waves, pulling on the tight cables in the stiffening breeze. The violently rolling seas strengthened, placing the cables under extreme pressure, and inevitably they snapped. The *Maurepas* crashed onto the half-submerged rocks with much greater force, as cries went up and splinters shot across the foam-soaked air.

This time the ship was badly damaged and almost immediately began to list, 'she went all to peeces, no boat daring to go near her', recorded Rose. Pennecuik stood by, waiting until Captain Thomas was rescued and then standing in his small boat, stripped off his clothes and swam for shore himself, only just making it, as the force of the waves kept him under for twenty seconds at a time, or so he recorded. Twenty-two of the fifty-six-strong crew drowned, many because they clung to their gold and silver. According to Rose, the ship went down with 60,000 pieces of eight and 30,000 crowns of goods.[8] A report from the Caledonians to the councillors in Edinburgh[9] was intercepted by the Spanish and sent by the Governor of Caracas, Nicolás Eugenio de Ponte y Hoyo, to the Spanish king; until recently it remained lost to historians of Darien. The report suggests the Scots negotiated a pact with their French visitors: they permitted the French to look for the treasure in return for one eighth of the silver, gold and other goods and one third of the cannons and anchors from the sunken ship. It seems Pennecuik did not permit the Frenchmen to take what washed up upon the shore.

The intercepted letter also explains that Captain Thomas introduced the Scots to Captain Corvette, an Indian *cacique* who had allied himself with the French. He asked the Scots for a commission to attack the Spanish, which had been denied him by the French. He hated the Spanish and their brutalisation of his people and was thirsty for revenge, but the Scots were anxious about inflaming their delicate situation, and settled on agreeing a pact. If either of them should be attacked the other would fight with them against the Spanish. The Scots cemented this further native alliance by giving him guns, ammunition and linen. When the time came and the Scots were attacked, there is no record of Corvette's men coming to their aid.

Understandably, the French had a bad Christmas. Pennecuik tried to make an occasion of the day and a feast was prepared aboard the *Saint Andrew*. But nothing would go right for the Scots. They failed to realise the Indian leaders Andreas and Ambrosio were rivals, and as ever, after much alcohol had been consumed the Indians started to argue and soon came to blows. Pennecuik, leaping from behind his brandy glass, intervened to pull them apart, settled them down and they regained their composure. But the sour note ensured the evening ended shortly thereafter. In the morning, however, Andreas was discovered in the hold below, unconscious and bleeding from the head. He was never mentioned again during the contemporaneous accounts.

Hugh Rose's journal comes to an end around this time too. It was sent to the directors in Edinburgh to provide them with a fuller picture of life in Caledonia and along with it the councillors sent the directors a 'Declaration of the Founding of the Colony'. With so little achieved physically, it was hoped their report would be better presented if it contained the façade of progress. To mark the occasion the Scots were gathered together around the few palm huts hurriedly constructed, with the Fort of St Andrew roughly hewn from felled trees to one side, a smell of newly cut wood mingling with the fetid smell of rotting jungle vegetation. The men stood solemnly around, encircled by the humid jungle, at places bright green and the dark grey-blue sea. They listened as the councillors reasserted the Scots' right to take possession of the land, punctuated by the calls of strange birds and the odd unintelligible insult of a curious monkey, as they recited parts of the Act of Parliament and solemnly added:

And now, by virtue of the before-mentioned powers to us give, we do here settle and in the name of God establish ourselves; and in honour and for the memory of that most ancient and renowned name of our mother Country, we do, and will henceforth call this country by the name of Caledonia; ourselves, successors and associates, by the name of CALEDONIANS.

The Scots may have achieved relatively little, but they had arrived, they knew where they were and what they were called. A cheer would go up in Edinburgh some months later at the thought of brave Caledonia, but doubts were beginning to enter the minds of those Scots at home, anxious for loved ones and concerned about the state of their investments. Included with the fine words of the declaration was a more alarming reality which would add to the concerns at home: a list of the dead. It already included seventy-six names.

SIX

THE REPUBLIC OF PANAMA

Lucho passed me the bottle of *seco* and winked before the first shot fired out. I fell to the ground and groaned as my suit trousers were covered in mud. Lucho was on his knees too as we turned around to the vast tenement behind us. The police were firing into the air: a warning to the *pandilleros* held up on the top floors of the squalid flats. The air smelt strongly of an unpleasant sweetness and the humidity forced sweat down the back of my white shirt. There was no return fire and Lucho and I laughed nervously as we stood up by the side of my car; leaning against it as we lightly ran to the flyover side of the road and further away from the damp building with its peeling paint and dripping brown water. Between the car and the building was a raised lot of around 100 square metres, caked in red-brown mud. The car was parked just off the road and we had come to get hold of documents from the PTJ – the Technical Judicial Police who provided accreditation for those who wanted to export their cars from the country.

This unfortunate incident was the latest hassle at the end of a long line of byzantine hoops that had dragged on for weeks as I attempted to organise the documentation to export my car back to London. I had been living in Panama City for over two years and had become attached to the blue jeep that had reliably taken me all over the mountains and jungles of the thin tropical isthmus which makes up Panama. The last few weeks had, however, tried my patience, jumping through the seemingly endless stages to complete the documentation to present to the customs officials at Colón, Panama's largest port, the Caribbean terminus of the Canal and home to the world's second largest free-trade zone. Paterson would have been proud to behold the direct physical manifestations of his entrepôt dream, if not the bureaucracy that lay behind it.

The Panamanian state does not, however, subscribe to any form of Presbyterianism. Corruption has permeated much officialdom and the process of exporting a car demonstrates the failings of the system. The car and the exporter are obliged to receive certificates called *paz y salvos* (safe and sound) both from the national transit authorities and also from the municipal authorities in Panama City. Further certificates have to be obtained from the PTJ and also from the directorate of customs. Each of these has to be obtained in a strict order and only within a tightly prescribed timescale from the date of exportation. The result is a mad dash from one office to the next with the attendant and necessary forms, copied twice, others three times, every time with signed, dated copies of the exporter's *cedula* (identity card) and if there is one slight error, the whole process has to be begun again. Given I had booked and paid for my car's passage from Colón to Southampton, and given there were only 48 hours before the departure, the crafty Panamanian state worked itself into a labyrinthian nightmare, and one only corruption could properly oil.

Some would say it would have been easier to simply hand over the necessary dollars when a gentle suggestion was made than to fight for integrity: integrity may have left your car on the quayside at Colón. There is in any event an inherent redistributive fairness about the Panamanian system: the country is one of the least equal on earth, worse in fact than Brazil. Multi-millionaires live cheek by jowl with people surviving on a few dollars a day in filthy wooden shacks. The streets of the city are testament to the inequality: brand new Range Rovers and Mercedes jeeps fight for control of the lanes with the worst beat-up cars imaginable, *'matracas'* as they are affectionately known locally. Children sell trinkets at traffic lights to families in Audis, BMWs, Porsches. The state employees are badly paid and they earn a little on the side by oiling the wheels of the system. Developing countries have to do with limited social security, so ingenuity and a robust capacity for survival take over. If the state cannot function effectively, people find ways to make it work for them.

So I had enlisted the help of Lucho to help ensure all the necessary documentation was in hand. As he lay laughing by the side of the car, his cheap *seco* firmly grasped in his hand, I was glad I had brought him; he was the epitome of the native Panamanian. Eagerly prizing his fingers from the small glass bottle, I gulped down the burning liquid although my watch showed it was not yet eleven in the morning. It was hard to believe the PTJ office was located by some of the worst slums in the city, slums known to be populated with *piedritas,* ghastly thin Panamanian crack addicts. Without his bottle and taking in the thunderous look on my face and the grimy sweat around my collar, Lucho decided to wade across the deserted lot and climb up the back stairs into the dingy police office. I got back into the car, locked it and looked across at the heavily armed police patrolling the base of the tenements. Panama was a safe place, but the district of Curundú was a hell on earth, a forgotten tragic corner of a city that tumbled forward, brushing aside the squalor into remote corners of a rapidly modernising city.

I hoped Lucho had the documentation as his short body clambered down the stairs. I had to be in Colón in four hours' time with the car, the paperwork and several bags, the collected items of over two years in this wonderful tropical country. The door slammed shut and Lucho turned to face me, his eyes bulging with victory and smiling, forcing his bottom jaw in front of the upper jaw, expelling an alcoholic burp below his short moustache. Lucho was in his early sixties, a widower, who worked at the same law firm as me. He was the man who sat as company director for endless thousands of off-shore companies. Lucho, it could be said, kept the tax man at bay. Lucho was reliable. He was also the office contact for dealing with the endless hassles of car registration and ownership and knew the people to speak to in the right offices. He held aloft the light pink bundle of papers that would allow me to export my car and take some of my life from Panama to the UK, back across the Caribbean and into the north Atlantic, following the path of the fleeing Caledonians and the path of modern-day international maritime trade, envisioned by Paterson and now a reality.

Relieved, we left the mud of Curundú and passed through the mysteriously named part of the city called Caledonia. I had asked and investigated but had never found out why this noisy, over-populated selection of streets was so-called. It had been named Caledonia since the days when Panama was a part of Colombia; a minor battle is recorded as having been fought between the Colombian Liberals and Conservatives at the Bridge of Caledonia during the War of a Thousand Days. It was the last major war Panama was involved in, before the US helped it secede in 1903. I fought my way through the crowded streets avoiding the eponymous *diablos rojos,* red devils, colourful decorated former US school buses, converted by stripping the yellow paint and replacing it with the Panamanian colours of red, white and blue and finished with a picture of a celebrity or politician or plain crook on the back door. The Panamanian bus drivers embrace a wide range of faces: from Shakira to Manuel Noriega, Che Guevara to Whitney Houston. The drivers race each other to the bus stops and are lethal. It is not advisable to get in their way. They crowd the poor streets of Caledonia as people jump on and off, paying the *pavo* or turkey, who takes the 25 centavos fares as they descend from the salsa fury of the inside to the noise of the streets, the colourful fruit stalls and cheap Chinese electronics stores.

My bags were sitting in the apartment in the colonial part of town, the 'Casco Viejo'. The apartment was on the seafront overlooking a dingy market and beyond that across the great bay of Panama to the towers of Paitilla and Punta Pacifica. It was sad to see the bags packed: the clearest sign of the end of a tropical adventure and my happy association with Casco Viejo. The neighbourhood had been forgotten by the city for years, but with the impressive renovation of the old towns of cities like Cartagena, San Juan and Porto Rico, the Panamanian Government now embraced renovation to attract tourist dollars. The original name San Felipe was ditched and the more tourist-friendly names Casco Viejo or Casco Antiguo were deployed to help transform the neighbourhood from a rotting slum filled with forgotten people to a showcase of colonial Spanish, French and early republican architecture.

Casco Viejo is located on a mini peninsula, entirely surrounded by the sea on three sides. It contains some of the most historic and important buildings in the Republic: the Palacio de Garzas, (the presidential palace); the national cathedral; the churches of San Francisco and San José and the former monastery of San Felipe Nerí. It houses buildings which were important to the construction of the Canal. The headquarters of the Compagnie Nouvelle de Canale are situated in the Plaza Catedral and have been transformed into the Interoceanic Canal Museum. The decrepit, vast Hotel Central, which housed engineers, architects, impresarios and others involved in the construction of the canal, stands perpindicular to the museum. And it is because of the French efforts to build the Canal in the 1880s that there remains to this day architecture that would not look out of place in Paris.

With mesmerising light bouncing off the sea on three sides, the sounds of salsa music drifting down the cobbled streets and the eclectic mix of buildings, Casco Viejo has the tropical charm so lacking in the other parts of the city, which now resemble Miami. Many Panamanians advised me against living in Casco Viejo, telling me it was dangerous, noisy, difficult to park, isolated. The guidebooks were less comforting: warning against walking after dark and even urging much caution during the daytime. And whilst some of the buildings have been renovated and dazzle with their fresh pastel colours and bright flower-strewn balconies, far more buildings are crumbling, dirty and half falling down. Bits of wood and corrugated iron woven together with string and plastic make walls and roofs. Large women with enormous curlers in their hair sit outside, sternly watching their thin children play in the street. Husbands in string vests and bottles of beer while away the time listening to salsa and Reggaeton. On every corner, a store run by Chinese families sells tinned sauces, papaya, lightbulbs and rum. And in among this tropical chaos expensive Spanish seafood restaurants sell overpriced lunches to the city's elite and to well-fed tourists.

Returning to London was a difficult proposition after two years of fun. Whilst the exhausted Caledonians were content to leave New Edinburgh, I had considerable reservations after becoming accustomed to sitting on the balcony watching sunsets turn the Pacific Ocean from murky grey to red. And there were *cuba libre* and fiestas to miss. Caledonians were certainly not the only visitors from the old world to enjoy strong liquor in the new.

With the car packed and pink documents safely stashed in the glove compartment, it was time to drive from one ocean to the other. Panama is the only country in the world where it is possible to swim in the Caribbean and the Pacific on the same day with ease. The Caledonians came to this part of the world and the Canal exists here because of the short crossing from one ocean to another. The drive from Panama City to Colón would take around one hour. It could be much shorter, but the impressive 'Corredor Norte', which cuts through pristine green jungle like a dark grey burn, is daily transformed into a congested route up and down the hills of the isthmus, passing dirty towns, overwhelmed with container lorries and weighed-down buses. The wonders of geography have made Panama what it is: a place of transit. William Paterson understood this very well.

For sentimental reasons I drove to Colón on the old road: better to see as much of the Canal as possible from start to finish and to add some sense of completeness to one of my final journeys on this isthmus of shady dreams. Panama was described by John Le Carré as being just like *Casablanca,* but without the heroes. Or as a prominent Panamanian politician joked with me at a party: 'in Panama nobody builds or loses a reputation'. It is a county of contradictions: Pacific and Atlantic; city and countryside; rich and poor; Panama City and Colón. The contradictions are not only geographical: cosmopolitan living jostles with untouched indigenous culture, modernity with lives unchanged for hundreds of years; friendliness goes alongside distrust, and a culture of close family bonds thrives within the fragmented society at large. Life here is all about the Canal and despair; the Canal and corruption. The Canal.

Does Panama exist because of the Canal or does the Canal exist because of Panama? *La Leyenda Negra* – the black legend – troubles Panamanians with the possibly true idea that Panama exists because its creation was a necessary step before the canal could be built. This idea, understandably, undermines Panamanian national identity. Panama was created by the machinations of the USA to prise the short ocean crossing from the obstinate Colombian government. But Panama had made itself independent from Colombia before it was created in 1903. During the nineteenth century Panama had ceded from Colombia, briefly, and styled itself *El Republico del Istmo*, a name which emphasis the importance of its geography and the importance of transit. As Panama celebrated the hundredth anniversary of the Canal in 2014, and as the expansion works on its new locks near completion, the continued importance of transit is readily apparent.

Certainly, William Paterson's project provides the underpinning of the modern-day economy of Panama. The Canal is a considerable employer, as are the free-trade zone, the substantial port facilities at both the Caribbean and Pacific ends and the vibrant service economy which aids, legitimately and otherwise, the worldwide flow of goods and capital. Banking is strong and Panama is full of lawyers. I found myself working for a large Panamanian law firm and was given a loosely defined role as a 'consultant'. The firm was established by a former president and at one time run by one of Noriega's former foreign ministers. It straddled the booming Panamanian corporate world dealing with securitisations, corporate mergers, franchising and the strong maritime sector, whilst looking beyond its shores to service a wide range of Latin American, European and North American off-shore clients in search of 'certainty' over their worldwide assets. The business of attending to the firm's impressive list of clients took me far from Panama: various Caribbean islands, Brazil, Chile, Colombia and beyond. Panamanian law practices are nothing if not international. Lucho was not the face of the law firm, but without his signature on endless directors' resolutions that kept nominee shareholders and directors behind a façade of impecuniosity, the law firm would be less profitable.

⌘

Lucho had been dropped off and richly rewarded in balboas to buy more *seco* before I turned out of the aptly named Area Bancaria and drove down Via España and continuing down Avenida Los Martyros, reflecting as ever how much history was reflected in the road names. The street I travelled down ran alongside two historical parts of town. On the right was the lush green of the former American Canal Zone, a strip of land which ran for a considerable distance either side of the Canal from Pacific to Caribbean. It caused tensions: the martyrs of the street's name were dead Panamanians who had protested against the Americans refusing to allow the Panamanian flag to be flown alongside the Stars and Stripes. By the time I first arrived the Zone had already been consigned to history, but the tensions remained.

The left side of the road housed a poor neighbourhood: Chorillo – a noisy, cluttered neighbourhood of rickety wooden homes and corner shops selling fried fish and cold beer. It was firebombed by the Americans when they invaded in 1989. It was easy for them to attack – they only had to cross Avenida Los Martyros. Their deadly pursuit of Noriega left hundreds dead. The poor suffered more than others. Chorillo still exists, defiantly facing the land that was once the Zone. Turning right I cut down to Balboa, the centre of the former Zone. Many Zonians still live in Panama, anxious not to return to the US but to continue their life of privilege in Panama. They grumble about the Panamanian government's failure to maintain their former home, but overlook the fact that the Canal functions very well. Indeed, the Panamanians were left with the major infrastructure task of expanding the Canal. A multi-billion dollar effort, which thus far has helped Panama enjoy boom times and the strongest economic growth in Latin America.

From Balboa the road passes the enormous Hutchison Whampoa ports and up the southern side of the Canal. The locks at Pedro Miguel and Miraflores were crowded with tourists. Overheated cars parked with happy freight-watching spectators sitting on the bonnets whilst ice cream vendors plied their trade as two enormous tanker ships rose out of the jungle and the muddy cuttings to gracefully slip their different ways through the locks: one heading to the Pacific and the other to the Caribbean. The sight of container ships or cruise ships in the Canal, particularly in the Gaillard Cut (now called the Culebra Cut), is magnificent. Towering manmade structures, rising red and black out of the verdant jungle, gliding silently forward, displaying a measured pace. The Canal creates a perfect harmony between man's technology and the throbbing jungle. The simple graveyard for the French who perished trying to build the first Canal in the 1880s sits beyond the locks in a shady green clearing. The failure of Ferdinand de Lesseps to emulate his Suez success in Panama was a crushing a blow to France. Thousands died. As the Caledonians knew, building reality out of dreams in this sultry corner of the Americas requires unmatched reserves.

Beyond the simple white crosses is the gleaming Puente Centenario: a bridge built by the then president to celebrate the country's centenary in 2003, but which lay unused for several years, abandoned, suspended over the Canal without the necessary lifeblood of approaching roads. The roads have now been built and the massive southern continent of America has a second link to the north.

I was now driving along a dark, well-made road in the midst of the Parque Soberanía. The park is one of the greatest places to experience in Panama: a dense, solid and wild jungle expanse which flows north from the city. It remains relatively untouched by the mass of civilisation nearby. As I drove, the disturbing growl of howler monkeys rumbled through the steamy air, gently at first, firming up and then ratcheted up, booming across the tree tops. Dead anteaters lay by the side of the road – large damp carcasses, a gleam of white and dark brown fur: exotic road kill. The road was quiet and the sweet jungle air rushed in the open window with a welcome cooling effect in the humid afternoon. The jungle air was fascinating: so different from the salty, polluted air of the city. It was rich and tasted of the dark soil. Within the jungle and away from the road it was heavy and cloying, the intensity of the humidity beyond the fringes of the jungle was shocking, even frightening, in its claustrophobic intensity. The humidity's power made me reflect how it would have sapped the energies of Caledonia's landsmen as they cut down the bush to make way for New Edinburgh. Thankfully, I had long since changed out of my muddy suit and grimy white shirt of earlier into Panama's favourite cooling linen shirt, the *guayabera*. I would have to find a taxi and then a bus in Colón to get back across the isthmus when the car was safely deposited on the first stage of its journey back from the old world to the new. For me this was a vivid example of William Paterson's 'door to the seas'.

The road neared the end of the Parque and climbed away from the Canal. A sign announced Camino de Cruces – a part of the cobbled pathway used by the Spaniards to extract their gold from the New World. Much of the loot was shipped from Lima, where it had been collected from all over modern-day Peru, Bolivia and Ecuador and shipped to Panama City. From where it was transported across the isthmus to the Caribbean where the great Barlovento fleet would gather from Cartagena and transport the gold and silver across to Cadiz once a year to fill the coffers of their Catholic Majesties in Spain. The Caledonians never appeared to understand the importance of this: the vital link in a vast colonial scheme run from Madrid for the benefit of Spain, which formed a vital resource for the Spanish kings to fight their holy wars in Europe. Panama was essential. Its geography was essential. Paterson was right, but misplayed his hand.

The Camino de Cruces can still be walked and the stones and the path literally take one back into history. Here Spanish and Creole forces had marched across from Panama City to defend the realm against pirates. Down this very path Drake and Morgan had stolen from the Spanish king. Panama might be small, but its importance in both the new world and the old cannot be underestimated.

The clean road emerged from the jungle abruptly ended by a 'push' – a hotel where very private rooms could be taken for an hour or a night for sexual encounters. Panamanians call them 'pushes' because they are entered by taking a car though a garage door and a button is *pushed* to close the garage door and summon the receptionist to pay for the room. Panama's very smallness has created a flourishing industry in such ventures, given the need for anonymity on the narrow isthmus. From the 'push' the road was once a mangled dirty squiggle across the isthmus. Reddish mud seeped down to the tarmac, with litter strewn everywhere. Vast hoardings cut into the jungle displayed scantily clad women advertising everything and anything from cigarettes to cement. The Corredor Norte has been expanded so the 40-mile transit across the isthmus is now a seamless blur of jungle from a sharply cut concrete line.

The car radio was throbbing to Panamanian music – *typica* – which is a brassy, folky music heavy on the accordion and guitar, mostly soulful laments to the *campesino* way of life and the countryside. Graham Greene, writing in *Getting to Know the General* (his account of the Panamanian dictator Omar Torrijos), complained that it was unpleasant and the hallmark shout, or *saloma*, sounded like dogs barking. Panamanians struggle to reconcile their desires to preserve an identifiable Panamanian culture derived from Hispanic traditions with the Latin American-wide desire to embrace all things from the USA. Music is an area where Hispanic culture holds its own against the northern invasion, and indeed had successfully fought back in the cultural wars. The numerous shopping malls and fast food outlets of Panama testify to a less successful attempt to preserve a distinct identity.

Closer to Colón the trans-isthmian highway passes the road to Portobello. Spanish forts and a great customs house still stand, keeping guard in a dreamlike forgotten dampness. Sir Francis Drake was buried in a lead casket somewhere out in Portobello bay. I had spent the night there once during the Festival of the Black Christ – surely one of the most intense evenings that Panama can offer.

The Black Christ is the patron saint of the *maliantes* – the evil doers. He is cherished by prisoners, criminals and others who have strayed. The festival involved many pilgrims walking on their knees as a penitent to seek forgiveness from the Black Christ at his church in Portobello. Hundreds of pilgrims hobbled along the side of the road, many would hobble on their knees for miles, some are even reputed to come on their knees from Colón. The night of the festival Portobello was lit up with lights and cheap stalls selling religious icons, food and drink. In the ancient church the Black Christ reposed in a large chair on a wooden plinth, a Christ not of the usual alabaster white but black, shrouded in a purple robe with angry black thorns on his head. The penitential crowd swarmed into the light of the church. The heat and stench of hundreds of squashed bodies suffocated the humid air. Burly men with blood flowing from their knees and wax dripping down their naked chests took the enormous wooden plinth and began slowly to take the Christ from his home around the town. At least fifty heaved the *Cristo Negro*'s mighty plinth on their bare shoulders, their legs scrambling and buckling under the weight. As a penitential act, they took three steps forward and two back. Progress was inevitably slow, as thousands followed on their knees with lit candles, through the squalid streets. The swaying procession reflected in the dark shore of the Caribbean. Joining the procession I was crushed by waxy black bodies and moved by their devotion and the mesmerising humming and swaying of the crowd. The heat, the intensity and the faith were overpowering.

❧

Maersk were shipping the car back from Manzanillo port in Colón. It had been arranged by a Scot in Panama City who worked as a shipping agent. A surprising number of Scots work in Panama. Not Caledonians, but Scots nonetheless, who are in Panama as the fulfilment of Paterson's vision, making a reality of Panama as the 'door to the seas and the key to the universe'. Shipping agents, maritime engineers, property developers, bankers and diplomats.

Colón is reputedly the most dangerous city in the world. It doubled up without any apparent disguise as Haiti in the Bond film *Quantum of Solace*. It is a squalid town, corroded and largely ignored by the government in Panama City. Panama remains made up of a diverse series of people. In and around Colón there are still large communities of West Indians who speak beautiful Caribbean English, the descendants of the West Indians who came to Panama early in the twentieth century to build the Canal. Many stayed and they have retained much of their culture and language. It is estimated that in 1920, 31 per cent of Panama's population was made up of West Indians, descended from the 130,000 who left the Caribbean to work in Panama between 1881 and 1914, and ended up making it their home. It is a population which could have been imagined by William Paterson: a hub of trading people from around the world. The Chinese, the Syrians, the Greeks and the Jews all have a considerable presence in Panama and all are involved in significant businesses in the 'key to the universe'.

Colón and its environs were said to be unhealthy by Lionel Wafer in

1699, and what was true then remains the case today. The Caribbean coast is poorly populated and it rains a good deal. The coast is more humid than the Pacific. Colón's colonnaded streets are damp and their colonial arches are crumbling, almost derelict in places. However, life, represented by drying clothes, noisy radios and eager-faced children, colourfully and clamorously emits from the dilapidated windows. Crime is a considerable problem and the Panamanian evening news is full of grainy shots of young, usually black men being pulled, bleeding, from the backs of pick-up trucks and dragged into accident and emergency centres. Gun crime is rife and deadly.

The road to the port passed a high wall topped with razor wire: a vast defence to protect the treasures of such a large and globally important trading area. Thirteen thousand ships pass through the Canal every year from more than eighty different countries. Panama has the world's largest merchant fleet. More than anywhere else, rotten Colón and its free-trade zone epitomise the trading post imagined by Paterson. Twenty of Panama's more than one hundred banks even have branches within the razor-wired walls, additional to those found in nearby Panama City.

Paterson's idea is most definitely alive, but not as he would have imagined it. The Zone, spread over 40 hectares, imports and re-exports more than $12 billion-worth of goods every year. Unsurprisingly, both brand piracy and money-laundering are particular problems. The British Embassy has operatives in town specifically to counter money-laundering and when I first arrived in Panama I was approached by someone working for a government agency at a diplomatic party who asked about my role in the law firm. Would I be prepared to assist with information gathering? It sounded too dangerous. Panama is rife with organised crime. The former drug king pin and dictator, Manuel Noriega, languishes in a jungle prison cell by the Canal outside Gamboa. A Presbyterian entrepôt might have been different.

Beyond the free-trade zone in Colón is the entrance to the Manzanillo port and I swung the car left and arrived at the gate, a fierce security checkpoint, a blaze of mirrors and machine guns glinting in the Caribbean sun. An English-speaking Panamanian appeared and uttered *que sopa?* (what's up?) – a corruption of 'que paso'.

Frank, the representative of Maersk, appeared and started sucking his cheeks in as he walked around the car, making almost imperceptible little shakes of his head. 'It's dirty,' he said. Naturally it was, how could the car arrive at the port looking fresh? He chose not to answer that question. 'We can't take it. We can't bring dirt onto the ship.' In Panama nothing is surprising. We then entered into a longish discussion about the logic of driving a car to the port without it becoming dirty and thus preventing it being boarded. The sun was still strong and sweat was pricking my skin: a solution had to be found, and of course it was simple. Frank suggested the car had to be washed and $30 would resolve the problem. We agreed on $20 for the car wash. The container ship would take twenty-eight days to travel from the Caribbean coast to the UK. Much faster than the dreadful journeys endured by the Caledonians who returned from New Edinburgh.

My taxi pulled up at the Bristol Hotel in Panama City. The Bristol is probably Panama's best hotel: a small, pink building in the Area Bancaria, with powerful air conditioning and dark mahogany public rooms with a self-consciously tropical feel. The days of the grand old Tivoli Hotel on Ancon Hill were well and truly over. I was shown straight through to the dining room where the British ambassador was meeting me at a quiet corner table. Jim stood up and we shook hands and quickly ordered drinks. I had been invited after helping him deal with some personal business in Panama; he wanted to thank me, but really it was I who wanted to thank him. Jim is a fellow Scot and has done more than any other person since Insh and Prebble to shed light on Caledonia. With the force of his own interest in the Scottish project he had encouraged interest both in the United Kingdom and in Panama, which had led to a series of exhibitions explaining the failed colony, which culminated in a glittering evening of lectures, drinks and the opening of a major exhibition in the Canal Museum in the Casco Viejo – the then president's wife, many of Panama's leading politicians, salsa singer and actor Rubén Blades, attended along with the diplomatic corp and several prominent British residents in Panama. It raised the profile of Caledonia far higher than ever before in Panama, where local people had no or only very limited understanding of the importance of their country's history in that of the creation of Great Britain. Jim was also instrumental in raising the profile of Panama.

Jim and I chatted about local people and looked through the menu, which was overtly Panamanian with a twist: lots of coconut, yucca, platano (Wafer's book was right) and seafood (Panama, after all means 'abundance of fish'). Jim was born in Edinburgh and attended the Royal High School before entering directly into the Foreign Service. His life had been a series of interesting postings between stints in London – Brussels, Burma, Kenya, Syria, Angola, Jakarta, Jamaica (as Deputy High Commissioner) – before ending up in the top job in Panama. He had visited the site of Caledonia before, including by helicopter, and also with Sean Connery. Connery visited Panama several times, enjoying the 2003 centenary celebrations, and somehow became mixed up with President Moscoso, Panama's diminutive former female president. He must have impressed her as she granted him a diplomatic passport, and so it was that he became interested in the history of Darien and the Scots' failure there; a difficult history for an ardent nationalist.

Jim would retire soon, after around five years as the British ambassador to Panama. He had been high profile and very successful; he was well known and well liked by the Panamanian elite and had done more than many to raise Britain's profile; he enjoyed informing people that Britain was Panama's largest investor. Cable and Wireless, HSBC and maritime companies had all made major investments in the country. Alongside the unseen hard work involved with being head of mission, the ambassador and his wife had hosted Christmas parties, informal dinner parties, Burns Suppers and occasional celebrations at their grand residence. There had been a rowdy party to celebrate the anniversary of the victory at the Battle of Trafalgar and a wild Burns supper with plenty of tartan, Scotch, haggis (which I brought from Scotland once, the poor-looking tinned variety), 'Highland' dancing and even a piper imported from Jamaica. That annually reconstructed picture of the Scots imagines a Scottishness that would have been alien to the good souls of New Edinburgh in 1699. Caledonia has resounded to the pipes and laughter of a Burns supper: the participants of Operation Drake held a supper at the site in the late 1970s, the then dictator, Torrijos, and his shady intelligence chief, Manuel Noriega, took part. I had met the ageing Colonel John Blashford-Snell in Panama. He had been looking for volunteers to help him with another expedition to Caledonia, and whilst these were not in short supply, his project could not get off the ground as the Kuna Indians had demanded an exorbitant fee for permission to visit the site.

Jim was organising another expedition to Caledonia. He wanted to take a boat from Colón and sail it down the coast and search for the graves or remains of the dead Caledonians. He enthusiastically explained this over lunch. As the ambassador he travelled to Caledonia with a military escort; New Edinburgh's closeness to the Colombian border made it dangerous, and everything had to be carefully planned. The expedition volunteers would live aboard a yacht and they would bring all their provisions with them. His enthusiasm was infectious, but as there was no way I could go, I would have to decline the fantastic invitation. Besides, I wanted to visit the scene alone and to make my own way to Caledonia, however difficult that might be. Jim warned me negotiations with the Kuna Indians was 'ball-aching' and I would have to be careful down there. We said goodbye. We would both be leaving Panama soon.

I was worried about getting to Caledonia. Jim was not the only one to have warned me about the Kuna Indians. They were the indigenous people who thrived in this land before the arrival of the conquistadors in Panama. Little is known about them, their history or their demographic patterns. Sadly, with the exceptions of well-known indigenous groups like the Maya, Aztecs or Inca, historians have a very limited understanding of pre-Colombian America. What we can be sure about, however, is that many Indians died because of war, slavery and the cruelty of the Spanish, while European diseases, which were often fatal to the Indians whose immune systems could not combat them, killed more than these three combined. A combination of those factors probably forced the Kuna to seek refuge on the northern Caribbean coast of Panama and the neighbouring islands. This is where they are based today and this part of Panama is known as the Comarca de San Blas in Spanish, or Kuna Yala in the indigenous tongue.

It is a separately administered province of Panama. During the early years of the Panamanian state, successive governments were intent on consolidating control of the national territory, a task much neglected when the province was ruled from distant Bogotá. Roberto Chiari, an early state-building president, was viewed as an aggressive colonist by the Kuna, who felt he was trying to impose Western values on them. In February 1925, under the leadership of their *cacique*, Nele Kantule, the Kuna violently rose up against the Panamanian police forces in the Comarca de San Blas, killing them. This event became known as the Tule Revolution. Panama at this stage was still a young country and the national government, like many in Latin America, struggled because of poor infrastructure to control events, which quickly led to talks and a peace agreement on 4 March 1925. This granted the Kuna people administrative control over their own lands which they maintain by means of a form of devolutionary agreement to this day. Through a combination of their geographical remoteness (until recently, the Comarca could only easily be reached by boat or air) and given their administrative independence, the Kuna have remarkably maintained their culture and traditional way of life. They do not, for example, permit the owning of private property on their territory; the leaders maintain the property for the benefit of all, and those who have tried to buy land or interfere with this system have met with grim consequences. A property developer who proceeded, against Kuna wishes, to build a hotel on the Caribbean coast returned to find it a heap of smouldering ashes.

There are many Kuna in Panama City living around the neighbourhood of Santa Anna, a poorer, atmospheric *barrio* in the west of the city. The women dress, more or less, just as they did when the Scots arrived over 300 years ago: with cotton dresses, a short mantilla over the head and shoulders, many beads and a distinctive gold ring through the nose. The men dress unexceptionally but are still striking, with short, thickset bodies, gleaming dark hair, clear, treacle-coloured skin and well-defined features. Many Kuna gather in the neighbourhood of Casco Viejo in Panama City to sell traditional Kuna handicrafts. The most important of these is the *mola*, a small square of fabric intricately sown with brightly coloured patterns, and often shapes of animals. Traditionally they make up part of the women's costume, as the *mola* is sewn into a dress or blouse, and these sell for considerably more. At sundown, as the red sun fades into the jungle on the other side of the canal, sinking below the span of the Bridge of the Americas, Kuna women sell their handicrafts along Las Bóvedas, the top of the walls which circle the seaward side of the crumbling old city and look out to the islands that make up the end of the causeway by the mouth of the Canal.

Modern-day San Blas is also occasionally populated with much less welcome visitors: Colombian guerrillas, drug smugglers and right-wing paramilitaries. The San Blas has become tangentially dragged into the violence because of its closeness to Colombia and its remoteness. Exhausted FARC guerrillas have occasionally sought refuge, both in San Blas and in Darien, from the fighting with the Colombian army and the paramilitaries. Both of whom, ignoring Panamanian sovereignty, have followed them across the border into Panama. Panama has no real army, and its Border Police Service is neither trained nor equipped to deal with resisting battle-hardened veterans from Colombia. In 1999 irregulars from the FARC's 57th Front threatened the Kuna in their communities of La Miel, Armila and Puerto Obaldia. Worse was to come, as paramilitaries from the AUC (Auto-defensas Unidas de Colombia) then entered a border village and over 100 villagers fled before them, fearful the paramilitaries would take revenge on those they suspected of aiding or colluding with the guerrillas. Added to this is the constant danger of violence from the Colombian drug smugglers who operate fast speed boats to ship drugs from Colombia to Central American destinations which are then smuggled into the United States. 'Homemade' submarines, light aircraft and clandestine airstrips are all used by the smugglers. It is dangerous to come across these people. Arms shipments going the other way for these various illegal groups also often pass through the San Blas. Who knows how many times smugglers have ducked, ignorant of its history, into Caledonia and rested a while in New Edinburgh, as patrol boats have passed by?

<hr />

My first trip to Darien was not to Punta Escocés, but to the community of Punta Alegre, a community of black Panamanians who reputedly take after the name of their community, Happy Point, and are perennially good-spirited. I was told this Afro-Darienite village was a great place to enjoy the sensual rhythm of the tambor and bullerengue music. The easiest way to get there is to fly to La Palma and then by small boat, but there are also the more interesting options of taking a boat from Panama City or driving to Yaviza and onwards by boat. My mind was made up when I learnt nine people drowned in 2001 on a similar journey from Panama City to Punta Alegre when their boat, the *Don Jaime III*, mysteriously flipped over. Road was fine. The Pan-American Highway runs from Alaska to Chile, stopping only for the 57 miles of impenetrable jungle that make up the Darien Gap. Two British orchid hunters ended up captured by the Colombian guerillas after ignoring very clear warnings to avoid this area. Punta Alegre has had its own Colombian problems. In 2001 six heavily armed Colombian para-militaries raided the town and violently held up the two local shops.

The road trip into Darien would take around five hours and after Santa Fé the asphalt road turned into a dirt track. It was the wet season and the road might have been impassable, but it was worth a try. The road out of the city begins magnificently on the Corredor Sur, a toll road that juts out from the coast across the sea like a long, grey bridge before shortly arriving at the international airport. Thereafter it is a different story: the road passes through 24 de Diciembre, the ugliest town in Panama; cramped in on either side of the Pan-American road, stained everywhere by thick, red mud. The town displays the worst signs of unsustainable, too-quick development – crooked concrete buildings and devastated greenery. At the far side of the town a different world emerges, of mature trees and well-kept fields, with, unusually for Panama, a rather European feel. Many of the people who have settled this part of what was once jungle are Santeños, residents of the eastern province of Santiago, who possess a deeper Hispanic culture and identity than many other Panamanians. How the Conde de Canillas must have desired a road like this when he made his attempt to marshal an army from Panama City across to Punta Escocés to rid himself of the Scots.

The car rumbled on past beautiful lakes near the internal border between the Panama and Darien provinces. As I approached the actual border a large sign blotted out the sky and obscured the dead-straight highway in front. It read *Bienvenidos a Darien* (Welcome to Darien) and was decorated with a poor picture of mountains. I stopped long enough to take a photograph then headed for lunch: a huge plate of rice, beetroot salad, lentils, fried platano and black, soggy meat. The *fonda* (inn) was typical: fly-infested, airless, with the oddest assortment of tables and chairs; it was very much frontier-land. The road outside was a thick, red, mud scar through the emerald jungle and the traffic was limited to the occasional passing pick-up truck, either with people swaying on the back or an impossibly high heap of furniture. Inside, a large glass-fronted display cabinet filled with traditional Panamanian-style hats, machetes, accordions and other self-conscious accoutrements of Panamanian culture tried to tempt customers. The traditional Panama hat is made in Ecuador. It was made popular by Ferdinand de Lesseps, the Frenchmen who failed in his bid to build a canal in the 1880s. The authentic hat worn by Panamanian *campesinos* is more yellow in colour, with brown swirls and a flat top, with a narrower brim worn turned up at the front. It looks rather odd.

After lunch I arrived at the unremarkable town of Metiti: a junction on the Pan-American Highway with a petrol station, a few basic shops, and a cluster of homes. There was no need to stop. From there the road forked down to the large estuary on the Pacific side and Puerto Quimba from where a *lancha*, a motor-powered wooden dug-out boat, would take us through the jungle to La Palma, the provincial capital of Darien. I could feel a vicious cramping in my lower abdomen and sweat began to form on my brow, and looking up I saw the sky darken in empathy. Moments later huge, slow drops of water began to explode on the windscreen, splattering the dust from the road, before gathering the full momentum of a devastating tropical downpour, blotting out the light and making driving impossible. The stomach cramps did not abate; they worsened and increased in frequency, the vast wilderness offered no respite as the rain crashed down. Pulling the car to a stop up against the grass verge, I grabbed my flimsy umbrella and threw myself out of the car into the downpour. Lunch had not agreed with me. I limped back to the car drenched in tropical rainwater.

When I reached Puerto Quimba some forty-five minutes later I had to go through the same, but this time was pointed in the direction of what passed for a toilet in Darien: a wooden shack the size of telephone booth, with shit-splattered walls, a soil floor and in the middle a hollowed-out tree stump with no means of apparent drainage. Three or four dilapidated buildings made up Puerto Quimba, mostly unkempt wooden affairs with corrugated iron roofs. There was no reason to hang around. On the *lancha* after the rain cleared, at the small quayside, I realised with some alarm I had no malaria prophylactics to ward off the malaria found in Darien. Pulling on a long-sleeved shirt, I sprayed myself in 50 per cent DEET. As our floating log sped through the evergreen jungle, the mist was rising from the treetops and I thought with little comfort how my ancestors must have felt coming to this vast jungle in seventeenth-century conditions. Here was I, with all the advances of the twenty-first century, only some three hours in Darien but already sick and fearful of malaria. As our drunk boat captain happily bashed the *lancha* into submerged logs floating under the surface of the estuary I began to fear more than simply malaria, but I was too tired to care. I longed to be in La Palma, in a clean hotel and close to a decent loo.

On all these counts I was to be considerably disappointed. La Palma may be the provincial capital of Darien, but it is little more than a small shanty town built around one main sort-of street on the jungle hillside, surrounded on one side by jungle and on the other by large homes and cantinas supported by large wooden pillars built over the river. I arrived late on Saturday afternoon and already the music from the cantinas was throbbing in the air. The only half-decent hotel was run by a bad-tempered middle-aged woman, who showed us a series of small, cramped rooms, divided from others by plasterboard and all far from immune from the Panamanian folk music. As night fell the main street filled with people sitting on little stools outside their homes, eating from stalls frying fish and *hoaldres* (deep-fried pancakes), drinking beers, the chatter of fast, unclear Spanish and the constant throb of the music providing an appropriate soundtrack. I walked the length of the town and found ourselves standing in complete darkness on the runway of the small airport that sensible people use to arrive in La Palma. Remote places are never without their advantages and La Palma's is the show in the sky. Never before have I been so mesmerised by stars: the sheer number and intensity set against the blackest of skies was beautiful. I stood with a painful neck gazing for an hour pointing out strange shapes and being forced to look away, close my eyes and then peer upwards once more to be impressed all over again by the milky spray of varying intensities of light and colour above. I had to lie down, such was the power of the beauty of the light and patterns and the impossibility of straining necks for such a prolonged period of time. I lay in the long grass and peered upwards; this was a scene unchanged over time, this was the same sky the Caledonians would have seen. Did they derive the same comfort, the same awe? I had to be dragged away to find something to eat.

In town I stopped by the large police station to find out the local security situation. En route to La Palma I had been stopped several times at police checkpoints whilst burly policemen asked many questions, checked my documentation and looked over the car. Whilst the police in the city look fairly tame in their lycra cycling shorts and sunglasses, the camouflage-dressed, machine-gun-wielding border police are clearly a more robust crew. They were bewildered by my idea of visiting the heart of Darien, La Palma and Punta Alegre and warned us against any deep forays further into the Darien jungle: Colombians from the various sides of the conflict were active and had been seen in the jungle recently, and were only thirty to forty miles away.

I rose early to discover breakfasting options were limited: *patacones*, thinly sliced fried platano, with black coffee. Over breakfast I felt four angry red mosquito bites. Despite my long-sleeved shirts and repellent, I had not factored in getting bitten so soon. I had little need to worry: the chances of contracting malaria or yellow fever are slim, but it did make me feel a certain affinity for the poor Scots more frequently exposed. It seemed somehow appropriate I should be in Darien feeling, in a more limited way, the same discomforts as the Caledonians so many years before.

Obtaining a *lancha* for Punta Alegre took some negotiating after breakfast: there was little enthusiasm amongst the boatsmen to head off such a distance on Sunday morning. The crossing, when it was eventually and expensively arranged, was a beautiful one: passing tiny islands by the mouths of the rivers, as dolphins appeared, nosily coming close to the boat, jumping over the waves playfully. The jungle an immense greeness, seemingly impenetrable and devoid of human settlements for miles on end. It was a rather Conradian experience motoring up the rivers with dense jungle on all sides, as what limited civilisation existed seemed to recede further away.

Punta Alegre itself was disappointing. Seen from the river it amounted to a collection of wooden shacks and a few concrete homes clustered around a dirty beach littered with small fishing boats and drying nets. I jumped onto the beach, thanked the boatmen and explored the small settlement on foot. The overwhelming impression was one of poverty. La Palma was rundown, but Punta Alegre looked desolate and ravaged. Many of the homes were little more than two-room huts made out of driftwood, obviously without running water or any amenities. The tracks between the houses were made of dirt, and none of the land was cultivated bar a few rows of platano plants. A few chickens pecked the dusty ground and fled before us. The residents were a mix of black Panamanians and on the far side in their homes on stilts were Indian families. Most were dressed with little more than a pair of shorts and were failing to live up to their jovial image. They were surprised to see me strolling through their village on a Sunday morning. I stopped off to buy root beer and chatted to a local man who said he used to travel a lot after studying fishing abroad. A young boy who followed us down to the beach told us there was a primary school, but the older children were taken by boat every week to the secondary school in La Palma. He liked his quiet life, he said, beaming, before darting off into the jungle.

The heat, the poverty and the sense of claustrophobia were stifling. There was no sign of African-inspired music, just more of the same Panamanian folk and salsa accompanying the men as they mended fishing nets and drank beer. Sometimes it's about the journey not the destination, but it was comforting to think this must have resembled a Cimarrón community hundreds of years ago. Cimmarróns were escaped slaves who lived in secluded communities in the jungle well away from the Spanish. They allied themselves with Sir Francis Drake during one of his adventures on the isthmus hundreds of years ago.

The journey back seemed faster, yet back in La Palma I messed up the times of return *lanchas* to Puerto Quimba and spent a miserable three hours hanging around the quayside waiting for a boat back. Just as I was about to leave the rain began, accompanied by strong winds, and the placid estuary was turned into a scene from *Moby Dick*. Already in the boat by this stage, we motored for one of the homes on stilts and took refuge under its creaking floor. The boat ride back to the car was stomach-churning and frightening. Six hours later, arriving in a darkened Panama City, I was grateful for pollution, traffic jams and bustling, aggressive human contact. The Scots, it seemed to me, had chosen a remote, dangerous but beautiful part of the world, where nature was more than able to hold her own against the attempts of humans to tame her. Several days later I woke with an aching body and a high fever: malaria? Fortunately, it was only a bad fever brought on by the constant climatic changes.

SEVEN

SETTLING IN

It is unlikely that the Scots celebrated Hogmanay in 1698/1699 in anything approaching style. Provisions were low and had been inadequate from the start. Much of the food brought by the Scots had also spoiled, probably as a result of poor storage and exposure to the hot, damp climate in Darien. Attempts at trading their goods for provisions with Caribbean merchants had been clumsily handled by the Scots, who seemed unbending on prices and ignorant of the realities of trading. Trading had taken place with the Indians, but there was limited agricultural land and the more than 1,000 hungry Scots soon ate up Indian supplies of yucca, platano (plantain) and bananas. Neither had the Scots arrived suitably equipped for large-scale fishing. Without an adequate diet, with the harsh climate and the prevalence of disease, the Scots became weaker and their immune systems suffered for the lack of decent food. Productivity began to slump, but worse, fear began to spread and the colonists began to doubt the rationale behind their orders.

However, the year 1699 dawned with optimism for William Paterson. He was intent on encouraging the mental and physical willpower required to turn the small settlement into the great trading colony he had imagined. He was the first councillor to leave the relative comfort of the ships behind and settle himself in a less than comfortable hut in New Edinburgh. Around him he must have heard the daily rhythms of the chopping and banging of clearing and hut construction, as the undernourished Scots sweated in the tropical heat, turning the jungle into a viable settlement. No easy task, as the verdant growth would spring up again almost as soon as it was cut down. There were frequent and persistent rains, which although beginning to ease in January with the onset of the dry season, still troubled the wetter Caribbean coast, turning the streets of New Edinburgh into a muddy mess.

Paterson was expecting the return of a young English merchant, Edward Sands, who had visited Caledonia from Jamaica in late 1698 delivering much-needed provisions in exchange not for money, but for a credit note for the Scots' goods, to the value placed on them by the Scots themselves. Along with the credit note, Alexander Hamilton, the colony's accountant, had left Caledonia for Port Morant with Sands (Port Royal having been destroyed by an earthquake and tsunami in 1692). Hamilton was set to return to Edinburgh to provide a full account of the colony's history to the Edinburgh directors. This was to prove to be a mistake, and was advised against by Paterson himself, as Hamilton was one of the few men with a grasp of trade and knowledge of the Scottish goods for sale. Two other colonists departed with Hamilton: James Cunningham, the ineffectual councillor, and Walter Herries, the mischievous and unreliable surgeon who would go on to cause much trouble with the publication of his account of the supposed stupidity of the Scottish colonial effort in Darien. The Scots would miss Hamilton's help when, instead of Sands, his boss Thomas Wilmot came to Caledonia some weeks later.

By late January Sands' provisions had run out and the Scots were cheered by the sight of a sloop laden with further provisions. Wilmot, owner of the trading sloop, disembarked in a bad mood. His employee, Edward Sands, should not have agreed to supply the Scots with the provisions he had at such prices; the Scottish goods, he claimed, were considerably overvalued. The Scottish councillors refused to negotiate seriously with Wilmot and offered only the smallest concessions on prices. Their pride, it seems was misplaced, as Scottish wigs, cloth and pans would not feed the hundreds of men in their charge. With such poor terms offered him, Wilmot left without selling the Scots any of the provisions he had brought. Paterson had tried in vain to seek a compromise on the price of the Scots' goods; he was well aware of the dangers to the mid-term prospects of the colony if English traders spread the word the Scots' goods were overpriced and they were unwilling to negotiate seriously.

The Scottish response was not to sit idle in Caledonia, but their efforts to relieve the want of provisions only resulted in more trouble. The quarrelsome council agreed the *Dolphin* should sail for the Dutch trading post of

Curaçao, taking with it the large sum of £1,400 in trading goods. Paterson opposed this decision, realising that the *Dolphin* was the least suitable ship in the fleet for crossing the Caribbean, and the error was compounded by the decision to send both Captain Pinkerton and John Malloch, the new captain of the *Dolphin*, on the same voyage. Paterson thought it foolish to send such a high value of goods, with two seasoned sailing officers, in such an unreliable boat. The council ignored him and so with a crew of around 25 men, Pinkerton set off in late January 1699.

We know from the councillors' letter,[1] carried aboard the *Dolphin*, that a mixed picture was emerging after the first month of 1699. The Scots had been told by their Indian friends the Spanish would come to attack them, but they had observed the Barlovento fleet sail in front of the great bay from Cartagena to Portobello, and no efforts had been made to attack. They understood this to mean that the Spanish were not capable of attacking them, which was a fair assessment at that stage. The letter reveals that considerable work had been achieved by the end of January. A 200-foot trench had been dug on the peninsula to turn it into an island, and this had been reinforced with a strong, high parapet, with bastions at various points. The councillors recounted that they had cleared space and begun to put up regular homes; they boasted the place they had chosen had, comfortably, space for over 5,000 men and could easily be expanded if required. They informed the directors they were building a port in which several large ships could dock. Despite this progress they included a plea for help at the end of the letter, hoping that it would not be required, given their last letter had surely arrived and help was on its way. They were not to know this letter had been intercepted by the Spanish and would arrive in Caracas rather than be received by the Company's directors in Edinburgh.

Meanwhile, despite the Scots' intransigence in the face of complaints about their high prices, more sloops had returned to trade. Edward Sands returned in one and a trader called Ephraim Pilkington in another. Both, it would appear, put their sloops at the disposal of the colony. They had also brought a small quantity of essential provisions to sell to the colonists. A few days later more merchants from Jamaica sailed into Caledonia Bay with provisions of beef and flour, but once again haggling over prices led to the departure of the merchants without purchases being made on the part of the Scots. Their departure was hastened when they began to inspect the wreck of the *Maurepas* and the Scots brusquely sent them on their way. Pilkington returned in his sloop, the *Maidstone*, at the end of February, but despite his best efforts he had been completely unable to sell any of the Scots' cloth, wigs, pots or pans. Better news awaited the Scots as Pilkington's ship brought with her a small coastal vessel, *The Three Sisters*, fitted out by Scottish sympathisers in New York, who had agreed to sell fish, butter and flour to the Caledonians, not in large quantities but extremely welcome to empty Scottish stomachs. Soon thereafter Wilmot returned with another trader, Moon, in a sloop called the *Neptune*, and they brought with them another merchant, named Matthias Maltman, to trade. They had no doubt noticed the hungry state of the Scots and assumed they would have been able to trade provisions for money and surely sensible men would have agreed. The council did not see things this way and not only decided against trading but acted in an extraordinary manner against these merchants, for leaders of a so-called trading colony. Pennecuik disliked Moon the first time he had met him and this time, idle and brandy-soaked, he argued with him from the very beginning. Instead of seriously negotiating reasonable prices to buy food for his hungry men, the commodore appears to have quarrelled with Moon over the fate of a homesick Scottish cabin boy named Skelton, whom apparently Moon had taken aboard his ship. Worse was to come with Maltman and his ship.

Councillor Daniel Mackay immediately took against Maltman, accusing him of sailing under a Spanish commission and travelling with several Spanish merchants on board. With Paterson protesting, he bullied the council into having Drummond arrest the ship. From the *Caledonia*, Drummond set out, boarded the *Neptune* and arrested the crew, but found no evidence of a Spanish commission, only two very scared Spanish seamen who had paid to be taken to Portobello. The Scots helped themselves to £100 which they had no right to and used it to pay for the goods their supporters in New York had helped to arrange. If the Caledonians were seriously interested in creating a trading colony, their behaviour was less than encouraging to those who might have been interested in trading with them.

Meanwhile, as the Caledonians set about destroying any disposition there might have existed to trade with them, Pinkerton, battling the seas in the *Dolphin,* was not fairing well. The ship, designed not unlike a brigantine, with a shallow draft and two masts with a square rig arrangement, did not sail well into the prevailing Caribbean winds and as a result Pinkerton and Malloch struggled to control her. Shortly after leaving harbour they were caught up in a storm and struck a rock off the coast. Pinkerton was injured and the ship began to leak quite badly. The Scots had little choice but to run her aground. The tide and winds pushed the boat under the fortifications of the Spanish port of Cartagena. The Scots had a lot more to fear than the modern-day visitor to that city. The Spanish were furious about the Scottish settlement in the heart of their empire and these Scots would not simply be punished as pirates. Interrogators were sent to obtain information from them. A crowd gathered by the walls of the beautiful city, its church towers gleaming above them in the Caribbean sunshine. The Scots came ashore in a small boat as the delighted Spanish governor was brought down from his residence in a grand carriage to oversee this small triumph personally. Pinkerton asked permission to return to save his cargo, but found himself and his crew put in irons and escorted to the vast dungeon complex below the Castillo de San Felipe de Barajas.

When the council heard what had befallen their compatriots, they were outraged. They sent a young Highlander, Lieutenant Maghie, with flags of truce, a drummer and a guard of honour to demand the return of the prisoners and the goods. Unrealistically, the Scots threatened the use of arms 'by sea and land' should the Spaniards not agree. Maghie arrived with the drummer beating and was escorted along the cobbled streets of Cartagena, past the brightly coloured houses with their large wooden balconies of tumbling flowers to the governor's residence. The impatient young Scot was made to wait. He presented the councillors' letter and a copy of the Act of Parliament creating the Company. The Spanish governor was appalled by the Scots' existence close to his city and affronted by the threats contained in the naive letter. He discarded the lot and was about to have Maghie placed in prison when the city's garrison commander interceded on his behalf. The next day Maghie demanded to see Pinkerton and his crew but was sent on his way to Caledonia. On his return from Caledonia, he came across the famed English admiral, John Benbow, who was attempting to rid the Caribbean of pirates and who would soon hunt down the famous pirate Captain William Kidd.

Some historians have singled out Benbow's decision not to help the beleaguered Scots as evidence of English anti-Scottish sentiment. However,
contemporary Spanish correspondence (see below) demonstrates that
somewhat later on Admiral Benbow did help the Scots around this time.
A letter written by the Conde de Canillas on 13 January 1700, when the
Scots' second expedition was trying to fortify its position, urges action to
be taken quickly to prevent their getting help from the English and Danish
ships that were then converged at St Thomas (probably in connection with
something wholly unrelated to Caledonia), reminding his correspondents
of the help that Admiral Benbow's fleet had previously been moved to give,
protecting the harbour with his fleet and seeking to obstruct the Barlovento
fleet 'giving heat' to the Scots. It is not clear whether de Canillas meant
Benbow had protected the Scots from the Spanish fleet in St Thomas or in
Caledonia, although the former is more likely. Confirmation that Benbow
lined up the fleet's ships to protect the Scots from Spanish attack presents
a very different complexion on Scottish–English relations. The Conde
de Canillas' letter, which is very hard to decipher, is roughly translated as
follows:

LETTER WRITTEN BY THE CONDE DE CANILLAS TO THE ROYAL ADMIRAL DON FRANCISCO SALMON COUNT MY LORD ON JANUARY 13TH 1700

My lord I'm replying to Your letter and hereby proceed to make you aware
of the arrangements I'm making at Cartagena for Governor Don Juan
Pimienta, who requests that the three boats that belong to Diego Peredo
will later join those of His Majesty to stop the actions of the Scottish foes,
before they are fortified and pose greater resistance. We must also be suspicious that time will bring along new complications and that they might
be joined by English and Danish squadrons, as it has been reported a new
arsenal is being created on the island of Saint Thomas, and although the
new findings indicate it's intended for the island of Puerto Rico, we must
be suspicious they might encourage the Scots, as happened with Admiral
Benbow's squadron when he went over to that port, giving strength to
the Scots and sought to impede, under several pretexts, the actions of the
Barlovento Fleet posted out at that port after 500 men had set off with me to

the Province of Darien. I am making you aware of all of this news so that in your capacity as great soldiers and subject to His Majesty's wishes, you might write on this occasion to General Pimienta all you find most necessary to alert him on this subject, and to the Governor as well as Don Diego Peredo and also to Captain Don Estacio, being well experienced in the matter, who is to stop by Cartagena and will give you further reasons so you resolve the matter in the best possible way. Once you have given me your resolution on the matter, I will align it with the orders I have to have arrangements made for Darien. By now you will have news that General Don Martin De Zavala has returned with the boats under his command to Spain and left Havana by mid October. He is one of those chosen by His Majesty to aid in the removal of the Scots, with the Barlovento Fleet, along with Don Diego Peredo's boats. All this you will learn on the copy of the Royal Cedula [orders] carried by Captain Don Estacio so you will be aware as well as the governor of Cartagena and Don Diego Peredo and having no other forces in the Americas other than yours and the ones in Cartagena we must work with them with the assurance that The Lord will help all the Holy and royal rulings of our King and Lord in order that heresy would not set foot in these domains with the obvious perils given the larger number of people. There are fewer Spaniards than the settled Scots. I hope you will provide me with reassurance and will inform me with news on the conditions of the boats from Cartagena and that they are ready to sail. May our Lord look after you for many years with kindness.[2]

There is little reason to doubt the veracity of Canillas' account, but it is surprising that it does not appear more prominently in Scottish accounts. The contemporary Scottish accounts fail to mention the help offered to them by their English neighbours when the first expedition made its way to Caledonia. When the scale of the Caledonian disaster became clear, someone had to be blamed. The directors in Edinburgh, Paterson and the councillors were those who were most to blame. It suited them very well to turn the focus of the blame for the disaster on the English. Nationalism had created the overenthusiastic response to the call for investment in an ill-thought-out scheme; nationalism was again used to deflect attention away from the failings of the Company of Scotland to the auld enemy. It is no wonder then that the account of Admiral Benbow helping the Scots against the Barlovento fleet was lost to historians, but it undermines the contemporary account that the failure of the Darien expedition could be laid at the door of the English. The Conde de Canillas' account to a fellow Spanish imperial office is undoubtedly reliable and evidences some of the fraternity that existed in the Caribbean between these troublesome neighbours.

Back in 1699, there was further interaction between the Scots and the Spaniards. The Indian allies of the colonists brought them regular information regarding imminent Spanish attack. The initial fear was of an attack by the Barlovento fleet. In mid January 1699 the fleet arrived at Portobello. The fleet's commander was Don Andrés de Pez. He immediately argued that his fleet was in no condition to mount an attack on the Scots; on the contrary it would need months of careening and refitting before it would be ready. The Spanish king had heard this before. When the Scots sailed through the Caribbean, the Spanish intelligence system had sent descriptions of the boats, numbers of men and their plans. Clearly some had too freely discussed matters in the taverns of St Thomas. The imperial intelligence-gathering system might have been cumbersome and slow, but it worked from St Thomas via Havana to the centre of the Spanish Empire in New Spain, now Mexico. There the Conde de Moctezuma, Don José Sarmiento y Valladares, the viceroy, issued orders to General Don Martín de Aranguren Zavala to dispatch the Scottish pirates from Caledonia. The Spaniards did not view them as traders or colonists. Zavala had actually arrived to deal with the threat of French pirates along the coast of modern-day Florida, but the Spaniards viewed the huge numbers of what they perceived to be well-organised Scots in the heart of their empire as a much more immediate threat. Zavala, however, complained his ships were far from seaworthy after the long journey from Spain and would need immediate careening before undertaking even a short voyage, never mind one that would take them down the coast to Panama to engage with the Scots.

So with all apparently available Spanish ships in desperate need of careening, the solution, as 1699 progressed, appeared to be a land assault on Caledonia. The man in charge of this was the Conde de Canillas, the president of of Panama, a man frightened by the possibility of a repeat of the events of 1681, when Henry Morgan had crossed the isthmus and sacked Panama City.[3] This had left an indelible mark on the Spanish psychology and certainly weighed heavily in their response to the Scots. The Scottish perspective appears to have ignored or been ignorant of the Spanish paranoia of pirates and obvious fear of the repetition of the disaster that Morgan had visited on Panama less than twenty years earlier.

Canillas knew he had to defeat the Scots before the newly rebuilt Panama City was threatened or attacked: an event which would have tremendous repercussion for the Spanish colonial system. De Pez agreed to provide Canillas with 500 men from his ship, who were marched across the isthmus from Portobello to Panama. There they joined the city garrison and some other soldiers Canillas had gathered. They totalled around 1,000 men. In early March 1699 barges were organised and the Spanish soldiers sailed for six days eastwards along the coast of Panama to El Escuchadero, a small port on the Pacific side of the isthmus. Such was the importance of this mission that both the Conde de Canillas and De Pez travelled with the men to lead the onslaught against the Scottish pirates.

Thankfully for the Caledonians the Spanish expedition was not a success. Indians were awaiting their arrival from the sea voyage down the Pacific and would transport the army from their ships to canoes to transport them up the wide rivers of the Darien jungle. The Spaniards had brought with them a considerable amount of kit, supplies and ammunitions to sustain them during the journey and to provide them with the energy and resources to take on the Scots in battle. As a result the canoes were quickly filled with equipment and there was no room for the soldiers. They were forced to walk alongside the rivers, hacking their way through the impenetrable green undergrowth. They entered deeper into the jungle as the river became smaller and eventually left it altogether, striking out on foot over the mountains that make up the continental divide.

At the base of the mountains they arrived at Tubuganti, a Spanish military outpost in the jungle which was used to bolster Spanish control over the unruly Darien province of Panama. It was overseen by Don Luis Carrizoli, a mixed-race servant to the Spaniards, who had a Spanish father and a Kuna Indian mother. It is claimed his father grew up with the Kuna Indians, taking many wives. Carrizoli's family had worked for the Spanish for many years. He would aid the Spaniards in their complicated dealings with the Indians: converting them to Christianity, forcing them to live in villages and bribing them with *paniquiris* (gifts). Much to the Spaniards' fury, the Indians had for years cultivated good relationships with the French, Dutch and English pirates who infested the waters off the Panamanian coast, and as a result were often highly inconsistent in their dealings with the Spaniards. It was a side to the Indians the Scots, like most Europeans, failed to understand. They assumed all Indians from Aztecs to Mayans to Kuna were in revolt against brutal Spanish colonial practices, but the situation was much more complicated than this. Carrizoli had mustered more troops, which brought Canillas' expeditionary force to some 1,500 men, a large army for the place and time.

The enlarged army set out to climb the mountains above Tubuganti, which would present a challenge for them over five days, but eventually they reached the top and were around five miles from Caledonia. They had fought their way uphill, through riverbeds and dense jungle to reach the top, but the men were exhausted, soaking wet from falling into rivers, and they found themselves with dwindling food supplies, wet ammunitions and aching limbs. Canillas, who was in his sixties, was exhausted and had suffered a seizure of some sort on the journey, temporarily losing the power of speech. His efforts to please his masters in Madrid were costing him dear. Fortunately for the Scots the Spaniards' timing was bad, and as they set up camp on top of the mountain that night a huge thunderstorm loomed overhead and the rain began, pouring for three days without stopping, drenching the army, their equipment and rotting their food. The slaves who followed the Spaniards and the Indians up the hills the next day were terrified and a mood of fear began to grip the flimsy mountaintop settlement.

Canillas, ill and exhausted, sought shelter under a poor covering of palm leaves, rattled every few hours by the boom of the cannon from Fort St Andrew on the coast below. In the face of battle with few supplies and nervous men, he understood his situation was a poor one. The men huddled around trees as best they could trying to keep dry, but with the incessant rain and never-ending drips from the branches of the trees, they were soaking, eating damp, rotting food and worrying about what they would do with wet powder in their muskets if the Scots should attack them. Canillas soon realised he had little choice but to turn back for Panama City. Laying siege to the Scots' encampment from a virtually unsuppliable position was a strategically foolhardy position to take. Canillas called a council of war and after much discussion within which everyone sought to maintain their all-important Hispanic honour, the Spaniards headed back to civilisation leaving the soggy, unpredictable and dangerous jungle to the Indians and the Caledonians.

The Scots were aware of Spanish movement in the hills around them: they were relatively well-informed by their Indian allies, who had rushed into Caledonia in early February to warn them of an impending Spanish assault. This was too early for the main assault party led by Canillas, but the Scots were not to know this and believed they were soon to be under attack. The council hurriedly met and agreed James Montgomerie should lead a party of 100 Scots to Pedro's village to assess the situation and repel any Spaniards they came across. Montgomerie set off from Fort St Andrew and led his column of 100 soldiers up the coastal hills into the green jungle. The Scots tired easily with the weight of their packs, rifles and ammunition, made worse by the clawing heat. Nevertheless, they arrived at Pedro's village in a matter of hours and were surprised to see the place abandoned except for a few women crying. The Scots decided to wait in the village and were soon joined by Pedro, who had been following a group of retreating Spaniards. He was delighted to see the Scots ready for battle and earnestly enjoined them to follow him to attack the 25 or so Spanish soldiers and their Indian and slave retainers, as advance party to Canillas' army, who he claimed were camped very close by. Nervously, the Scots followed their Indian hosts and arrived upon the encampment around dawn, spreading out in a line with bayonets fixed and muskets at the ready, but the Scots were themselves ambushed as the Spaniards shot down upon them when they came into view, killing two and injuring fifteen, including Montgomerie. Bravely, the Scots stood their ground and regrouped, but by the time they were able to try to press the advantage of their numbers the Spaniards had long since gone, taking with them intelligence back to Tubuganti to inform Canillas of Scottish strength. Nonetheless, the Scots claimed it as a victory and it was written up to please the directors and the masses in Edinburgh. Montgomerie himself hobbled back to Caledonia to receive a hero's welcome, and had the shot wound he had suffered in his leg treated.

Alarmed by the military engagement, the Scots sent letters of introduction

to the Spanish authorities in Panama and also to the governor of the province of Santa Maria. They explained the Act of Parliament, which they
claimed provided them with the legitimate right to settle in Darien, and
earnestly sought to convince Spanish minds of the lawfulness and justice of
their presence on the isthmus. They truly believed the Spaniards could be
won over by their logic and reason and invited a Spanish representative to
come and negotiate with them, offering safe passage. The Indians took the
letters to Tubuganti, where Carrizoli received them and forwarded them
to his boss in Panama. He responded with all politeness, stating he would
await further orders from his superiors before considering any attack on the
Scots and would leave them in peace in the meantime. In the custom of the
days he ended with, 'God preserve you, Illustrious Council, whose hands I
kiss ...' The Scots were buoyed up by this, little realising Carrizoli was also
receiving correspondence ordering him to prepare what troops he had and
await the arrival of the president himself with an army to evict the Scottish
heretics.

During these various tensions and excitements which punctuated the
first few months of 1699, life toiled on in Caledonia. Thomas Drummond,
the overseer brother of Robert, had been working his men hard and by
April Fort St Andrew was a gleaming circle of fresh wooden palisades with
around thirty guns mounted in its defence. Other guns had been taken up
the hill to fortify the bay and a large moat had been dug across the spine of
land upon which they were settled to turn it into a fortified island. More
and more huts had been erected in New Edinburgh and the colonists had
become more accustomed to living ashore, although the hardcore seamen
would not abandon their ships (with hidden food supplies) for palm-branch
covered huts. The reprieve of the dry season between December and early
April had resulted in some substantial progress, altering the face of the settlement. With blue skies, light breezes and the impressive green jungle, many
were moved to write home of the beauties of the land. Robert Turnbull
wrote to friends in Scotland describing the green paradise and the abundance of wildlife and fruits that made up Darien. Despite these fruits hunger
was still a significant problem in the colony; the inept approach to trading
taken by the council and their unwillingness to compromise on prices had
resulted in a failure to trade goods for provisions. Every day someone was
sent to Point Lookout to try to sight the relief ships the Scots had asked be

sent to aid them from Madeira months ago. They waited and waited, yet they did not come.

They sought solace in one provision they did not lack: strong liquors. Drunkenness was a refuge for many of the men and one of the only forms of bribery the council had left. With fears of Spanish attack by sea mounting, many drank too much. Paterson, the teetotaller, devised a scheme to offer additional Company shares to any man who joined him in taking the pledge. Only one took up his offer. The ordinary planters and volunteers were living on two pounds of flour a week, occasional beef or salted fish and whatever else they could buy or catch or find. But with so many men hemmed in by the jungle on the coast, there were limited opportunities to augment their meagre rationings. The flour was of poor quality and apparently made up of one half maggots and dirt. With the heat and the prevalence of disease it was clearly an inadequate diet for men to work day after day to build fortifications, clear land and sow crops. One Scot mournfully describes his compatriots as 'so many skeletons'. The rate of death from disease, probably yellow fever and malaria, continued, picking up as the rainy season developed later in the year.

All this led to a certain mutinous menace around the colony and the remaining councillors realised they were viewed as part of the problem. Paterson had been lobbying hard for an expansion of the council and at last it appeared he would be able to achieve his aim. After the debacle of the *Dolphin*'s capture in Cartagena and the imprisonment of the crew, the Scots were determined to make some sort of a response. With a misunderstanding of the global geopolitics, they thought a petition to King William might result in him instructing the Royal Navy to blockade Cartagena, demanding the release of the Scots. This required the services of a courier, and since three councillors (Robert Jolly, James Montgomerie and the young lawyer Daniel Mackay, all of whom had previously rejected the proposal to expand the council) had already had enough of Caledonia, Paterson, who did not get on well with any of them, sensed an opportunity to have one of them agree to the proposal in return for carrying the reports and the letter for the king back to Edinburgh. Mackay was the weekly chair of the council when Paterson took him aside to tempt him with the deal. Mackay agreed and allowed Paterson's proposal to be debated, which Pennecuik now supported, probably because he disliked Montgomerie. Jolly argued against, but when the motion was carried he left too. Jolly and Mackay shortly thereafter abandoned the colony, taking a sloop to Jamaica and from there they travelled onward to Bristol and Edinburgh.

Paterson ensured the men he wanted were then placed on the council: Thomas Drummond, Samuel Vetch, Charles Forbes and Colin Campbell. Pennecuik must have regretted his support of the motion and became isolated as the only sea captain on the council. His power had come to an end and his mind turned towards how he might best exit the colony. Panic spread through the colony when Pennecuik refused to provide information about what stores he had aboard, and this was made worse when he began to take on board casks of fresh water and ballast. No sooner had he done this for the *Saint Andrew*, than the captains of the *Endeavour* and the *Caledonia* followed suit. The planters looked on in dismay from the shore.

Towards the end of April as authority, morale and the cohesiveness of the colony continued to deteriorate, the council decided to call elections and call into existence a parliament to aid them in governance. It seems clear this was not something they embraced, but felt was necessary to provide, in today's terms, a sense ownership to the planters, who were wondering why they were suffering, starving and dying painful deaths in this strange jungle. New Edinburgh was divided up into eight wards and elections took place to find eight representatives of the people to aid in government. The council's candidates faired very badly and the planters took the opportunity to elect people from amongst their own position to give themselves a better voice in the decision-making process.

The new mini-parliament and the councillors soon met in New Edinburgh's largest building and in the damp heat set about drafting a series of new laws by which the colony would be governed. The '34 Rules and Ordinances' were discussed, amended, refined, voted upon and thereby enacted. Some must surely have come as something of a surprise. Blasphemy and disrespect to the colony's officers was punishable by hard labour and a diet of bread and water. The penalty of death was enacted for murder, rape, burglary, robbery and treason and, more usefully for the nervous leaders of an increasing desperately band of hungry men, death was also enacted to be the just penalty for mutiny, sedition and even disobedience. Other laws were far more liberal and attempted to describe the civil rights to be enjoyed by the Caledonians. No man could be detained without trial for more than three months, courts, juries and laws against bribery, partiality and corruption were all established. The election process and the laws passed showed a certain maturity in the colony. To underline this, the first measure taken by the new parliament was to appoint a committee to undertake a full inventory of what provisions were left, much to the fury of some of the sea captains, who refused to comply when ordered to transfer their far better-stocked stores to the shore.

Tensions between landsmen and seamen continued and were exacerbated as conditions worsened for the first expedition. Food and hunger dominated men's minds and desperate but very limited trading took place with the few boats that passed by. The Scots were perplexed and no doubt angry at the failure of the directors in Edinburgh to send relief ships. Daily, men peered across the horizon hoping for what the colony needed most: supplies and the enthusiasm and energy of well-fed, fresh recruits from Scotland. Day after day, they waited and retired disappointed.

The directors in Edinburgh were in financial difficulties, but had managed to fit out one ship and send her to Darien. Luck was against the Scots, however. She was shipwrecked off the coast of Jura and the provisions she carried sank to the bottom of the cold sea. The hungry Caledonians would have to wait.

EIGHT

DARIEN

Caledonia is slightly more accessible today than it was in the days of William Paterson. Travelling alone to the area is difficult. Other than the native Indians who live there, few people go there. There is no form of tourism and those who have visited have formed part of official expeditions. Logistically, at last, Caledonia can be reached by taking a small plane from Panama City across the isthmus, then down the coast to the remote south-west corner of the Caribbean, close to Colombia. From a small landing strip the trip involves continuing by boat down the coast for another 20 miles.

The Kuna Indians are organised into tribes and each tribe is based on a particular island or series of islands. The tribes do not always cooperate or get on well. Each tribe or village is ruled by a *sahila* and sometimes by a committee of wise men. The *sahilas* take part in the 'Congreso General de Kuna', effectively the Kuna parliament, which meets several times a year, mostly at El Porvenir, but also in other locations and in response to incidents or problems.

The Kuna of Mulutupu consider they have some control over the area in which Caledonia is situated. In preparation for my visit I spent considerable time liaising with the Institute Panameño de Turismo about visiting Punta Escocés. No help was forthcoming and no Kuna would organise anything from outwith the area of Punta Escocés. As troubling as it appeared, the only solution was to fly down the Caribbean coast, grab a boat and hope for the best. It seemed a very unimpressive plan.

Early one morning, the busy airport on the canal side of Ancon Hill lay in early morning darkness. The departure area was brightly lit and full of brightly dressed Kuna Indian women and their small husbands. Air Panama advised me to wait and assured me I was first on the cancellation list. It was so early the restaurant was not yet open, so I found a quiet corner and sat down to wait, watching the endless bustle of people and the heavily taped together cardboard boxes and selection of plastic bags that served as luggage. By 5.50 a.m. the flight had been called and the passengers had trooped through security, but I was left behind. I went in search of a greasy Panamanian breakfast and my last cup of coffee for a few days.

By 7.30 a.m. another flight was called and around twelve people trooped through. Queuing, I stood a foot above the rest of the passengers, Kuna Indians surprised to see me taking their flight. Whilst some San Blas islands cater for tourists and some have small hotels, these are found further away from the Colombian border and are closer to Colón. Mulutupu, my destination, has no infrastructure for visitors and its closeness to the Colombian border discourages the development of any such facilities. It is not unknown for there to be attacks by both guerrillas and paramilitaries in Panamanian territory, the border between the two countries being porous and difficult to control. The plane was an uncomfortably small twelve-seat propeller plane, painted in bright red and white, the livery of Air Panama. The plane coughed into life and we taxied around before heading down the runway and after what seemed only a very short distance, pulled up and flew over Ancon Hill, the Casco Viejo and the shimmering tower blocks of the modern city. The normally grey-looking Bay of Panama appeared blue in the morning sun.

The flight from the city took an hour and crossed the isthmus further east of Mulutupu, crossing Lake Bayano in the middle of Darien before finding the Caribbean coast and following it down towards Colombia. From the window, once we had cleared the city, the view was a mass of green, an enormous spread of broccoli-like treetops and canopy cover of intense, remote cloud- and rainforest with brown-stained gashes of river or lakes breaking up the emerald monotony. Near Lake Bayano square, brown, Indian settlements nestled in roughly cut clearings: cut off completely by road, but well supplied by Darien's own network of rivers and streams. The monotonous hum of the propellers reinforced the sense of far away; of time and distance travelled from the modernity of the city to a pre-modern world, captured in time, protected by its own remoteness.

The turbulence was unpleasant. Travellers in Panama are warned to fly in the morning before the hot afternoon air makes journeys more challenging. The turquoise streaks of coastal waters were a welcome sight as we neared the Caribbean, the clouds above the sea less menacing than the angry grey cumulus the plane fought and bounced through over the Darien mountains. The little plane swept down and low to the right and descended several thousand feet, flying low to the coast. Ragged yellow beaches passed below, deserted except for stray logs and dry coconuts. A considerable amount of coral protects the beaches from the heavy seas, keeping a beautiful range of blues spanning out from the coast to the deeper waters, but most eye-catching were the small, densely populated islands and on-shore settlements – home of the Kuna Indians. Each island is small and often perfectly formed. In the centre, spanning out to the coast of each island, small palm frond-covered wooden huts appeared, tightly packed together, like a monotonous patch quilt. Small boats paddled their way around the islands and the occasional white sail stood out against the blue background.

Before arriving in Mulutupu, the plane swooped down and bounced hard onto a small concrete landing strip on the mainland, close to the island of Ustupu, from where many little *cayucos*, small canoes carved out of tree trunks, were furiously paddling across the water to meet the arriving passengers. A few passengers were getting off, and a series of soggy cardboard boxes held together by string, old plastic bags and boxes of doughnuts were carried down the steps to the waiting *cayucos*. From the landing strip the mountains provided a sharp contrast to the lazy blue sea and the angry sky. The Scots would have sailed down this coastline before they arrived at Punta Escocés. It is not physically beautiful in a conventional sense, but the dramatic, distant atmosphere holds a power, a sense of authority, something similar perhaps to the quiet majesty of Glencoe or the western coast of Sutherland. With so many coral reefs, the Scots would not have dared sail close to the shore. Hidden reefs break the water hundreds of metres out to sea, and a palette of blues spills out from the beach, hinting at the varying depths: treacherous sailing for the inexperienced.

Much remains unchanged from the late seventeenth century, with one major exception: 300 years ago the Kuna Indians lived mostly in settlements on the mainland. Today, the islands hold most of the 50,000 population of

Kuna Indians. Historians are unsure why they moved, but many consider that they abandoned their traditional way of life on the mainland because of unrelenting pressure from the colonial authorities and efforts to make them conform to a modern way of life. The Indians' fiercely independent streak continued well into the twentieth century, and they have been prepared to spill blood to preserve their culture and way of life. Island living offers greater safety, further remoteness and greater control over their own affairs.

The plane took off again within five minutes of landing and carried on down the coast, flying over more cluttered islands and the occasional, smaller, mainland settlement. Within fifteen minutes it banked steeply to the left and turned low over an island to land at an airstrip located on a small, well-kept island, dedicated to the runway. The plane bumped sharply down on the concrete strip and sped alarmingly towards the sea before pushing its nose down and braking violently, swerving side to side furiously before pushing hard around to the left, where it shuddered to a halt beside a small wooden *bohio* (palm-frond hut). Sliding down the stairs first, I was greeted by a smiling girl asking for the $2 in airport taxes. A grinning young Indian in an enormous yellow and black cagoule stood by a *lancha* gesturing me to get in, to travel from one island to another.

At the bottom of a small path a wooden jetty snaked into the calm seawater and tied to it were three or four dug-out canoes, some with outboards, some with only paddles. The boatman headed for a motorised launch and the engine coughed into life, straining to pull the dead, hollowed-out tree away from the airport island towards nearby Mulutupu. Mulutupu is perhaps 700 metres across and long, and from the sea a variety of small wooden homes huddled together on the waterline were visible. The water was like oil, smooth and rippling heavily against the heavy wooden *lancha*, gentler than the fierce seas beyond the reefs. The Indian homes are made out of wood, mostly white cane and topped with palm leaves, orderly and clean from a distance. Sandwiched between the houses and the shoreline are a series of tall structures with long legs suspended over the water – these serve as toilets, and were doubling up as climbing frames for the small children who perched from the sides and top, playing and jumping in and out of the water. Occasionally a modern concrete building appeared from between the curtains of white cane, but the overall picture was of a way of life unchanged in hundreds of years. Besides the plane, outboard motors seemed to be the only significant change to the Kuna way of life, and these were far from common, outnumbered easily by sails and paddles. Before reaching shore, the canoed paddled closely down the side of the island, stopping occasionally to drop off large yellow tubs to smiling women who poked their heads around the doorways of their tidy homes when it pulled up, and the yellow-cagouled Indian whispered something strange in the melodious, soft Kuna language.

Once on the island I found myself facing inland and looking at a neat row of densely packed white cane homes, mostly oval in shape with large overhanging palm-frond roofs. The doors were made of tightly packed wooden slats and there were no windows. By each hut was a clearing with a space for an outside fire, and smoke was drifting from a number of fires and from the roofs of several huts. The paths between the huts were very narrow, made of sand, and walking between the Kuna Indians' homes involved carefully bending over to avoid a mouthful of palm frond. The cagouled boatman enquired in Spanish of the purpose of my trip, but wary of specifically mentioning Punta Escocés, I offered a vague answer about better understanding Kuna life and seeing some of the coast. He looked perplexed. Before I could progress further into the island I was shown into someone's home and asked to sit on a very low wooden bench. I found myself in a damp space between a traditional hut and a modern building, in which were slung several bulky-looking hammocks. A little woman stuck her head out of one and gave me a quizzical look. Relying on Lionel Wafer's guide to the Kuna language I pointed to her hammock and said, 'cappuha' she stared back, puzzled, slowly smiled, nodded and went back to sleep.

Before long the boatman returned with an older Indian, short, with a round face and the distinctive Kuna features of a long nose, droopy ears and a wide mouth. Most Kuna are very short, with thick black hair and a waxy complexion, given added distinctiveness by the stretched, elongated pull on their features. He spoke limited English, and although keen to practise, the conversation was smoother and made more progress in Spanish. Straight to business he extracted $10 for the boat ride across from the landing strip.

Sitting on the low bench and trying desperately to be casual but caught by a strong and somewhat impatient desire to get to Punta Escocés, we talked. Trying to sound vague about boat trips around the area and visits to other

Kuna communities, some nice beaches were discussed. That was possible. There were facilities for tourists, he explained. The cagouled boatman looked on intently, sensing money might be about to change hands. All commerce on the Comarca is used for the overall benefit of the community and the *sahila* determines how it is spent and on what, I was told.

My trip involved seeing two different parts of the Comarca de Kuna Yala: Caledonia and, of course, Punta Escocés. Caledonia is a Kuna community based on a small island near Mulutupu. The name is an obvious interloper. The names of the other islands and Kuna communities are distinctive and similar: Mulutupu, Tubuala, Mamitupo. The difficulty was the visit to Punta Escocés.

Sitting on the low wooden bench the heat was oppressive, and a salty dampness oozed from everything. Flies and chiggers were hungrily buzzing around bare ankles. This was not a place to spend too much time. The conversation turned towards a possible itinerary and the best approach was to be as nonchalant as possible about Punta Escocés, given the apparent sensitivities around visiting the lost Scottish colony. But it did not work; as soon as these words were out, albeit carefully camouflaged in a string of other possible destinations, the older Indian immediately picked up on the significance of Punta Escocés; he began repeating the words *patrimonio historico* and looking at me meaningfully.

The dilemma was whether to break cover and plead to be taken to Punta Escocés or continue to plead ignorance about the special nature of this destination and continue to push for a *lancha* to cover the general area with a short time there. The conversation moved naturally on to discuss the price of an undefined day-long or two-day expedition, but it was immediately obvious this would be a lengthy negotiation and he declared he was not able to decide, only the *comisión* could organise a trip and only they could set the price.

Who were the *comisión*, and could he explain to them about the expedition? He gravely shook his head: they could not meet until sundown at the earliest; they were at sea, fishing. There were several hours to wait, but there was time to pursue a different course. I was taken across the island to the only shop. Housed in a dilapidated concrete building surrounded by cane huts, it was a sorry store selling old cans of tomatoes, candles, rice and beer. Politeness dictated something was purchased and a lukewarm can of Balboa lager was the least bad of the available options. The older Indian, who would not divulge his name, headed off rapidly across a wide open space on the island, littered with fishing tackle and rusty cans. The far side led to a rotten building with a broken door. Inside a musty dampness caught at my throat and upstairs a filthy room with a broken bed was proudly shown to me. A small wooden sign shamefully announced this was a guest house. It had all the appearances of a failed attempt to encourage tourism twenty years ago. On the mildewy mattress on a rusty iron bed I placed my bag. This was a diplomatic coup and afterwards there was much slapping on the back, smiles and rubbing hands. A small hammock in the corner of a Kuna family's hut would have been more comfortable, cleaner and culturally more enticing. Friendships had to be formed, however, and if the cost of visiting Punta Escocés was a dishevelled night here, then it might be worthwhile.

Outside on the increasingly muggy island, small crowds of children played football amongst the puddles; some went totally naked and a few wore underpants. There was little to see on the island apart from endless rows of white cane homes, small winding sand paths, puddles and the rocky shore with the raised toilet structures. Men wandered around without much direction and there seemed to be a real scarcity of women on the island. As we wandered in no apparent direction I returned to the issue of when the community elders who make up the *comisión* might meet. Could a message be sent to them, to ensure they would meet this afternoon? As we walked, the unnamed Indian talked in a strident manner about how much money other visitors had paid to visit Punta Escocés: thousands of dollars to anchor their yachts in the bay to carry out research or just to have a look around. Colonel Blashford-Snell had had his ambitions for a new expedition down to Punta Escocés ruined because he could not afford the price tag the Indians had put on granting him access to the area. The British ambassador had issued me stern advice that negotiations with the Kuna Indians were going to be difficult.

In the centre stood the island's largest structure, an open-sided hut with a large roof made of palm fronds. It was the size of a basketball court, with wooden supports around a sandy floor. The mystery of the scarcity of the women was resolved: around 200 beautifully dressed Indian women, with their distinctive red mantles, bright mola blouses, beaded legs and glinting gold nose rings crowded in the semi-darkness, engaged in discussions under the thick roof. Bowing low to enter, we stepped into the community hall and sat down carefully on a low wooden bench at the back. The smell was strong and the light was bad under the heavy roof. The women were speaking excitedly in their delicate, high-pitched voices in the Kuna language, their rapid hand movements and animated gestures and occasional sharp screams undulated across the midday heat and gloom. It was impossible to understand anything of what they said but in the intensity of their voices and the ripples of indignation and dismay that travelled under the roof I could tell something was being keenly debated. I asked why the discussion was so heated. My companion was uncertain whether to explain their cause for concern and was soon joined by another, younger Kuna. They laughed quietly then sat in silence.

One of the women had been disciplined by the *comisión* for using bad language. She had been overheard swearing in Spanish and as a result had been condemned for this by the all-male *comisión* and sentenced to having her hair shaved off. I looked around in the murky half-light for the cruelly marked victim but she was not present. She was in a period of shame, and it was not thought appropriate for her to be present before the proceedings, my companions explained.

The discussion turned more generally to the nature of the disciplinary system on the Kuna islands. From what I understood, they appeared to apply their own laws, pre-modern, non-state customary laws, an anthropologist's dream. Various punishments could be applied to the Indian community by the *comisión*, whose decisions appeared to have no formal safeguards, appeals or court systems. The Kuna islands were part of Panama, but the state's institutions did not penetrate the rainforest which separated the communities from the rest of Panama, with the exception of immigration law. The Kuna regulated behaviour as they saw fit and had rules developed by the *sahila* to cover the difficulties of regulating behaviour on the island. Property was communally owned and everybody worked together for the benefit of the community. Fines were imposed for drinking outwith designated Saturday and Friday nights; for fishing without permission; for sleeping with another man's wife without his permission; or for challenging the authority and will of the *comisión*. It was obviously a substantial power on the small islands and mainland of the Mulutupu Indians. This explanation of the unaccountable power granted to the Indians who sat on the *comisión* provided a stark warning not to step out of line, emphasised by something powerful reflected in the remoteness and unchanging nature of their way of life on the sandy little island. Panama City might only have been a short boat ride and flight away, but the guarantees of Western culture and civilisation were too far away to provide either comfort or protection.

Returning the focus to the objective of visiting the Scottish colony, the conversation was pushed back to the theme of a boat trip along the coast. I realised that the more this agenda was pushed, the more obvious the importance of it would be apparent and therefore the more would be the cost, in all sorts of ways, of getting an expedition together to visit Caledonia. On the other hand, it was easy to foresee a torpid, uncomfortable three or four days marooned on the islands with only promises of a future trip. This was not an easy place to be. At a diplomatic party the evening before, I had joked with the British consul to make enquiries should I not return within three or four days. Visitors had gone missing in this part of the world before and I had already spotted several Colombians hanging around boats on the little quay when I arrived. Their presence on the island was hard to explain.

Smiling at my impatience the younger of the two Indians, now with his yellow cagoule draped over his shoulders like a cape, was dispatched to find a member of the *comisión* and within an hour they returned with a smiling Indian with clear features and much better Spanish. He introduced himself and small talk was exchanged at the back of the large hall, as the musical discussions drifted over the wood smoke from the exasperated Kuna women. Within fifteen minutes or so, the conversation was pushed back to the possibility (never mind further necessary discussions about the cost and logistics) of a boat trip down the coast. He nodded and said yes this was possible but would have to be arranged by the other members of the *comisión*, that I had arrived without notice, that I would need to spend a few days on the island with them, and that there would not be a problem, but a formal decision would be taken tomorrow or the day after and I would be able to get over to Punta Escocés and the other places within the week. 'The week!' I repeated to myself, reeling.

This was disheartening. It was apparent Punta Escocés was being used to maximise profit for the island, a noble enough reason, but spending four or five days would ensure my money would run out, it would be difficult to arrange a flight back to the city, there were few flights and of course there was no guarantee a visit would be arranged at the end of that day. There was also a safety issue; it would soon become apparent a gringo was marooned on an island. It was far from sensible to be stuck in the wilderness off the coast of Darien, a few miles from the Colombian border, with no means of communication. Needless to say, my Panamanian mobile phone was dead.

Punta Escocés was *patrimonio historico* for the Indians and they must derive some benefit from it, plenty of people had visited and paid thousands of dollars to do so, but look, he exclaimed, waving his hand around generally, where were the benefits for Kuna children, for Kuna women? There was no option but to agree with him. But paying thousands of dollars was not an option. The conversation was all negotiation, part of the bluster and the attempt to drive up the price. Little progress was being made and the afternoon trundled on with its oppressive heat and a dank smell of bad seawater and acrid smoke. The Kuna women were tiring of their heated discussions and some were bundled together, sleeping around the outside of the hall. A small Kuna male sat unmoving on a small chair in the middle listening.

Frustration was starting to take hold and a firm programme for visiting New Edinburgh had to be developed fast. I asked the Indians to reconsider and agree to put together a trip for the next day and to agree the price and the logistics, but they would not, their decision reinforced by a fear of the authority of the *comisión*. 'When might a decision be taken?' Alarmingly and dishearteningly the recently arrived Indian stated it would not be today, probably not tomorrow either, because one member of the *comisión* was in Panama City, one was sick with malaria, one was collecting fresh water on the mainland and the rest were fishing. Advance notice should have been given, he reproached me. There was little point explaining contacting the island was impossible, IPAT (the Panamanian Tourism Agency) was not interested and the Kuna representative at the tourism ministry did not return calls. He smiled broadly, leaning forward and nodding and with his hands outstretched told me 'stay, enjoy the island, make your home in the hotel and buy what you like at the shop'. The cagouled boatman moved closer and, speaking softly in my ear, asked if would I like to spend the evening in his hut.

I sat feeling distinctly uncomfortable. I had spent all day on one small island, with no prospect of leaving. I was stranded. The Indians would not let me leave until I had spent a few days spending money. The thought of the run-down hostel with its rusty bed, unfinished windows and lack of plumbing was unappealing. The member of the *comisión* then played his best negotiating card, 'you have arrived without permission, you shouldn't be here. Everyone needs permission. Anyone leaving the island needs the permission of the *comisión*,' he told me gravely, nodding, without a smile across his broad mouth. It appears I was being both propositioned and threatened by the Kuna Indians of Mulutupu within the space of a few minutes. The Caledonians had received a better reception 300 years earlier.

Leaving them, I wandered along the sandy paths to decide the best way forward. The poverty on the island was oppressive, the heat was unavoidable and insects had found a new target. Perched on a slippery rock, gazing out over the sea beyond the island, I could see the landing strip and further down the coat, the route that would take me back into the history of my fellow countrymen. Caledonia lay less than an hour away but the reality of actually visiting was now in doubt. The Indians could refuse to take me, and more likely yet, they would ask me to return after keeping me on the island for a few days. I was in effect a prisoner, unable to leave and with no means of communicating with anyone off the island. The price tag the Indian chiefs would place on my simple trip down the coast might be extortionate. I had brought $200 with me and would pay more if necessary. Some Caribbean Colombians watched me suspiciously from their coconut boat. They were trawling the coast, buying coconuts from the Kuna and taking them the 30 miles down to the Colombian border to sell them. They were known to trade goods other than coconuts the other way. They did not like foreigners. This was not a place to be hanging around. I went back to the crumbling hostel, picked up my bag and returned to the waiting Indians.

The motorised *lancha* glided across the still water, leaving Mulutupu and the threatening Indians behind. On the boat was a bigger Indian who had been told by the *comisión* member to take me for a tour of the bay, but not of course Punta Escocés. Permission had been granted to visit some neighbouring islands and beaches. I had negotiated to pay $40 for a trip to some of the neighbouring islands. The boatman was given instructions not to let me leave and that I should be brought back to the island before it got dark. My guide was twenty-four and unmarried, he had left the islands only once several years ago for Panama City and held no curiosity about the wider world; it was not necessary, he said, he was happy. I explained the history of Caledonia, which he knew nothing of, but was interested to know about the history of his people and appeared sad. He was not aware of why the neighbouring Kuna community was called Caledonia. The little boat stopped at a few beaches and I feigned interest: they were beautiful, calm and peaceful, protected behind the underwater fortress of coral that made the seas easy to traverse in our dug-out tree trunk, but treacherous for larger ships.

I had to reach Caledonia. I had prepared myself to part company with the Indians of Mulutupu. This was not a decision easily arrived at, but the entire day the experiences on the island were at best frustrating and difficult, and at worst threatening. The over-interested Colombian coconut traders talking swiftly into their radios confirmed in my mind I was not going to languish on the island for four or five days. It would be better to find other Indians, on another island, and ask them to help. Tubuala was ruled by a different *sahila* and was close enough to Punta Escocés. I prepared to jump ship and find another route to Caledonia.

The boatman had no problem when asked to travel close by Tubuala, but cautioned he could not land there because he was from a different community. He pulled close to the island. Unsure how I would get off the boat and on to Tubuala, I had taken off my boots and tied them to my rucksack, which was firmly on my back. I would swim if I had to. From the sea, the island looked much like Mulutupu: a dense patchwork of white cane huts crowding down to the rocky shoreline. The largest island was joined to a smaller one by a long, low footbridge. Before the boatman could speed up to pass under the concrete bridge I stood up and placed both hands on a steel rail coming out of the concrete pillar. Lifting myself up, almost falling back into the water, I managed, just, to pull myself up the side of the pillar of the bridge. The engine cut out immediately and the boatman looked up at me in alarm. I apologised, paid double, waved and turned to go. He was unhappy and cursed me as I made for the centre of the little island. Looking back, he stood, uncertain, in his wooden boat, bobbing up and down, drifting further from Tubuala.

As I turned away from the shore and into the maze of cane huts I was met by the sudden appearance of bare-chested women running from their homes to watch me and smile. They had exposed small breasts and broad smiles, replete with beaded legs and delicate sandals. The Kuna women reverse the rules of nature; they are exotic, colourful, unlike their surly male partners. Smiling heavily, I asked them where I could find a boatman, but they spoke no Spanish and returned my words with beautiful smiles and fey glances. Waving, I moved on only to be lost between a maze of white cane and palm-frond huts, with paths narrower and windier than Mulutupu. Worse, the houses were closer together and the palm fronds extended further, almost sheltering the pathways from the rain which was beginning to fall, forcing me to double over as I scurried along the darkening paths, uncertain what sort of reception my unannounced invasion of this most remote place would generate, the sweat beginning to pour down my back, forehead and into my eyes.

Within 100 metres of the sea I was lost and turned to an open-sided hut where a skinny man lay in a hammock, surrounded by young women on plastic stools. He jumped from his hammock at the sound of my strange voice, picked up a hat and bounded over to me, invading my space with his strong, unwashed smell and curious eyes. I was after a boat and driver to take me down the coast for a couple of days. He was unfriendly and suspicious. He eyed me slowly as he backed off and pulled on a shirt and led me from his home along more back-breaking paths through sandy puddles to the home of an old Indian man, wearing no more than what looked to me like old gardening trousers and a battered trilby set at a jaunty angle. This man, I would later discover, was the *sahila* of the Indian community of Tubuala and at the same time as being autocratic, he also ran a more liberal regime than the *comisión* of Mulutupu.

We sat down on plastic chairs in the narrow path outside his wooden home. The light was beginning to fade and my body ached from tiredness and stress. At first we sat in silence as watched me. It was unclear whether he even spoke Spanish. He gave the impression I may as well have been from Mars. Eventually, he spoke slowly with a measured Spanish. He wanted to know my background: who I was, where I was from, the size of my family, how I had arrived. It was getting darker and I had no idea where I would spend the night or whether I could eat, but the old man was not to be rushed. He wanted to know the measure of me. He fell into a silence, digesting the information I had given him, motionless. I feared he was on the verge of falling asleep on the torpid island. I asked him if he knew of

Caledonia, not the island, but the former Scottish colony. 'Si' he responded, 'it's close.' I smiled widely and asked would he take me there for a day or two? He nodded, yes, he could. He then offered to provide me with a boat, boatman and a hammock for two nights. Without drawing breath I agreed, overwhelmed at the escape to Tubuala and some considerable levity at the thought of not having to deal with the men who made up the *comisión* of Mulutupu. The *sahila* coughed loudly, stood up and asked for $50. He was clearly embarrassed. The money was handed over without hesitation. It had taken a day, but at last a route was established which would take me in the steps of the Caledonians back through history to New Edinburgh.

Tired from the early start, the heat and the negotiations, a shower, food and sleep were essential. The trilby hat-wearing *sahila* whispered some orders and another Tubuala Indian appeared and took me to a cane hut. The door creaked open to reveal a mess of jumble, old clothes, fishing tackle and assorted shoes. In the middle, strung from pillar to pillar was a sturdy hammock. In the musty light I could see a litter of old batteries, artificial flowers and rusting knives and machetes. Near to the hut, by the sea, was what looked like a pig pen, which turned out to be a raised platform surrounded by waist-length white cane, with a large hole in the floor. Washing involved clambering over large stones on the raised platform and pouring water from a plastic tub with a small pot. The cool water refreshed and helped flush the stress of the circular negotiations and the threats of earlier in the day. A Kuna family sat only a few metres away, eating fish and rice from bright plastic plates, listening to some unidentifiable music on a radio. Back in the hut, with the door wedged closed with yet another plastic chair, I ate two cheese sandwiches brought from the city, and remember kicking the pillar to rock my hammock from side to side before falling asleep, surrounded by a strange way of life similar to what the Caledonians must have experienced.

The next morning began early. The Indian guide and boatman stood by the hammock as the moonlight bounced in from the open door. He wanted to know whether I would like some coffee and fried fish; I grunted a yes to the former and shook my head vigorously to the later. Pulling on clothes without washing, I hopped across the earthen floor to find my shoes before entering outside a world of remarkable bustle. Children were playing, women busying themselves with large steel pans, and men were generally sitting outside their huts on small plastic tubs, or wooden chairs. Exchanging a *buenos días* I went in search of water to splash over my sleepy face and to gingerly mount the overhanging wooden lavatory. Biscuits and hot coffee comprised breakfast and, so very different from Mulutupu, there was already much activity taking place as the man with the battered trilby directed a series of young men to ready the boat, find petrol, and prepare the outboard for the trip down the coast. I tagged along lamely behind the different young men, watching what was happening and hoping to offer some help, but with great efficiency and within only thirty minutes of my having woken, a large *cayuco* lay in the bay with a full tank of petrol and a purring outboard. The *sahila* and three others watched us depart as we rounded the headland and headed across the bay towards a series of other islands and towards the Colombian coast.

I asked the boatman's name three times and remained unsure each time; it was a mixture of Spanish and Kuna and sounded like 'Willen'. Afraid to ask again, I stuck with Willen and he did not demur. We skimmed across the turquoise waters of the inner bay out towards the coral reefs and the heavier waves beyond. He was married with children, but it sounded like he had separated from his wife and I had been given his hut and hammock to sleep in the night before and he had gone back to sleep with his wife and family. He seemed a bit crabby and quickly fell into a silence behind his large mirrored imitation Oakley sunglasses. We were heading east along the northern coast of Panama, but still within calm waters; we were on the safe side of a reef and further Kuna islands were out to our left-hand side. The Caledonians would have sailed on the further side of the reef, as the coral and islands would have been too dangerous to navigate with large ships and unfamiliar pilots. The old buccaneer they had picked up in St Thomas struggled to find Golden Island and the bay, so it is unimaginable he would have known how to navigate these shallow waters along the treacherous coast safely. The coastline was little changed: an untidy dark beach with ragged-looking green foliage, which led back to some flat land with relatively thick jungle before mountains soared up from the plateaux covered with thick, dense jungle overlaid with heavy mist and topped by a thunderous grey sky. Out to sea the sky was blue, and above the sandy, coral, shallow waters there gleamed picture-perfect turquoise water leading out to the deeper blue sea.

The outboard made a gentle humming noise against the quietness of the relatively still sea and the *cayuco* made good progress. I could see several other islands quite close by to my left and asked Willen which was Caledonia. He pointed out a medium-sized island which was far less cluttered than the others. He did not know why it was called Caledonia. Unexpectedly he launched into a tale of the inadequacies of the Kuna education system and his disappointment not to know more about his history, his people and his culture. He clearly wanted to and explained a future for himself as a tour guide, despite the dearth of tourists in these isolated parts. He talked nostalgically of some Dutch visitors who had arrived many years ago and promised to send him some photographs of him and their trip, but these, he said sadly, had never arrived. The name 'Caledonia' was a thrilling testimony to the Scots' presence and its utter incongruity made it very special as we sped past. The Kuna had the name right: many call it New Caledonia, another place entirely. That island was at least fifty minutes by *cayuco* from the site of the original Caledonia, which is now known as Punta Escocés on modern maps.

The safety of the natural barriers of the islands and coral reefs was left behind and feelings of both nervousness and excitement surged at following in the footsteps of Paterson and the rest of the other tired but excited Scots who had travelled down these same waters with expectant eyes. These visitors, who had seen neither television documentaries nor photos of far-flung places, marvelled at this strange coastline, a happy but unsettling occasion. Their memoirs and letters do not record their emotional responses, but undoubtedly it was an extraordinary experience for them over 300 years ago. The relatively abandoned nature and remoteness of this wild place and its forgotten souls had converted my journey into a pilgrimage commemorating their bravery and suffering.

The water soon began to swell and the waves crashed over the front of the *cayuco* bringing a nervous chill to me and a wide grin from Willen. He enjoyed my unease as we headed into rougher waters and the outboard had to be cut and revved up and down to hit the waves at just the right time to ride over them in our flimsy wooden canoe. The swell became so deep the *cayuco* was at real risk of being swamped by the oncoming waves, but Willen had a sure touch on the outboard and just as the next wave would crash into the bow of the long boat, he would immediately rev the engine to its full capacity and push the boat up the wave and over it and would immediately cut the power again to avoid the *cayuco* hitting the bottom of the next wave at the bottom of the swell. The whole process slowed our journey considerably and I nervously eyed how far from the coast we were, probably too far to swim there safely, given the size of the swell. There was no lifejacket in sight.

Willen was pointing and telling me to look straight ahead, where the mouth of the great bay that could hold 1,000 ships was located, but with the mass of greenery and our angle of approach I could see no more than mountains and green shore, as I held tightly to the sides of the wet wood. The sea became rougher the closer we came to our destination, and distinguishing more from the mass of green in the distance was challenged by the constant whack of the waves on the boat and the shattering bounce of the wood up our spines. As we ploughed up and down, the mouth of a bay became visible; as I looked at my map of the colony this was clearly the wide mouth of Caledonia Bay, and the land that crept out from the mainland coast like a long arm formed the formidable position the Scots took. Not far off some sharp black rocks, sticking out of the sea like rotten teeth, revealed themselves when the swell fell back. These would be the rocks that shattered the hull of the *Maurepas*, drowning several Frenchmen in the process and causing Pennecuik to strip off his clothes and jump into the sea to make for land. Contemplating the swim from my wooden bench underlined for me his bravery, as the *cayuco* bobbed in the churning waters.

We pulled further away from the rocks and began to enter the wide mouth of the bay. At the left-hand side behind the rocks was a gradual round headland set in from the mouth and bulking out in a circular fashion into the bay. At its base were large rocks and the circular section was slightly inclined, like a mound, and covered with foliage and large palm trees in the centre. It was immediately obvious this was the site of New Edinburgh. Maps from the time place the settlement there, and it would seem to anyone arriving in the bay a natural place for a fortified settlement, given its sheltered and slightly higher position, with its hills to the seaward side. From the sea nothing of any form of settlement was visible, but most striking of all was the size of the bay; it looked to my inexpert eye at least a mile across and several deep, with no islands, except what looked like manmade outcrops upon which some small Kuna Indian settlements were positioned. There was no way out of the bay at the far end and whilst the rocks protected one side of the mouth of the bay to the open sea, the other side was sheltered by a steep hill, which loomed menacingly over that side of the mouth. The Scots had indeed found a 'crabbed hold'.

Further back the bay was long and narrow and surrounded by vegetation on all sides, with steep hills pulling up from the immediate flat land on the mainland side of the bay. There was clear room for a considerable settlement on the flat land before the mountains on the landward side of the bay, and some room for a smaller settlement on the seaward side, but this was restricted by a considerable hill which rose from further back behind New Edinburgh, more towards the sea. On this summit Point Look Out was positioned and the mountains on the far side contained the path up through the forest which would lead to Tubuganti. Under a heavy grey sky the overall impression was impressive, but not beautiful.

Willen had begun to be nervous some time back and when we entered the bay his agitation increased because of the Indian village in the bay. The village, he told me, belonged to the chiefs from Mulutupu. He revved the outboard down and I noticed one side of the bay was quite shallow as we quietly cruised along the coast towards the Indian village. It was several hundred metres from where the Scots had settled New Edinburgh, and consisted of little more than four or five white cane and palm huts on the side of the bay and two huts built on the artificial coral island 100 feet from the coast in the shallow waters. With the engine cut and both of us silently propelling it forward by paddles, we approached and sat quietly looking and listening for signs of life from the village. After five minutes of silence he nodded gravely at me and the engine softly purred into life as we turned and made for a small yellow sandy beach near the headland of New Edinburgh. Willen was bemused at the suggestion a town called *Nuevo Edinburgo* was ever settled here, and yet more amused to hear it had contained over 1,000 northern Europeans.

The *cayuco* took us over the flat, sandy seabed close to a small beach on the right-hand approach of New Edinburgh. This was an obvious place to disembark, and it must have been where the Caledonians ferried their goods back and forward between the fleet and the settlement when they arrived. It would have been here where the Indians allies would have seen the ships of the first expedition try to warp themselves out the bay, bringing a sudden halt to the new Scottish colony.

Rolling up my trousers I jumped into the shallow water and felt warm, sandy mud ooze between my toes; grabbing the front of the boat I pulled it up onto the beach. Willen was keen to spend as little time as possible in the bay and looked alarmed when informed we would be there for the rest of the day and possibly the night. Armed with nothing more than a machete I turned to face the overgrown streets of New Edinburgh. From the beach there was no sign that anyone had ever lived here. The fertile soil, the humidity and the amazing resilience of the rainforest ensured any wooden construction would soon be rotten, broken down, turned into mush and displaced by green shoots and new jungle. Even the Caledonians of the second expedition complained Fort St Andrew was overgrown by the time they arrived.

Walking from the beach into the light forest felt like walking into a sauna. Within metres the trees and the heavy growth blocked out the shoreline breeze and sealed in the moisture. After only five or six swings with the machete, sweat oozed from my forehead. The rainforest was much like any: bushy and thick on the ground, laid over and sprawling around tree roots, puddles of mud and higher mounds of more solid ground. Thick white cobwebs hung between branches, reeds, tree stumps and anything else that would support them. Spiders sat with bodies around eight centimetres by eight, their overall span with their long legs was around 15 centimetres across. The machete had to be used to clear the foliage and webs immediately in front of my face. The spiders were not dangerous but they could bite. That would be unsettling. Only minutes into the jungle and already orientation was difficult, the beach was long gone and even the sea could not be seen. A hush, a sort of vacuum effect, muffled the sea noises and replaced it with damp drips, bird noises and the mechanically repetitive call of jungle insects.

Heading towards the outcrop of what had been New Edinburgh, it was difficult to make fast progress, largely because, in addition to the foliage, it was not easy to walk anywhere in a straight line: prickly bushes, fallen trees and particularly large spiders all diverted me from any obvious route to where I wanted to get to. There were no paths and no rivers or streams to walk alongside. Looking at the various drawings and maps of the lay-out of the settlement, I remembered the drawings I had seen of Colonel Blashford-Snell's expedition, but everywhere was a heavy curtain of damp green with no obvious signs of a former settlement. The Scots had chosen a hard place in which to convert themselves into Caledonians.

The temperature was easily somewhere in the high 30s Celsius and the effort involved in walking through the jungle was shattering. Within an hour of being inside the jungle I had consumed over a litre of water; my limited supplies would not last the day at this rate, and I scanned the jungle for decent-looking fresh water supplies. Some brownish water in a muddy stream appeared to be the best available. The humidity was intense; the change in humidity between the shore and behind the heavy curtain of jungle canopy was surprising. It was little wonder the Kuna chose to live on islands to receive the benefits of the cool sea air. The humidity, more than the temperature, made the jungle suffocating and for those Caledonians detailed to clear land and construct huts, the cloying dampness presented a major challenge and explains why many council members and the officer class amongst the settlers chose to remain accommodated aboard their ships in the bay.

It was well documented that there were two lasting physical manifestations to testify to the Scots' presence around the bay: one was a stone oven in New Edinburgh and the other was a long canal the Scots dug out at the end of the seaward arm of the bay to better protect themselves from Spanish attack. Fort St Andrew, the living quarters and huts and the defensive walls, have not survived, partly because they were burned down by the victorious Spaniards and partly because wood simply rots in the jungle. Earlier visitors to the bay were fortunate to come across clay pipes in the mud: these were part of a consignment of pipes brought across on the second expedition aboard the *Olive Branch* and were lost to the Caledonians when the ship sank. Delicate, pale pipes, quite small, that have survived better than the colony they were supposed to be sold from.

There was no chance of finding more pipes, so the obvious goal was to find both the oven and the ditch. The oven was close to where our *cayuco* had landed and I began to search through the jungle to find it. I had read it was a low, circular oven made of brick, and earlier archaeologists at the site have concluded it was used for making bread. It may have been when there was sufficient flour, but the accounts given by Scots who betrayed themselves to the Spanish suggest there was only fish and hard biscuit left to eat as the colony progressed towards the end of the first expedition's time on the isthmus. In an effort to find the oven, I had both to scan across the heavy growth and slash my way through it with a machete, whilst avoiding the gruesome spiders. After a close look at the maps produced by the earlier twentieth-century expeditions, I found it: a low circular mass of what looked like brick covered in moss and other greens. The brick was damp and warm, the moss oozing but clearly visible. I crouched low and imagined a sweaty Scottish baker toiling away. Bread-making would have been hard work here.

I crossed the ground surrounding the oven, circling outwards, hoping to find other remains washed up by the rain or dislodged in the mud. It was a fairly forlorn hope, given the fairly intensive searches carried out by Blashford-Snell in the 1970s and more recently by Mark Horton of Bristol University for a BBC documentary. Any easily discoverable remnants had long since been bagged up. I walked through the jungle from the site of New Edinburgh down to the Kuna Indian village. Heading down a slight slope walking towards the sea and towards the hill which would once have housed Point Look Out, it was clear how difficult it was to orientate oneself in the jungle when there were no distinguishing landmarks and worst of all when the sea was obscured by the trees.

Progress was helped by finding a small path which appeared to lead from the Indian village round the back of New Edinburgh towards the open shore. I headed down the path towards the village, pausing to look back up to where the bulk of the settlement would have been. Today where there is crowded jungle there once stood several hundred huts with palm-frond roofs, cleared streets and communal buildings. The council in their letter of 20 January 1699, which was intercepted by the Spaniards, boasted that the settlement could conveniently hold 5,000 men, with space to expand if necessary. The letter also claimed a port was being created in which large ships could dock. The picture painted of this activity, of the progress made and the attempt to turn a wilderness into a settlement, is of a successful development. Both the climate and the terrain would have been major impediments to completing such plans. Carrying water and fighting through the undergrowth would have been utterly draining: the Caledonians are sometimes described as a disorganised, badly led crew who achieved very little, but standing on the soil of New Edinburgh showed me, in a way no history text could, just how difficult their task was, and how extraordinary their achievements were for the time, or even for modern times.

The path meandered through the jungle and in most places was neat and tidy with hard-packed black soil; it was clearly well used by the Indians who lived nearby. As the path took me further from New Edinburgh it curved down closer to the sea and once again it was possible to see the wide expanse of the bay and feel the cool breeze from the sea. As the Indian village came into view I approached slowly and carefully, in case the villagers had returned. Willen's anxieties had made me feel a little jumpy. From closer up it was apparent the village was a smaller version of what exists on Tubuala or Mulutupu: a series of small white cane homes with dried palm-frond roofs. Some of the homes were on the coastline and others were 20 metres out, delicately placed on top of an artificial island. Crouching in the long grass with a machete in my hand, I peered hard to see if anyone was around. The village was empty and silent. As I wandered closer a small dog barked and skirted the side of the village. It is unlikely this settlement would have been here in the days of the Caledonians, certainly there is no record of there having been a village close by. The village is where the Spanish eventually advanced along the coast and down the hill from Point Look Out as they breached the Scottish defences and got closer to Fort St Andrew. From here the Spanish would have been able to have a clear aim at the Scottish boats.

It seemed inappropriate to snoop around the empty village and I headed back to New Edinburgh. By this time the afternoon sun was strong and I lay down under a thick palm to rest for some time and ate. Here in Caledonia there was little evidence of any cultivation. I could see a few platano trees at the back of the Indian village, but there was little evidence of the usual variety of fruit trees found in Panama: mango, grenadilla, avocado, sea grapes. The soil was certainly too wet to grow crops like wheat or oats, which would have traditionally been relied on, and the Caledonians would have been very heavily dependent upon Indian help to cultivate fresh fruits and vegetables in this area.

I fell asleep in the jungle and woke around 4pm, anxious to get back to Willen. Before leaving, I gathered some of the wild hibiscus and other tropical flowers in a small bundle and tied them firmly with a piece of tough grass. There were a number of other things to see before we headed back and it would have been uncomfortable to do that in the dark. I headed back down the path and rather than follow it over the hill down to the open Caribbean, I tried to guess where it cut down back to the beach where Willen was waiting. Standing in the dark jungle the correct direction appeared to be somewhere midway between the village and the end of the peninsula. I calculated that walking down from the path would lead me to the boat. Hacking my way through the undergrowth I was soon drenched in sweat and desperate to reach the coast to swim in the water to cool. The particular bit of jungle I found myself in was strewn with little streams and several large fallen palm trees; keeping in a straight line was almost impossible. The further into the jungle from the path I got, the more uncertain I was as to which direction led to the boat and the beach. Placing the machete and my bag on the ground I looked around for the deep blue colour of the sea, but it was not visible. Looking up I hoped the thicker clouds would point to the coast and the lighter ones out to sea, but as luck would have it, the sky was blue with only very few unremarkable dotted clouds. A slight feeling of panic began to rise from my stomach.

Trying again to orientate myself, it was impossible to see the sea and the path was long since lost in a green morass behind, or in front, of me. I attempted again to keep in a straight line and fight my way forward in the hope of finding a clearly distinguishable landmark to act as a guide, but this impossible. I was exhausted, and looking at my watch guessed there would be an hour before sundown. It seemed incredibly stupid to be lost in the jungle, in the wilderness of Darien, in a place known to be occasionally frequented by drug traffickers, guerrillas and paramilitaries, without a compass, a phone (one that had reception), a radio or any other appliance which could help. Despite the passing of over 300 years I was no better prepared than the Caledonians. Overcoming a considerable fear of bullet ants, I tried to scramble up the nearest tall palm tree. It was useless and there was no chance of reaching high enough to see over the overgrown jungle to the sea. I came crashing down with skinned shins and thorns in my palms.

In desperation I began to call out Willen's name, loudly. At first, there was no response but I persevered. Faintly at first I could just hear a response, he was shouting back. Another human voice was comforting after a day spent in the lonely jungle, but at first it did not help much as divining the

direction of his calls was difficult. Eventually, after considerable concentra-
tion, I was able to work out where he was calling from and, continuing
to shout out his name, I could head towards where he was shouting back.
After less than five minutes like this I emerged, exhausted, onto the beach.
I had never been far away, but the density of the jungle made getting your
bearings very difficult.

We pushed the *cayuco* off the beach and clambered back into it. Willen
was keen to leave immediately but first we had to try to find the trench
the Scots had dug for themselves a little further down the peninsula. The
light was starting to soften and a rose colour was gathering in the clouds,
above the mountains on the mainland. Dusk brought a certain tranquillity
over the bay, as the wind softened, the birds chattered less and the surface
of the sea became smoother. We glided a little further down the coast with
the outboard making a gentle 'phut, phut' sound and I felt able to relax.
As we came round the headland, we could see where the land narrowed
and followed closer in to the shore and there the narrow canal dug by
the Caledonians remained: one of the few monuments to their doomed
armed stand against the mighty Spanish Empire. It was long and narrow,
probably 50 metres or so long by about 2–3 metres wide, with thick bushy
undergrowth coming down the sides. Clear water ran over a soft-looking
sand base. In this very spot Caledonians sweated hard to clear the channel
of soil and despite their hard work this defensive measure helped very little
at the end of the day.

The council, in their letter of 20 January 1699, wrote that the channel
was at least 200 feet long, and that in addition to the channel a strong, high
parapet had been built with several strategically positioned bastions. There
was nothing left of the parapets or bastions. The permanency of the canal
suggests a fairly solid defensive structure was put in place here by the first
expedition. By the time the Spaniards attacked from this very approach,
they had already destroyed the fortifications after New Edinburgh was
deserted for the first time, and these had not been rebuilt by the men of the
second expedition. I looked wistfully down this flawed defensive position
and paused to wonder: what if? What if the line had held and the Spaniards
had been repelled at this very place?

Willen revved the outboard up and spun us back round and into the
centre of the mighty bay. As we drew level with where Fort St Andrew

had stood, he slowed the *cayuco* down and to his surprise I stripped my sweaty clothes off and leapt from the side into the cool water, washing away layers of grime, dirt and sweat from my day in the jungle. Staying under for as long as I could, I burst gasping back to the surface, drinking in the cool evening air and the beauty of Caledonia from the sea. In the soft light and after the adventures and emotions of the day, the 'door to the seas and the key to the universe' had taken on a special quality it had lacked when I had first arrived. Buried somewhere here were the bodies of thousands of dead Scots men and women, and many other nationalities; the Greeks, Venetians and English who had joined the expeditions. And the bodies of dead Indians and Spaniards. Crossing paths in this strange far-away land.

I pulled myself back into the boat and dragged on my clothes. We motored to the mouth of the bay and Willen turned the *cayuco* around to face the bay and cut the engine completely. Silence almost reigned against the soft sloshing of gentle waves on the boat. Carefully I took out the homemade bouquet of wild flowers and kneeling on the side of the boat slowly and carefully recited the Lord's prayer before gently placing the flowers on the water. I prayed for the souls of all who had died in this place, brought together by the necessities of trade, of empire, of war and peace, of freedom and of violence. Opening my eyes, I stood at the end of the boat looking for the last time on Caledonia, on the place upon which a proud nation had projected its hopes for economic salvation and global success. The outboard roared into life and we turned sharply out of the mouth of the bay, and it was not long before the waves pounded the bow of the *cayuco* and the night came racing down from the sky to greet a silent Caribbean.

The stars were bright above the coast, as we slowly made our way back up towards the distant island of Tubuala. The half moon helped light our way as we followed the shore west. Exhausted but exhilarated from spending the day in New Edinburgh, I regretted the impossibility of sleeping in the settlement, but the Indian leaders had warned it was not safe at night and at dawn the chiggers were said to be unrelenting. Willen lay low in the boat with his baseball cap pulled firmly down on his head. He appeared to cheer up as the tiny lights of Tubuala began to flutter above the waves on the horizon. We returned late enough that very few people were sitting outside their huts. A few men helped us pull the *cayuco* clear of the water and take the outboard off the back. We trooped back exhausted down the narrow path from the island's shore to Willen's hut, and with relief – and without eating or washing – I threw myself into the hammock.

The next morning I woke before dawn. As with the previous morning, I appeared to be the last person up and the paths bustled with Indians in the last of the morning's darkness. Today Willen and I planned to visit the Kuna island called Caledonia, equidistant between Tubuala and Punta Escocés. Before that, however, I was desperate to eat breakfast and asked around where something could be bought. There were no cafés or restaurants on the island, but Willen told me his wife would make me something. I hoped for platano and coffee, and was not to be disappointed. Watching the sky burst red, drinking sour black coffee on a small plastic stool, resting my head against the white cane of the hut, I was glad breakfast did not consist of mouldy goods from a ship's store and brackish water. Despite the very early hour the island was already warm and mosquitos were beginning to dance around in the early light, the *cayuco* was on the shoreline, outboard roaring and Willen was ready to go.

As we crossed the Caribbean to head out to Caledonia I asked Willen what Caledonia was called before it was given its strange name. He did not know, nor was he sure why one of the neighbourhoods in Panama City was also called Caledonia, a name that dated back to Colombian control of Panama and the Thousand Day civil war. The journey across to Caledonia was much shorter than to Punta Escocés, largely because it did not involve straying beyond the protective wall of underground coral. The sun beamed down as we arrived at a small wooden jetty on the shore of the island.

Caledonia looked different from both Tubuala and Mulutupu: it was less crowded. There was either more space or less crowded accommodation on the island. The boat pulled into an impressive-looking solid wooden jetty, far larger than anything found on the other islands, and we tied it up before leaping onto the wood and heading onto the island proper. The largest building before us was a two-storey modern building with a large verandah painted in blue and white. Willen called up to somebody and an animated young Indian leaned over, smiled widely and called us up to the first floor. I was introduced to him and whilst he softly chatted in Kuna with Willen, I sat enjoying the breeze, looking over modern-day Caledonia from this relative vantage point. It was quite large, with open green spaces, a green area in the middle with a basketball court and a large palm-covered hut which was probably the *congreso*.

I offered to buy some beer, and unlike some of the other islands, there appeared to be no prohibition or requirement to seek consent from a *sahila* or *comisión*. There was lukewarm Balboa and we drank it slowly in the mid-morning heat. I asked this modern-day Caledonian about the name of the island. He wasn't sure why it was called Caledonia, maybe one of the elders would know. I asked him about Scotland and Punta Escocés and whether he was aware of the connection between the two places, but again he just shook his head, took a slug of beer and smiled widely.

We headed down into the community and over to the main hut to talk to the Indian elders. I would need to pay a small fee for visiting the island. The *congreso* was much like the one in Mulutupu – a large, cool hut with a high ceiling made of palm, although the sides were open, which allowed the breeze to cool the hall and kept the heavy air found in Mulutupu away. The elders were relaxing in hammocks strung along the centre of the hall, some four or five small Indian men in ragged long trousers and open shirts. They looked a lot less surprised to see a Westerner than the other Indians. Yachts stopped more often at Caledonia than the other islands in this part of the Comarca, I was told later. They looked back blankly as I explained the original Caledonia in Spanish to them and the links between Caledonia, Scotland and Punta Escocés. They were engaged by this discussion of their ancestors and talked of the oral tradition of history of the Kuna Indians, of their respect for their forefathers, of their relationships with visitors to their lands. Answers to specific questions about why the island was called Caledonia were not forthcoming and it seemed impolite to push. I asked them about the modern-day relationships between the different Kuna villages or communities and they shook their heads: 'Some are very difficult and don't take part properly in a community spirit,' said one.

The Kuna feuded amongst themselves when the Scots arrived in the late seventeenth century, so it was unsurprising tensions remained and the Indians of Tubuala and Mulutupu seemed very different. Despite their interest in their culture and their impressive efforts to protect their culture and identity from a variety of external factors, I was sad that nobody on the island was aware of the historical links to the Caledonians of centuries gone by. These wiry Indians in their hammocks were the modern-day

Caledonians, living a life not wholly dissimilar to their Scottish namesakes' 300 years earlier, and yet the history which binds them together appears to have been forgotten. I bade the *sahilas* farewell and paid $5 for my visit to the island.

Back in the now bright light the temperature was rising and the island seemed less busy than it had when we'd arrived. The Kuna women who bustled around cleaning the paths between the houses had taken shelter in their homes and an early midday peace descended on the island: it was hammock time. The only people still out were a large group of small children, of around ten years old. They came galloping over, all cries of *hola* with arms thrown into the air in excitement. These young Caledonians crowded round and demanded to know why I was so white. I told them I too was a Caledonian, which produced bafflement in their tiny faces as I attempted to explain I was from Europe, far away. They liked that and asked me to come with them to a special place. I reluctantly agreed only to discover the 'special place' was a tiny shop, and handed over a wad of dollar notes to buy them all sodas.

There was little else to see on the island, and it is unclear from the historical accounts whether the island was populated when the Scots arrived in Darien. It was also unclear whether the original Caledonians had ever visited this island. It was time to leave and as I headed back to find Willen I passed a telephone booth. Leaning in with the intention of reporting back to Panama City and explaining I would try to return on the plane tomorrow, I discovered the line was dead. The booth, a much-vaunted tool of modernity, served no purpose in this strange pre-modern world. Willen was ready to go and we sped off. Caledonia stood on the horizon with a group of small children holding their soda bottles aloft in one hand, waving furiously with the other. I waved goodbye to these descendants of Caledonia: a living monument to the failures of my ancestors in the new world.

That evening on Tubuala, Willen suggested a beer in the local cantina. The night was cool and bright and the entire island had taken on a ghostly white colour as the nocturnal light from the moon and stars reflected back from the white sand paths and white cane walls of the huts. We strolled through interminable paths to the far side of the island, to the shore where what looked like a large cardboard box stood – the bar. Inside, a few morose-looking Indians sat huddled over bottles of beer. We ordered some and chatted quietly in Spanish in the corner. Willen talked about tourism development on the islands and how they could encourage visitors to come. I thought back ruefully to the Kuna representative with the Panamanian Institute of Tourism and how hopeless he had been. We talked about infrastructure, hotels, restaurants and guides, about the obvious appeal of the countryside and the tremendous interest in Kuna culture itself. Willen was keen to improve his life and the life of his community. The beers were having a soporific effect on me, and the plan was to leave early the next morning. Thanking Willen, I paid for the beers and asked him to show me the way back to my hammock and some much-needed sleep.

Settling into my hammock there was a gentle knock on the door and the trilby hat-wearing *sahila* came in. He asked how the trips had been and whether they were enjoyable. There was a problem, however, he said: a member of the *comisión* from Mulutupu had come to the island to speak with him today and complained that the Tubuala Indians had taken a *gringo* to Punta Escocés. The *sahila* had denied this and explained there would be trouble, he asked me when I was leaving and how. I explained: by plane tomorrow morning. He looked glum and shook his head; the Mulutupu control the landing strip he said, I might have problems with them. He was sorry, he said. I asked him why and he explained he should not have agreed to take me to Punta Escocés, and ruefully I reflected I should not have asked him. Feeling a little alarmed, I asked him what sort of trouble I might expect. He looked forlorn and said they might not let me board the plane back to Panama City or they might ask for more money. If there was trouble at the Mulutupu airstrip tomorrow, he said, I was to get word over to Tubuala and he would try to help. He then paused and asked me for more money to smooth out the problems. I handed over the agreed $50 and offered another $50. He accepted it happily, shook my hands and wished me good luck for tomorrow. Lying back in my hammock I felt alarmed at the thought of a confrontation with the Indians of Mulutupu.

Just as I was about to drift off to sleep there was another knock at the door and a thin Panamanian policeman in battered camouflage fatigues appeared. He introduced himself and explained to me he had heard on his patrols there was alarm on the part of the Mulutupu Indians that a *gringo* had travelled to Punta Escocés with an Indian from this village. A feeling of panic began to form in my stomach. He understood I was leaving tomorrow and warned me there would be trouble at the landing strip. With a weak smile of assurance he told me to contact him tomorrow, he would be on duty, and if things got out of hand, I was to get a message to him and he would sort things out. My increasingly troubled mind worked through the logistics: the journey from the island on which the landing strip was situated to Tubuala must be around fifteen minutes, I would not have a *cayuco* tomorrow, nor did I have a working mobile phone or any other way of contacting him. As I explained this to him, he said, 'Not worry *hermano*, just send someone for me'. With this weak reassurance he told me once more to be careful and left.

I lay back in the hammock in the candlelight of the damp-smelling hut feeling a little anxious. The last few days had taught me just how remote the Comarca was. I had been warned there might be a conflict tomorrow and felt wholly unreassured by tonight's visitors. With little idea how to respond to what might happen I blew out the candle and settled back into the hammock hoping, at the least, sleep was possible before dawn.

The next day, the door was roughly pushed open by Willen. It was still dark. He stood with a torch and an anxious grin. There was no time for breakfast and he appeard to be keen to get to the landing strip and back before the trouble began. The *sahila* had spoken to him. The *cayuco* made the journey across to the island in less than fifteen minutes, as Willen remained tightlipped, with an anxious hand gripping the outboard. As we neared the small jetty where I had found the yellow-cagouled Indian several days ago, I leaned over and shouted my thanks to him over the roar of the outboard. I pressed money into his hand to use in case he should have difficulties with the Mulutupu Indians. As we came closer his face tightened as he scanned the horizon, I turned to see what was causing him alarm and made out a series of objects lined up on the beach by the small jetty; it took me a moment to realise the beach was covered in *cayucos* like a colony of long brown seals. Willen killed the outboard and let the boat glide in towards the jetty, he leaned over, shook my hand and wished me *buena suerte*; it was obvious from his eyes that he was afraid, and it was contagious. As soon as the *cayuco* made its wooden clunky contact with the jetty I jumped off to the sounds of the outboard revving and the spray of Willen as he took off as fast he could.

Feeling like a condemned man, I turned and looked up the sandy path into the rainforest. Before me were hundreds of Kuna Indians with machetes. A sense of disbelief descended as I tried to figure out how I had placed myself in this tricky situation. This sort of confrontation seemed as far as it was possible to get from a desire to see the remains of a 300-year-old colony in a forgotten corner of the jungle. To my left and right on the jetty were dozens of immaculately carved wooden *cayucos*, with their paddles carefully placed at an angle over the sides. Behind me was the rapidly disappearing outline of Willen and his transport back to safety. How would I now get hold of the policeman on Tubuala? Who would I send? The sun beat down on the path as I was swallowed up by emerald jungle. Confession and mercy were the only possible strategies: fight or flight was impossible. The Indians stood to look at me, but ignoring me turned and knelt down to cut grass and chop back at low-hanging branches. With relief I realised the massed numbers of Indians had arrived, not to confront me, but to take part in a day of communal labour to maintain their airport island. They were more interested in raking the sand and doing countless other maintenance jobs than haranguing me.

The entire island of Mulutupu was engaged in a huge gardening exercise, a sort of parody of a television makeover show, with a chorus of snipping, cutting, brushing, sweeping and trimming. The path had been reclaimed from the overgrown jungle and freshly demarcated; the grass on the landing strip dazzled several shades of green lighter than its surrounds and the overhanging branches had been trimmed and tidied. The path had by now returned me to the small *bohio* were I had paid my arrival tax, and a smiling young girl wearing an Air Panama jacket asked me for a departure tax of $5. The sight of her red and white official jacket was a shot in the arm, and I wanted to stand beside her, a representative of the modern world, where I was not at the mercy of angry Indians and their machetes. Sitting down to wait I consulted my watch, hoping the plane would soon arrive. There were at least 30 minutes to wait and no guarantees the plane would be here at all, never mind on time. If it picked up enough passengers on the islands it visited before arriving here, it would simply return to Panama without stopping here, I had been warned.

Keeping a wary eye on the Indians, I noticed they remained engrossed in their slow but steady massive gardening project and their only distraction from this was a two-minute break when they converged on two older Kuna women who handed out some sort of juice from two vast containers, served in sliced coconut shells and plastic bottles cut in half. The Caledonians had spent a lot of time drinking with the Indians 300 years ago and managed the diplomacies of the day better than I, and it would seem the Indians were still as suspicious of each others' communities as they had been then. I hoped there would not be difficulties between the Tubuala and the Mulutupu because of my desire to see Punta Escocés.

I was stirred from these thoughts by six Kuna Indians. Each of them quite old, easily as old as late seventies. They wore rubber boots, plain trousers and ragged shirts open down their sinuous short bodies. They carried long silver machetes and looked down at me. The Air Panama woman had disappeared and the sky did not announce the imminent arrival of the plane. 'You have cheated us,' shouted one of them in rough Spanish. As I attempted to respond, the eldest one cut me short and smacked the back of my hand with his machete. 'You went to Punta Escocés without our permission.' Staying silent on the thorny issues of Punta Escocés, I explained my interest in Tubuala, but suggested some compensation if they felt aggrieved and a return trip, planned and organised with them over several days. Ignoring this, they demanded I open my bag and hand over my wallet. My wallet was taken and forty dollars pulled out and placed in a stained pocket of the eldest Kuna Indian. Gently taking my wallet back, I pulled out a business card and explained to them they should come and visit me and we could talk about a further expedition, with more people, properly funded. They talked amongst themselves in Kuna. This idea proved popular, and the angry confrontation with the semi-circle of irate Indians appeared to lose its heat. I kept one eye on the sky, searching for a sighting of the small red and white propeller plane.

It seemed the worst had passed as they engaged me in a discussion about a return trip. I asked for telephone numbers and names of people on the island who could help me return. As this took place a distant buzzing sound began to roll down the coast and across the sky to where we stood, something of a relief. The girl in Air Panama colours returned. Having pocketed the $40 from my wallet and with discussion about a further planned trip the Indian elders visibly relaxed and began to fade away from our confrontation. The plane's engine roared above our heads and the little plane bounced several times on the asphalt runway before turning hard left and coming to a sudden halt before the *bohio*.

I shook hands with the Indians and exchanged smiles, whatever difficulty had been ironed out and we parted on good terms. Bags were loaded on. Running up the stairs I grabbed a seat and pulled the seatbelt on immediately and fastened it extra tight, lest anyone try and take me off the plane. Minutes later I heard the welcome thump of the door being shut. Engine noise filled our ears and after a jolt the little plane went tearing down the strip and lightly and very gently lifted us off the island before we banked steeply over Mulutupu, and settled on a course up the Caribbean coast. An hour later we would be in Panama City. One hour in time, but a journey through several hundred years from a pre-modern world back to modernity, I ruefully reflected, as the plane banked to the side and left the Caribbean, Caledonia and the Kuna behind me.

NINE

THE FIRST EXPEDITION DEPARTS

Back in Edinburgh, all Scots, but particularly the directors and shareholders, were anxious for more news of the colony. They knew sloops could easily cross to Jamaica and from there parcels and letters could be sent home to Scotland via London or Bristol. The lack of news alarmed the directors and made them sensitive to rumours emanating from London. There had been dark whispers of disease, death and even, as time wore on, of abandonment. The directors were in a difficult position, they had sought a third call on their stockholders and apart from the construction of the ships had little to show for eating up so much Scottish capital. A small dividend had been provided, but given no profits had surfaced from the colony in Darien, this was unlikely to be repeated. The directors' response to news was in any event slow: they had received the letters desperately asking for more provisions from the first expedition's council in late September, and had begun to prepare a ship with provisions of biscuit, oil, flour, pork and more alcohol. Despite the letters, the directors were not to know such provisions were in urgent demand and that young men were dying for want of a nutritious diet. Lionel Wafer had at last published his account of the isthmus of Darien and anyone who read it was led to believe fruits and vegetables grew in abundance in that distant paradise.

Nonetheless, by January 1699 a brigantine, the *Dispatch*, was ready to set sail, provisioned with a modest amount of victuals and stores. Her captain, Andrew Gibson, was told to make directly for Darien by the shortest route, the concerns over privacy no longer important, despite the fact the directors were still unaware whether Golden Island had been taken and a suitable settlement made in Darien. The *Dispatch* did not get far; in squally weather it was wrecked off the coast of Jura. All provisions were lost, and the hungry men of Caledonia would have to wait. Most of the men managed to struggle ashore.

This bad fortune was soon forgotten in Edinburgh, when Alexander Hamilton arrived at Mylne's Square on 25 March 1699. Hamilton had left New Edinburgh just before Christmas and did not yet know of the hardships his compatriots were to endure. With him he brought the optimistic accounts and journals of Hugh Rose and letters from many of the settlers. The directors were relieved the colony had been established. In Edinburgh, the whole city was ecstatic, the taverns and coffee houses of the High Street were crowded with talk of the vast trade that was soon to begin and the money the merchants would make. Families discussed sending their younger sons to the colony to extend the family name and dwindling Scottish fortunes. The Scots enjoyed their good news amongst the poor weather, failing harvests and talk of yet more famine to come. People's minds drifted from the grey weather and failing crops to imagine the wooden homes of Caledonia, the lush jungle, the blue skies and Scottish hopes reborn across the seas. The Castle guns were fired, bells rang out across churches in Edinburgh and riders were dispatched across the kingdom to spread the good news. Hamilton was handsomely rewarded with 100 guineas and surely did as well again as he was lauded and celebrated in the taverns. For other families the news was painful: the list of those who had already died was published at Mylne's Square. Some would have to mourn without a body and imagine their loved ones buried far away, never to return to their homeland. In the midst of these enthusiastic celebrations, Councillor Cunningham arrived from London. He was annoyed to realise Hamilton had beaten him to be the first back. Upon his promise to return to Caledonia the directors resolved to pay him £200, but he took the money and disappeared to his home in Scotland, never again to gaze on the palm fronds of Caledonia.

In April and May of 1699, the sentries on Point Look Out were becoming more and more frustrated and disillusioned that resupply ships would ever arrive from Scotland. They had been scouring the horizon in vain with empty stomachs, dreaming of well-stocked ships on the horizon. Desperate for good news, in mid May the council sent a *piragua* (type of canoe) out along the coast to speak to some passing sailors and to find provisions. They encountered an English trading sloop and asked its captain to come to Caledonia to trade some provisions for their goods. The captain refused, and as the Scots pleaded for him to come, he stood firm, handing over a copy of a small piece of white paper, which would deal a blow to the morale of the colony. Acting on orders from King William's Secretary of State, James Vernon, Sir William Beetson, the Governor of Jamaica, had published a challenging proclamation:

IN HIS MAJESTY'S NAME and by command, strictly to command His Majesty's subjects, whatsoever, that they do not presume, on any pretence whatsoever, to hold any correspondence with the said Scots, nor to give them any assistance of arms, ammunitions, provisions, or any other necessaries whatsoever, either by themselves or any other for them, or by any of the vessels, or of the English nation, as they will answer the contempt of His Majesty's command at their utmost peril.[1]

All English colonies in the Americas acted in a similar manner, but it was Jamaica, the hub of Caribbean trade, that inflicted the most significant damage on the Scots. The Caledonians stared at the soggy paper in bewilderment and were taken aback by the date, 9 April 1699: a Sunday. The governor had taken the unprecedented step of publishing the proclamation on the Sabbath in order to ensure large church audiences were aware of the governor's intentions and, more importantly perhaps, to prevent the departure of two fully provisioned English sloops for Caledonia the next day, Monday. These ships might have provided sufficient supplies to ensure the Caledonians survived until July, when the second expedition was due to arrive.

Wider European concerns played a significant role in the English response to Spanish outrage over Caledonia, but it should be noted that the formal complaint from the Spanish king did not reach James Vernon until 3 May 1699. The Jamaican governor had his own local concerns, he had argued: 'If they settle there and are healthy, the noise of gold (of which there is great plenty in those parts) will carry away all our debtors' servants and ordinary people in the hope of mending their fortunes, and will much weaken what little strength we have.'

The Caledonians were shocked and appalled. They had been underfed and ill for months and had long hoped for fresh food and provisions to fortify themselves against the incessant rains. Work had dwindled to a trickle as the landsmen's strength weakened and the crews of the ships rarely ventured beyond their decks. The creation of laws and a parliament had done little to inject enthusiasm or a greater sense of morale and common undertaking. As provisions diminished suspicions grew amongst the men about the levels of food being hidden on the ships and worse, fears began to spread that some of the ships would leave without the landsmen to begin a career of piracy. Many Caledonians concluded the directors would not send any help or assistance to them now as King William's displeasure was evidenced by the proclamation, and proceedings in Edinburgh must have been sabotaged too. Hope had kept the Caledonians united and in place, toiling away, dreaming of reinforcement, fresh men, ideas and enthusiasm from Scotland. At a stroke, with the publication of the proclamation all this seemed a distant and unlikely prospect. What morale that had remained in the sticky jungle soon began to evaporate.

Paterson's health also began to falter, his body racked by fevers sending him into long periods of delirium. As the endgame for the first expedition approached, Paterson was less and less able to take a leading role, confined instead to his hut, sweating and hallucinating from tropical fever. He was largely ignored, as the rest considered how to depart the wretched isthmus. Many planters feared the return journey, the boredom, the disease and the terrifying, unpredictable seas. They also feared their reception in Scotland, being shunned as deserters and cowards, returning to their families, bitter with the shame brought to the family name, darkened by retreat and dishonour. Few in Scotland would understand the demands on the colonists; the incessant rain, stinking mud, oppressive heat and fear of attack.

Amid this fear, the parliament met and the Caledonians' representatives pleaded for the abandonment of the colony. They made their speeches below a rain-soaked palm roof, gesturing around them at the miserable state of their condition and their failure to achieve real progress. Hundreds of men had died and so little had been achieved. Were a small wooden fort and a few streets of palm-frond houses worth so much sacrifice? The men openly doubted how New Edinburgh could ever be converted into the 'door to the seas and the key to the universe'. They began to question their leaders and Paterson had himself bled to weaken the grip of his fever, and on shaky legs spoke to encourage the men to stay. He made little progress convincing his men that a route across the isthmus and a path across the mountains were essential to the success of a port that would then be able to trade both east and west. If more had already been achieved, the rousing words in the parliament might have encouraged the colonists to stay. Few agreed with him and in an atmosphere of confusion and fear, preparations began to ready the ships for departure. Paterson became further marginalised when on 5 June his fever worsened and his mind drifted far from reality. He lay in much discomfort in his soggy hut, ignored. Only Thomas Drummond visited him; he admired the older man's courage and determination to stay put and see his project carried out. It was not to be and, still very ill, Paterson was carried aboard the *Unicorn*. He would never again return to the damp soil of his much dreamed-of noble undertaking.

The parliament did not meet again to formally decide whether to leave and the council offered little information as to what had been decided. New Edinburgh was awash with uncertainty and gossip. Many believed Pennecuik was considering taking the *Saint Andrew* and departing with men to become pirates. Leadership had effectively broken down and the colony was in chaos. Sickness had become more acute and the Scots realised they were unable to properly defend the colony. There was panic as the evacuation became a headlong rush to cram people on board. Tired bodies wanted off the isthmus and to find a secure place on board a ship, whilst the crews struggled to ready their boats for the gruelling journey from Darien. Many planters feared the journey. Some had not even the strength to make it aboard a boat to be rowed out to the ships and others simply decided to stay. Around twenty remained on the shore to watch as the once mighty fleet bobbed up and down in the bay, anxious but unable to leave because of the wind direction. The Indians watched too. They were not surprised, they had seen over 1,100 healthy and determined men and women sail into the bay just over eight months earlier and had watched as their condition deteriorated from idleness, fear, in-fighting, fevers and lack of proper provisioning. The Indians had seen many white men come and go, but had known very few who could remain for long in their lands.

Did the English proclamation deliver a fatal blow to the colony? It is hard to account for the two-month gap between the arrival of news of the embargo and the departure from the colony, one quarter of the time the first expedition spent on the isthmus. Seventeenth-century sailors in the Caribbean were expert at getting round embargos, evading inspecting ships and the general business of being a pirate. If there was money to be made, English and other foreign merchants would have continued to trade, but they were mindful of the unsuitability of many of the Scots' goods, which were in any event highly priced. The high-handed and illegal manner in which they had treated some of their customers had come back to haunt them. An essential part of Paterson's project had been to trade westwards, New Edinburgh was not intended to be simply another Caribbean trading colony. Squeezed between Cartagena and Portobello, at the far end of the Caribbean surrounded by mercantilist Spaniards, it was ill-placed for such a role and yet, in all the time the Scots were there, there is no record of efforts to take goods across the isthmus to sell them on the Pacific coast or to take Scottish ships around the cape to trade from the Americas to the Indies. When William Murray and Lawrence Drummond reported to the directors in person in late November 1699, they blamed a number of factors, chief among them being the 'scarcity of fresh provisions and strong liquors'. They blamed the abandonment on the proclamation. They could hardly stand in front of the directors and accuse them. The directors in Edinburgh had been too slow in provisioning the colony. If the second expedition had arrived a couple of months earlier, there is little doubt that, proclamation or no proclamation, the Scots would have remained for longer on the isthmus and it is clear the second expedition remained hopeful of further establishing Caledonia notwithstanding the proclamation.

With little concern for why they left, a few days after boarding the ships the sailors took advantage of the wind to get themselves out of the bay and set sail, leaving behind very little. Thomas Drummond had the foresight to take the guns out of Fort St Andrew and have them taken aboard. The Spanish would arrive shortly after and complete the process of destruction, knocking down the rest of the fort and the miserable huts. The council provided sailing directions, ordering the ships to sail together for the New

The beach at Punta Escocés: this is where the Scots would have come ashore when they first arrived at Caledonia. (Jim Malcolm)

Punta Escocés from the bay: the view of the headland and entrance to the bay from the sea. (Jim Malcolm)

Arriving by plane to the Kuna Yala: the aeroplane travels across the Cordillera from Panama City to the Comarca of Kuna Yala, from where one must proceed by boat to Mulutupu and from there to Punta Escocés.

View of the island of Mulutupu and the Indian residences on the shoreline.

Mulutupu houses.

The *cayuco* that took me to Punta Escocés in the bay where the Caledonians would have arrived.

View of the bay from New Edinburgh. (Jim Malcolm)

The site where Fort St Andrew would have stood, jutting out into the bay to protect the entrance. (Jim Malcolm)

The defensive canal dug by the Caledonians. (Jim Malcolm)

Artefacts recovered at the site of Caledonia. (Jim Malcolm)

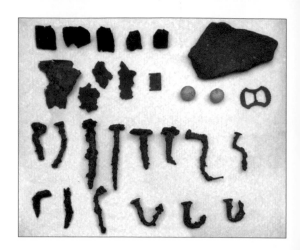

Aerial view of Punta Escocés. (Jim Malcolm)

Port Royal, Kingston, Jamaica, where the Caledonians fled to seek help from the English authorities.

St Andrew Parish Church in Kingston: the Scottish church existed around the time the Caledonians visited Jamaica.

Admiral John Benbow, who protected the Scots when he could. (© Getty Images)

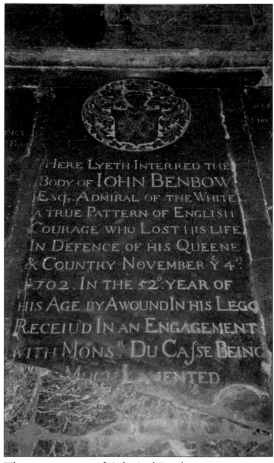

The gravestone of Admiral Benbow in Kingston.

A water tank in the small town of Darien in rural Georgia, named by colonial Scots to commemorate their ancestors.

James Island Church, Charleston, South Carolina: founded by Rev. Stobo when he fled Caledonia with the second expedition. He would become a very successful minister.

The Stobo Bible, beautifully preserved to this day and available to see at the South
Carolina Historical Society. (Courtesy of the South Carolina Historical Society)

Carlos II, the Spanish monarch who opposed the Scots in Darien. (© Getty Images)

The author in the Darien province of Panama. (Vladimir Bernal)

England coast and from there to Ireland or the Galloway coast of Scotland. They were to stick together and if they were separated they were supposed to leave word at a resupply port with their location. Upon arrival in Scotland they were immediately to send word to the Court of Directors and then follow their orders.

The order to abandon Caledonia and return to Scotland via Jamaica were given on 20 June 1699 whilst the ships jostled in the bay, waiting for the wind to change. On 22 June they got out to sea and soon split up; getting the wind into their sails to allow them to sail involved 'much a doe' and the *Saint Andrew* and the *Unicorn* were obliged to anchor off Golden Island. The journeys were dreadful, and the travellers endured the worst suffering of the entire expedition. In early July, the ailing *Endeavour* began taking on board water from leaks, the captain abandoned ship and ordered everyone on to the rowing boats, desperately signalling for the *Caledonia* to return to collect them. Robert Drummond did so and continued for the New England coast, where they arrived on 3 August 1699. During the forty-two day voyage, one hundred and five people died. Drummond was disgusted. He wrote:

In our sad and lamentable condition, we all embarqued upon the nineteenth day of June; having equally divided our people and Small Stock of provisions we had: with orders from our Council to make the best of our way for new-England, or any wher else upon the Main, where we might have provision to get home to Scotland ... in our passage from Caledonia hither our Sickness being so universal aboard, and Mortality so great that I have hove overboard 105 Corps. The Sickness and Mortality continues aboard. I have buried 11 since I came heire already. We have never heard so much as one silible either by word or writing from any in Scotland since we were come from hence. I am afraid I shall have a hard pull to gett the Ship home for my people are still Dying, being all weak: and Men is very Scarce heire to be had ...

Sir, I am not capable by writing to give Yow ane account of the Miserable condition we have undergone first before we came off from Caledonia, being Starved and abandoned by the World ...[2]

Conditions were no better aboard the *Saint Andrew* and the *Unicorn*. Captain John Anderson took over command of the *Unicorn* (its original captain, Pinkerton, remained a Spanish prisoner), but the crew's condition was desperate: so many men were ill, others were ravaged by the hardships in New Edinburgh, the fevers, poor food and hard work had taken their toll. The ship's provisions were spoiling and little fresh water or food was left aboard. To make matters worse, many of the planters who crammed aboard were ill, forced to live in unsanitary confined conditions below deck, creating a breeding ground for the rapid increase of illness and fever. Unlike the journey out, the men were simply too weak to scrub the decks with vinegar to maintain hygiene. The number of men available to crew the ship was limited and Anderson had to drive them hard; fewer men, they each had more work and the ship was in a poorer condition than during the outward journey, while in the panic before the departure, the ships were not properly careened. Tired arms had to work the pumps and weak bodies tried to control the lines, as the ships were buffeted by strong Caribbean winds and rolling seas.

South of Jamaica, the *Unicorn* was caught up in a raging storm at night: she lost her foremast and mizzen top and the ship was so battered its creaking wooden frame began to let in more water. Those who were able manned the pumps and the ship tried to ride the night out and by dawn, the exhausted men collapsed, delighted to have survived and surprised and pleased to see help at hand. The *Saint Andrew*, captained by Pennecuik, who by now had become sick after his months on the isthmus, was on the horizon. Anderson signalled for help and the flagship slowly came over, its crew uneasy at having to expend effort that did not lead them closer to safety. Anderson rowed across and met the gravely ill Pennecuik, who ordered a small sloop to remain with the *Unicorn* and sailed off. Anderson realised he was in a terrible state: he had few able men, a severely damaged ship, few provisions and little useful help from the Company. The sloop designated to help him sailed off shortly after. Showing considerable courage and determination, he had his men cut down the damaged masts and rigging and erect a jury-mast, a temporary mast to replace one that had broken. In the calm weather he ordered his men to pump water out of the hull and fix it up as best they could to slow the leaks. With increasing sickness, worsened by the long periods the men spent listlessly aboard ship, the *Unicorn* made slow progress up the Caribbean, but the crew had only limited control over it.

Winds buffeted the vessel around Cuba, too close to the great Spanish harbour at Havana, and sailed further east along the northern Cuban coast to the port of Matanzas, where Anderson ordered men ashore to find fresh water. It was a calculated and necessary risk, because men were dying for the want of fresh water, but it was also a hazardous one. Cuba was a key part of the Spanish Empire and a strong military base, strengthened because of the English occupation of Jamaica. The Spanish feared losing Cuba and ensured it was well protected. The Scots had chosen quite the wrong place to land: Matanzas was protected by a Spanish fort with twenty-four guns, the commander of which was horrified to see what he assumed was a pirate ship come ashore. The Scots knew they were taking a risk, but their dry throats and aching limbs sorely needed clean, fresh water. They ran across the bare green scrub which led down to the shore searching for springs or streams of fresh water, trying to drag heavy wooden barrels behind them. Those ashore soon abandoned their search for water and made for their boats as canon and musket fire angrily began emanating from the fort. The Spanish would not contemplate pirate raids and opened fire on the Scots, who had neither the firepower nor the strength to engage the Spaniards. In their haste to leave, they left behind their interpreter, Benjamin Spense, who quickly realised the game was up and took the opportunity to practise his Spanish, surrendering to the yellow-and-blue-uniformed Spanish soldiers.

Spense was taken to Fort San Severino, where he would spend some time in the darkness of the freshly built cells, grateful at least for food and fresh water and for being removed from the damaged and disease-ridden ship. The Spaniards realised the importance of their captive: he was no mere pirate and he was taken along the northern coast to Havana, where he was tortured and interrogated. He provided an intricate account of life in the colony and about the military make-up of the planters. A detailed account was taken down and sent to Madrid, where it was to be studied by the Council of the Indies. Apart from this questioning, his lengthy incarceration was both dull and nerve-racking, endless stuffy days in a darkened dungeon but always in fear, knowing the likely outcome of his adventure would be a pirate's death at the hands of his captors.

The monotony was broken up in September 1699 by the arrival of some old friends: his fellow Caledonians, Robert Pinkerton, James Graham, John Malloch and David Wilson, the valiant crew members of the *Dolphin*. They arrived in Havana weak and painfully thin. They had been poorly treated by the Spanish authorities in Cartagena, but they were the lucky ones; some had died and others had been sent as slaves to man the Barlovento fleet. It was routine for the Spanish fleet to sail once a year from its colonies, from Cartagena, stopping at Portobello to pick up the gold and silver, then go from there to Havana to reinforce the fleet and from there back to Spain. It was the well-worn treasure route that the pirates of earlier decades had chased after. These men would soon be bundled aboard a ship in the great fleet and arrive to be imprisoned in Cadiz, where they were visited by the resident English diplomat, who was horrified by their suffering and pitiful appearance and tried to intercede upon their behalf. Before progress could be made they were taken away to Seville to stand trial for piracy. Unsurprisingly, they were found guilty and sentenced to death, but they had a persistent and highly vocal champion on their side: Mrs Pinkerton was daily haranguing the Company's officers to petition King William to ask the Spanish monarch to show them leniency.

Meanwhile the *Unicorn* continued its precarious voyage north with the ailing Paterson aboard, his mind weakened by high fevers and the disasters that had befallen him. His wife was dead, his body weak and, probably worse than everything else, his project had failed and in the process, he would have been aware, he had cost the lives of hundreds of Scots and squandered the much-needed capital of a poor kingdom. He had few reasons to survive the journey home. The name Paterson would no longer be eulogised in ballads, men would no longer queue to buy him drinks in Edinburgh's taverns. The directors would demand a long explanation from him, and this, perhaps, is what kept him going, suffering in his stuffy cabin as the *Unicorn* slowly made its way up the eastern seaboard of the United States: the need to explain what had happened.

Ten days after the *Caledonia* arrived in New York, the *Unicorn* miraculously made it too. Around 150 men died and of the remaining 100, 60 or so were ill. They were a ragged, yellowy bunch, poorly clothed, with few resources. They were to receive a less than welcoming reception: the proclamation had also been published in the English North American colonies and everyone was nervous of providing help. There were many Scottish traders in the colonies, but they were often viewed as interlopers and alleged to be involved in piracy. Since Cromwell had passed the first Navigation Acts in 1651, which mandated that only English ships could transport goods from outside Europe to England, the Scots had been further marginalised. The legislation was extended, banning all foreign shipping from English colonial trade, and the colonies themselves were banned from exporting their goods to non-English customers. These measures were initially taken to limit the rapid expansion of Dutch shipping and trade, but hurt Scottish trade too, dependent as it was upon the larger consumer market in England. This led to large-scale resentment and increasingly placed the Scots in English colonies on the defensive. After the proclamation was passed against Caledonia, the Scots in New York were fearful of acting. The patriotism and concern that had led to the dispatch of the *Three Sisters* was unlikely to be repeated.

The Governor of Massachusetts was Richard Coote, the Earl of Bellomont, an elderly man and relatively new to the post when the Scots arrived. He was born in Ireland and had served in parliament and had served the queen as Treasurer and Receiver General before. He worried what the trade commissioners in London thought of him and was anxious always to do the right thing for his masters there. His track record was a little patchy: he had become mixed up with another Scot, the famous pirate William Kidd, whom he had sponsored as a privateer before the politics of the Caribbean changed, and he felt obliged to arrest the Scotsman when he returned to New York. He was no doubt troubled to read more Scots had arrived and would have known how seriously the government in London would have viewed his handling of the matter. He suffered from bad gout and had to endure the discomfort of leaving his comfortable quarters in New York to travel to Massachusetts when the Scots first appeared. Bellomont was in Boston when the Caledonians arrived in New York and the Lieutenant-Governor of New York, John Nanfan, was in day-to-day command. Soon after their arrival the Scots petitioned him for help. Sam Vetch and the Drummond brothers wrote:

> Unto the honorable Mr. Nanfan Lieutenant-Governor of New York the humble request of the Scotts Gentlemen belonging to the Colony of Caledonia humbly sheweth:
>
> That whereas the want of provisions and sickness of their people having obliged them to abandon the same and return home to Scotland and being putt in here in the most miserable can be expressed thro sicknesse and famine they not haveing money to purchase provisions for victualling them for their

voyage, begg they may have liberty to dispose of as much of their stores which they have aboard as will purchase provisions for two hundred men for ten or eleven weeks and they shall ever acknowledge the singular obligation done to your humble Servants.[3]

The request agitated Nanfan; on the one hand it was very tempting to agree to help – if the Scots were provisioned they would sail away and an awkward problem could disappear – but the proclamation made clear no assistance or provision were to be given to the Scots. Nanfan must have been a humane man too, as he was shocked and saddened by the terrible state of the Scots. He called a council on 5 August 1699 and with four other officers he decided the Scots should be allowed to sell goods to buy provisions until the Earl of Bellomont's decision was known. He then hurriedly wrote to Bellomont on 7 August:

On Friday arrived here the *Calledonia* of 60 guns, one of the Scotch ships went downe hither. They have been forced to abadon the Settlement being reduced to the Extreamity of famine and buried a great part of their men … They brought 300 and odd men out of Calledonia and in their voyage have thrown over 103 men and the remaining 200 so weak (not with any contagious distemper as I am informed by Coll. Morris who has been on board, but pure fatigue and famine, they have been forced to short allowance only of salt provisions since they left Scotland) they are not able to get up their small bower anchor … They have no money therefore I desire your Lordship will let me know by thy first opportunity how far the Law will allow me in this their necessity which is very miserable, the Barter of Stores of war, arms and powder, Instrument for Labour etc. for provisions, with a direction how to act therein. I have been very cautious in the Minute of Council, but their miserable condition and their now haveing abandoned their settlement and returning home is enough to raise Compassion if the Law will allow it, but I will do nothing further till your Lordship order.

And again on 14 August 1699:

There is another Caledonian arrived, lost his Masts and half starved; he has thrown over 160 men since he came out.

The Earl of Bellomont responded:

> You know how strict my orders are against furnishing the Caledonians with provisions, yet if you can be thoroughly well assured that these ships will go directly for Scotland and not return any more to the place whence they now come (called Caledonia by them) without doubt you may safely furnish them with just provisions enough for their voyage but no more.

Ominously for Bellomont, the Lieutenant-Governor responded only some days later:

> I wish your Lordship had been more plain about the Scotch ships, but I will advise with the Council and take all safe measures possible.

Understandably, Bellomont was baffled by this cryptic response and wrote back sharpishly:

> I wonder what I writ about your furnishing the Scotch ships with provisions should puzzle you, for I thought I expressed myselfe in plain termes enough that I would have you suffer them to buy provisions enough for their voyage to Scotland but not to carry them back to Caledonia; which latter was the thing I apprehended if you let them take away abundance of provisions, especially upon the Newes of the Recruit sent them from Scotland of men, armes and all other provisions.

It is interesting to note from this last letter that the English knew the second expedition was well equipped and very much on its way. Nanfan responded:

> The Caledonians by and with the advice and assistance of their Countrymen etc. have plaid us not fair, but your Lordship in a little while shall have the particulars.

Bellomont was far from pleased and wrote on 16 October:

> I wonder how you could pretermit the account of the behaviour of those Scotch from Caledonia, which is more moment then all the rest you have

writ of, ten times told: pray faile not to give me a perticular Relation of them and what you mean by saying that by the assistance of their Countrymen they have not plaid you fair. I wish you have not burnt your fingers with them, and broke the instructions I sent you from the Secretary of State. Pray doe not fail to write me all the particulars about them next post.

Still in the dark, he wrote again, on 23 October 1699:

I wonder you have omitted send me word what the misbehaviour of the Scotch from Calledonia at New York has been. 'Twas worth all other advices you have given me ten times over.

Concerned by what had happened, with some knowledge but not the full picture, he wrote directly to the Lords Commissioners of Trade and Plantations in London from Boston on 26 October 1699:

… I am the more particular in this account of the ships from Caledonia, because I apprehend the Scotch that came in them, from a starving condition they were in at their first coming, grew very insolent while they were at New York … but the Lt. Governor has not as yet taken pains to inform me of their behaviour particularly, and only gives me a hint in the last extract … … I have writ to the Lt. Governor … to explain the hint he has given me and… Their not playing fair with him: and the next post I expect an answer. Your Lordships will see that I have been cautious enough in my orders to the Lt. Governor if New York not to suffer the Scotch to buy more provisions than would serve to carry them home to Scotland, and if he has suffered them to exceed that he is to blame.

Nanfan had indeed burnt his fingers and was less than keen to own up to his bad-tempered boss. The Scots had taken advantage of his generosity and he was alarmed to see Bellomont reminding him of the proclamation, which did after all warn English subjects against breaching it 'at their utmost peril'. When Bellomont died in 1701, after a brief spell as Acting Governor Nanfan was not confirmed in the post.

The Scots had indeed been making mischief. If the English knew of the departure of the second expedition, then the Scots must have heard of it too. Some felt their duty obliged them to return, although most, after their gruesome experiences, had no intention of ever returning to Darien, putting a foot aboard a Company ship, nor, if they could help it, returning to Scotland. Thomas Drummond felt he should return to Darien, his soldier's training and his sense of honour made him feel he had failed by leaving. Not unreasonably he also felt there was considerable hope for a successful return, as New York buzzed with gossip about the well-armed, well-stocked Scottish ships that had sailed directly through the Caribbean to Darien. Drummond needed a ship and a crew to take him back. The *Unicorn* was in poor condition and would eventually be beached and abandoned near New York, a rotten monument to failed Scottish dreams. The *Caledonia* was set to return to Scotland.

Drummond talked his brother and Samuel Vetch into helping him take another ship and with some justification they believed the charter of the Company entitled them to commandeer another Scottish ship. It was clear, however, with the proclamation and the clear political signal from Whitehall, that such an act would be viewed most dimly by the colonial authorities. When a Scottish ship named the *Adventure* limped into port, unable to continue with its voyage to Glasgow because of the deaths of several mariners, the Drummond brothers seized their opportunity. The ship's captain, John Howell, was invited to dine aboard the *Caledonia*, and as he toasted the Scots he found himself imprisoned and his ship arrested and taken as a prize, on the grounds that it was Scottish and the Company officers had the right under the Charter to take her. Armed men departed for the ship to bring her closer to the *Caledonia*. The pilot, Peter Wessel, concerned for his job, headed to the town to inform the authorities and make a deposition on 12 September 1699:

> ... Captain Drummond's boat came on board ye said Ship againe, then under the care of her deponent (who was then preparing to carry her into the road) and with armed force their Cutlasses drawne in their hands Commanded this Dept. [Wessle] to bring the said ship under the reach of their Guns, who refusing they weighed the anchor of ye said ship themselves and brought her under the Sterne of ye said Ship *Caladonia* ...

Howell meanwhile was a prisoner and as soon as he could escape, he too made a deposition:

> ... the said Capt. Drummond, Commander of the *Caladonia*, kept him [Howell, writing in the third person] a prisoner on board the said ship *Caladonia* for the pace of Tenn hours or more and afterwards went with the dept. on board the ship *Adventure* whereof the dept. was Master and kept the dept, Prisoner all night, having posted several Centinells armed with drawn swords in his ship. That the next morning the dept. was sent for on board the *Caladonia* when he saw Capt. Drummond and severall other Gentlemen, who asked the Dept. what he though of it, or whether he would goe to town: that he answered him Yes, very willingly ...

As soon as Howell was ashore he sought help from the authorities and from Nanfan. The Drummonds had lost their courage and, despite having taken the *Adventure*, decided against departing there and then with the ship for Darien. They no doubt knew they may well have been tried as pirates and the consequences would have been severe. The Scots had panicked and were soon summoned. The ringleaders of the plot were told to 'personally appear before the board to-morrow morning at tenn of ye clock (all excuses laid aside) to answer such things as on his Majesty's behalf shall be objected against them'. The Scots knew they were in trouble and if they were imprisoned or arrested they would be unable to make their way back to Darien. Showing some considerable native wit, they concocted their defence:

> That whereas we are informed that either by misrepresentation or misunderstanding the said honourable Council have conceived an opinion that we should have seized a Scotts ship within their harbour which was comeing up to towne and that it was done either by assumeing to ourselves an unlawfull power or to affront the Government, Wee therefore do hereby declare upon honour that we never had any designe either to seize ye ship (but only to delay her coming up until we should give the Master and Captain advice who was incapable of it by reason of his drunken-nesse) far lesse to affront your government under whose protection we at present are and from whom we have received so many favours and do stil expect more, therefore as we

extreamly regret there ever have happened any thing that should have given the least umbrage to a misunderstanding betweixt us and the Government for whom (as our duty is) we have all the respectfull deference imaginable so do hereby declare our Innocence in this affair whatever rudenesse might have happened through the indiscretion of sailors and in testimony of the truth and sincerity of the same have subscribed this at New York September 13th 1699.

Seriously ill, Paterson was talked into agreeing to this version of events and he signed his name agreeing to the 'submission'. Nanfan was furious and wanted to take further action. He tried to take legal action against them, but this was not encouraged by the Attorney General (apparently a Scot) and he was left to fume. The Scots' oleaginous description of what had occurred managed to get them off the hook. Vetch and Paterson were forced to ask Nanfan for help about ten days later to help apprehend Scots who, sick of disease and hunger on board the ship, had succumbed to the allure of life on land and slunk down the anchor rope and swum to shore to seek a better life. The Scots were aware they needed as many men as possible to get the *Caledonia* back to Scotland.

The Drummonds, despite this setback, were still determined to head back to Caledonia, and hatched another plan, this time using more orthodox principles. Thomas Drummond teamed up with local traders Richard Wenham and Stephen Delancey, whose pasts involved pirating off the coast of Madagascar and who were more than happy to become involved in some risky business if it could pull in a good profit. Thomas arranged that he would transfer the remaining Scots' trading goods over to Wenham and Delancey and in return they would provide him with a small sloop, the *Ann*, and provisions for the return journey to New Edinburgh. He transferred the goods to a bonded warehouse on the shore, renamed the ship the *Ann of Caledonia*, and quietly weighed anchor and slipped out of the harbour without asking permission on the evening of 20 September 1699. He sailed with orders from the Council, with around twelve sailors and some landsmen who wanted to return. Meanwhile Robert Drummond remained in New York with the *Caledonia*, which was being careened.

If the Scots who set sail in the *Caledonia* and *Unicorn* did not fare well in New York, the Scots who sought salvation in the *Saint Andrew* had a much worse time. After it had sailed off without offering the *Unicorn* much help, Pennecuik demanded the ship make for Port Royal in Jamaica. He would never see the island's green shores; fever carried him away before they landed. His body was heaved overboard with limited ceremony. Colin Campbell, a soldier and not a sailor, took command and with his weak and ailing crew struggled to make progress towards Jamaica. Sickness and death were everywhere. One hundred and forty men died on the terrible crossing from New Edinburgh and the ship was harried by a cruiser from the Barlovento fleet.

To much relief on board, the ship eventually anchored off Bluefields Bay, in south-western Jamaica, a port used by pirates like Henry Morgan some years earlier. Campbell, knowing the desperate condition of his men and suspecting them of mutiny, was keen to get to Port Royal to organise provisions. He hired some horses when ashore and rode directly to meet the governor, Sir William Beetson. As could have been expected of a man so keen to thwart the Scots by publishing the proclamation on the Sabbath, he was unenthusiastic about helping them now they had fled New Edinburgh. He offered Campbell an audience and refreshments, but was determined to enforce the letter of the law. He would not be moved like Nanfan and Bellomont by the Scots' terrible condition. He was also nervous, however, as the Spaniards had begun to take reprisals, viewing the English and the Scots as one and the same. The English on Jamaica feared a Spanish attack, so it was with some relief that Beetson could report to his masters in London that the Scots had left Darien. Campbell was dispirited and rode to the quayside in Port Royal to seek help from Admiral Benbow. He could not help and was not interested in taking the *Saint Andrew* as a prize. He had his hands full preparing his fleet. In the conflict-ridden waters of the Caribbean, war and danger were never far away: he would be dead by 1702, the victim of a Caribbean engagement with the French.

The few Scots who had survived as far as Jamaica had poor options: they could sell themselves as indentured labour to sugar plantations, beg or steal to survive on land, or remain on the rotting ship where more and more men were dying. A nasty yellow fever epidemic swept the Caribbean that summer, killing many from different islands and the Scots too succumbed, weakened from their journey and months of malnutrition. They were a sorry bunch, a group of yellow-faced, thin survivors clinging around their rotting boat. They were shunned and ignored and left to die. With so few men Campbell had the *Saint Andrew* run aground and left to rot. It was a sad end for the flagship of the Company of Scotland. Campbell went ashore to try as best he could to make a living.

Of the entire first fleet, only one ship returned to Scotland: the *Caledonia*, captained by Robert Drummond. After his brother's departure in the *Ann of Caledonia*, he knew the Scots' luck was running out and his ship was as ready as it was going to be. He had finished careening it as best he could and his men were in a better condition, if not healthy. They departed New York on 12 October 1699. She carried only 300 men and not all of these would sail up the Clyde, but mercifully the journey was a brief six weeks. Drummond brought the ship up the Clyde and riders were sent to inform the directors in Edinburgh. Paterson was helped ashore and spent two weeks getting across to the capital, where he met the directors and sat down with shaky hands to write his report. Drummond received orders early in December to keep the men aboard ship, which must have come as a blow to them. The directors were more concerned to ensure the remaining goods were 'laid up carefully in the Glasgow warehouse'. With shareholders incandescent over the failure of their investments, the directors were more concerned to protect the remaining value of the goods than get their employees off the ship and have them properly looked after. There were few goods left, as they had been exchanged for the *Ann of Caledonia*.

The *Caledonia*, sole survivor of the first expedition, would languish in the docks near Greenock for some six years before she was put up for sale in May 1706. The Glasgow merchant, Arbuckle, who had become rich fitting out the second expedition, bought her with a Mr Mackenzie, who might have been the former secretary to the Company. Nobody, however, wanted the arms she possessed, some 400 fire-locks, 800 pistols and 500 swords. Some years later, in a letter to the Commissioners for the Union, the Company warned that whilst these arms would remain in Port Glasgow they could be used by people 'who are disaffected to the Government'. The failure of the colony at Darien was to have huge and sometimes bloody ramifications for Scotland.

TEN

HOPE REBORN: THE SECOND EXPEDITION

Some months before the *Caledonia*'s arrival in Greenock, the directors took lodgings in Glasgow to be nearer the second fleet and oversee its provisioning. Paterson's advice was to be followed, at last, and the four ships of the second expedition would save time by leaving from the west coast. However, the resupply ships for the original expedition, the *Olive Branch* and the *Hopeful Binning,* left beforehand from Leith and arrived too late to sustain the members of the first expedition. William Jameson and Alexander Stark, the captains of the respective relief ships, were horrified to find lush greenery sprouting through the charred ruins of Fort St Andrew and the dilapidated huts of New Edinburgh. The men from the resupply were concerned as to what course of action they should take and were relieved when the Indians and a former Caledonian who had stayed behind approached them in the bay and breathlessly explained all that happened. At least they understood their predicament, but such a tale could hardly have filled them with enthusiasm for the task ahead.

As so often was the case with the unfortunate Scots, events would take their own course. After they landed, the men raised the Company's flag and fell into the pattern of hard drinking their fellow Caledonians had been so fond of before. This time around such a practice was to have more direct consequences aboard the *Olive Branch*; a crew member stumbling below decks during the dead of night in search of more brandy tripped and with his naked flame set the store of brandy alight. The fire soon spread and very quickly burnt the ship down to the waterline, sending a ghoulish light across the bay, and throwing long dark shadows from the men gathered at the water's edge, into the intimidating bush. The poorly provisioned and meagrely armed Scots were, overnight, made much more vulnerable.

Sensibly, Jameson and Stark ordered the *Hopeful Binning* to Jamaica with the majority of the men, whilst a dozen stayed at Caledonia to try to hold the colony against any further possible Spanish advances. The few men left behind were cheered in November when two small and ragged sloops sailed into the bay: they were the *Ann of Caledonia*, captained by Thomas Drummond and sailed from New York, and the *Society*, a sloop chartered at St Thomas. Drummond's command limped into the bay in poor condition: en route she had come under attack from a Spanish gunship, but despite her small size, limited arms and crew of a dozen or so, Drummond, the stubborn fighter, would not surrender her, defiantly battling on until he could escape under cover of darkness. His men were delighted to see they had not been forgotten by the directors in Edinburgh and were much cheered by the news that a sizeable second expedition would be arriving with fresh provisions and men. Caledonia remained in Scottish hands.

Meanwhile back in Scotland, Glasgow was enjoying the generous attentions of the 'African' Company, as provisions were organised for the journey to Darien from this western city and not the capital. The directors had taken an office in Glasgow, in Stockwell, and had rented some warehouses. Glasgow was just beginning to embark upon its transformational role from small town to Second City of the Empire. Its position had already guaranteed that the directors took advantage of the city's better location to locate and provision the new fleet. We know from a detailed ledger kept by Peter Murdoch[1] just how extensive the goods brought aboard the ships were. It covered everything from groats to gravats; hemp to hair; combs to cabbage and brimstone to beeswax. From early May until mid August we have a detailed list of who provided what and to which ship it was sent, with details of exactly in what quantities the items were delivered. Much of it was basic food, delivered in large quantities: 19,903 pounds of biscuits from various suppliers; over 80 skins of dressed calf; and over 22,626 pounds of stockfish. Other food items were delivered in smaller quantities: cinnamon; cloves; nutmeg; raisins; casks of lime juice; and casks of muscovado sugar. Other items were there for trading and included more 'hair coverings', bonnets and plaid, whilst the Scots appear to have realised fishing lines were a good idea and some 538 pounds were delivered. More armaments were sent: boxes and belts of cartridges; coils of cordage; barrels of powder and bags of flint and boxes of knives. These would all be needed in due course against the Spanish.

As the goods piled up, they were soon transported aboard the Company's fine new ships, and there was none finer than the new flagship, the *Rising Sun*. She had been built in the Netherlands and Peter the Great had taken wine aboard her on his peregrination through Europe before returning to found St Petersburg and set Russia on a western-bound course. John Prebble lovingly describes her:

Made of good Berlin oak and 450 tons in burden, she was more than 150 feet long from her forecastle head to the carved caryatids on her stern. She was armed like an Indiaman with thirty-eight guns, twelve, eight and four-pounders, their ports painted red and encircled with golden laurels on the after deck. She glowed with the gold of her name. One rising sun burst into gilded rays beneath her sprit, and another below her stern. All her golden carving was rich, elaborate, curling leaves, convolutes and whorls twined about her windows, poop-deck rail, roundhouse and captain's barge. Her yellow-panelled cabin was luxuriously finished – bed curtains of Bengal cloth, fringed, canopied and tasselled with gold, gilded handles to the doors, five tablecloths and yellow damask in a chest of orange wood, eighteen ells of linen napery, two large looking-glasses framed in gold, dark red earthenware, blue cups of polished pewter, and spoons of yellow horn.[2]

Despite, or perhaps because of her splendour, she nearly remained in Amsterdam, as the Company failed to meet all its debts and she was arrested and kept in the port city over the winter of 1697–98, and only released after some shareholders ensured the money was found to release her.

She would be joined in her voyage from the Clyde to Darien by the Company's other, smaller, vessel, the *Hope*. It was estimated these two ships could carry another 500 colonists to Darien, but because of the number of people who wished to settle in Caledonia the Company decided to charter two other vessels to carry around 1,300 people in total, of whom around one third were Highlanders who spoke only Gaelic. The chartered ships were the *Duke of Hamilton* and the *Hope of Bo'ness* (Borrowstounness). These four ships gathered by Greenock, were stocked, and excitement began to mount as the summer of 1699 wore on. Feelings had been riding high in Scotland since news of the colony had trickled back to the mother country, tempered by irritation and anger as the Scots heard about the proclamation. This appears to have been treated less as the deathblow it came to be viewed after the collapse of Caledonia and more as a challenge: a sign of English fear of the success the Scots would soon have. Other news from the colony clearly angered the directors. In the summer of 1699 they received a glum letter from some of the colonists complaining of the supposed plan to take the *Saint Andrew* and use her for pirating. The directors shot back:

> We must say it cannot but grieve us to think that when your settlement alarms, in a manner, most part of all Europe, and when the eyes of men are intent upon the event thereof, we should be alarm'd, on the other hand, ever since December last with continued Reports of your jealousies, animosities, factions, heart-burnings and disagreements among yourselves ... nor can we attribute it to anything else but to your people being penned up in a corner close together, in a state of lazy idleness, as we are informed.

However, a much more serious and darker rumour was finding its way north: the colony had been abandoned. The directors were furious. We can fully understand their anxieties from a survey of their orders to the ships' commanders, as they changed as summer turned into autumn. They wrote in their sailing order to the *Rising Sun* on 17 August 1699 that:

> When you make Golden Island and come within a convenient distance of the said Company's settlement, you are to open and use the enclosed signals, and if you should happen not to be duly and exactly answered as the said signals do prescribe, then you are to spread the Company's colours and come to anchor about the middle of the Bay opposite to the body of the said Island, and at the same time you are to give a signal to them ashore by firing of a gun and making a whef with your ensign for a pilot to conduct you into the harbour.[3]

All of which assumed a level of organisation and structure in the colony that had never existed even when the Scots were in possession of Caledonia. At this stage in August there appears to have been little understanding in Scotland of the repeated messages revealing hardship in the colony, or knowledge of the eventual abandonment of Caledonia. However, the directors had recognised the challenge the second expedition would face and the increased hostility to their project. Their 'directions and advice' to the *Rising Sun*'s captain ordered him to ensure all men were taught 'the use of both great and small guns' and that the men were organised into fighting units. Just over one month later the directors would write again to the second expedition's leaders, but this time with much more concerning news:

> And whereas we have received information from London of a very improbable story that those of the said Colony have wholly deserted their settlement there, for fear of the preparations that were making against them at Carthagena, and gone where nobody can give account of them, we can give no manner of credit to the said story, all circumstances relating to it appearing inconsistent and fabulous that we can believe not set of men in the world of any reasonable measures of discretion and resolution, and much less those in whose fidelity and courage we have placed such an entire confidence, could be guilty of so much groundless cowardice, folly and treachery. Yet in case it should happen that through any unforeseen and unexpected accident you find the Colony removed from their said settlement (which we cannot suffer ourselves to believe upon any account), then you are to use all means possible for re-possessing yourselves (even by force of arms if need be) …[4]

The directors were to receive the confirmation they could not suffer themselves to believe shortly thereafter and sent further instructions to the new council members now making their way to Darien, having departed on 24 September 1699. The new instructions blamed one man:

> In regard that Captain Robert Pennicuik, one of the former Councellors has not only all along since his first going to the said Colony, held an undue correspondence with several persons, both here and in England, concerning the Colony's proceedings and circumstances, to the manifest prejudice and discredit of both the Company and the Colony … you are hereby ordered upon meeting with him, on the Colony or elsewhere, to run him out of all his offices and commands, both by sea and land, with disgrace and infamy; and punish him otherwise as upon examination you shall find his crimes deserve

This harsh indictment would not bother the already dead Pennecuik, but it did seek to shift blame from the directors and provide some form of an account to the furious stockholders, reducing the heat in the boardroom in Mylne's Square. It remained to be seen whether the directors themselves had done a better job in the selection of the four new council members. The captain of the *Rising Sun* and commodore of the fleet was appointed to be one of them. He was James Gibson and was a wealthy Glasgow merchant who had been the Company's agent in Amsterdam, where he watched his ship built and in whose cabins he shared wine with Peter the Great. He had bought £500 of stock in the Company and had been made a director. He was more a merchant and money man than an adventurer but he had proved his worth to the Company and was a capable seaman. Still in poor health, and in fact forced back to his sick bed after nearly drowning during the wreck of the *Dispatch,* was William Vetch, one of the original council members. With his poor health he was clearly a bad choice, as poor health in Scotland would only worsen in tropical Panama. Major John Lindsay was also chosen, but little is known about him. The Edinburgh merchant James Byres was the fourth choice and he too had been with the Company from the outset, being one of the first to subscribe his name for stock.

The second expedition also brought together a more varied group of would-be Caledonians. There were, for example, over 100 women amongst the 1,300 people crowded aboard the ships on the Clyde, although this is disputed by the testimony of men who deserted Caledonia, who informed the Spanish there were fewer than ten women. Most were wives of men then departing or, although they did not know it, widows of husbands they hoped to meet upon their arrival. Whilst we have recorded the disappointment of councillors who were perturbed to find only ruins upon their arrival in New Edinburgh, we know little of the reaction of these brave women who sailed across an ocean to be with their husbands, women who found themselves not just alone in a foreign land but forced to grieve their loss under terrible circumstances.

The directors also sent along men with particular skills to help build not only a colony but also a real community: John Wallace and Thomas Kerr were sent as engineers; John Jaffrey was to be the fire master; Robert Keil the goldsmith; James Hunter the blacksmith; and David Dovale 'who professes to understand and speak Spanish, Portuguese, Italian, French,

Dutch, English and the Indian languages' was sent to join Benjamin Spense – not knowing that Spense was languishing in Cuba. He would be alone in communicating with the strange people they met and it seems clear he did not survive long, or was sent elsewhere, as when the time came to capitulate to the Spanish, the communication was carried out in a mixture of French and Latin.

In addition to caring for the technical aspect of the new colony, the directors were also keen to look after the spiritual welfare of their charges and four new ministers were sent along with the second fleet. They were sent with an ambitious commission by the Church of Scotland. It was grandly and optimistically entitled 'The Commission to the Presbytery of Caledonia, July 21 1699' and named Archibald Stobo, Francis Borland, Alexander Shield and Alexander Dalgliesh as the four ministers who would 'be sent to Caledonia, to labour in that pious, necessary and glorious work'. The moderator was keen for them to be busy and laid out detailed instructions for constituting a presbytery, electing a moderator and clerk and from there progressing to 'divide the whole inhabitants of the colony, according to their local residence, and the best conveniency their present circumstances can admit, into so many Districts or Parishes, that each Minister may have a particular charge … and then increase the number of the Elders and Deacons …' The Church was also keen to save souls and when the ministers were not dealing with the Caledonians, they were to 'labour among the Natives for their instruction and conversion, as you have access'. They were also encouraged to stay as long as possible and on no account abandon the presbytery. Later, Borland, Shield and Stobo (Dalgleish was dead) gave notice to the moderator in a letter 'from the woods of Caledonia' written only two months after their arrival that none amongst them wished to remain in Caledonia. The Reverend Francis Borland was the only one to return to Scotland and wrote a mean-spirited, priggish account of his time, which, even so, serves as a useful guide.

Both the moderator and the directors were trying to turn their small part of Darien into a permanent settlement. These tradesmen, ministers, additional planters and above all the women were being sent to build up the colony and turn it into a viable trading post. They hoped children would be born in Caledonia, coins would be minted and issued, bridges built over ravines, roads constructed, leading to ports and docks, and that warehouses and official buildings would be put up in a flurry of activity to hold the spices and trading treasures and count the tariffs and customs due. This was the door to the seas and the key to the universe, after all.

With these grand hopes and to the noise of uncertain goodbyes from the quayside, the fleet left the Clyde and slipped out slowly past Loch Long, the Holy Loch and the Cowal shore, only to stop and anchor by the Isle of Bute for the next month. Gibson was unhappy with the winds, and so the fleet wasted a month's worth of provisions just off the Scottish coast. The directors wanted the recently returned Daniel McKay to return to the colony and Gibson was told on 23 September 1699 to await his arrival with further provisions. For whatever reason, he slipped anchor the next day and the fleet sailed for Darien. McKay would have cause to regret not being aboard for reasons other than his irritation that the fleet had sailed without him. He travelled instead on the *Speedy Return* some weeks later, but as he sailed down from Jamaica to Caledonia, he fell overboard whilst fishing sharks and the hunter promptly became the hunted. He was not to see the muddy pathways of New Edinburgh again. But his visit to Scotland would produce one definite bright spot to the whole sorry saga. He arrived in Edinburgh in the middle of September, as rumours of the abandonment began to circulate, but he denied this was the case and naturally, as he had just come from there, his version was readily believed. As we have seen, the second fleet sailed with knowledge of these rumours, but they were widely believed not to be true. It was not until 9 October 1699 that Mylne's Square received letters from New York, written in August, which confirmed the news nobody wanted to hear or believe. However, as a result of this the directors were determined to respond and made it clear to the new Council of the Second Fleet that there must be no abandonment of the colony. This too would be ignored, but the man who was dispatched to deliver the letter was Alexander Campbell of Fonab, a man who would score a small victory at Tubuganti on behalf of the Caledonians and restore a little pride in sorry Scottish hearts.

There were few writers aboard the ships of the second expedition so we know less about it. From the orders sent to the ships' commanders we know the directors asked the councillors to make good use of their time on board training the men, but warned the surgeons to be diligent in looking after the sick and also advised that an eye be kept on the stewards to be sure they did not help themselves to more brandy than they were entitled. Borland tells us they first saw land on 9 November 1699, as they passed the island of Antigua and sailed on to Montserrat, where Gibson sent his long boat ashore for fresh water and provisions and some intelligence. The first two they were to be refused by the English governor, but were informed their comrades had deserted Caledonia: Borland tells us the councillors did not believe it. Not long afterwards the Reverend Dalgleish perished, lamented as a good man of God by Borland. He was one of 160 who died between the Clyde and Darien. They arrived on 30 November 1699: St Andrew's Day, but Scotland's patron saint was not looking out for them in Panama. Borland gravely intoned:

> Upon our arrival in this new world, we met with a sorrowful and crushing-like dispensation, for expecting here to meet with friends and countrymen, we found nothing but a waste, howling wilderness; the colony deserted and gone, their Huts all burned, their Fort most part ruined, the ground which they had cleared adjoining to the Fort all overgrown with shrubs and weeds. We looked for peace, but no good came; and for a time of health and comfort, but beheld trouble.[6]

Once settled in the bay a familiar pattern descended upon the Caledonians: poor leadership and bickering. Thomas Drummond had himself rowed across the bay to the *Rising Sun* to meet with the new councillors and impart some advice. He presented letters from Paterson and Samuel Vetch and asked to be appointed to the council: a request James Byres looked upon with incredulity. He would soon attempt to browbeat the others into his having sole command of the outpost; he was not about to have the upstart, stern soldier telling him what to do. Drummond, volatile at the best of times, was furious, and with good reason after his efforts to return to Caledonia, to hold the settlement, bring further provisions and establish lines of credit with merchants in New York to ease problems of resupply. Drummond was passionate about the colony and made it clear to the other leading Scots that the only option was to begin rebuilding the huts and more importantly Fort St Andrew before the Spanish attacked. The council and many colonists did not like this advice: they had come, after all, to reinforce an existing colony, not to build a new one. The thought of the clashes and struggles ahead clearly scared them and they were horrified by Drummond's suggestion that he lead men against Portobello in a pre-emptive attack. Byres was a merchant, this was a trading colony and he was not for the 'taking of towns'. Drummond was of course correct and it would not be long before the Spaniards would come to them. Byres wanted to leave several companies of soldiers in the bay and recommended the rest sail to Jamaica: a proposal for abandonment without quite abandoning the colony. In the end it was a report by Gibson which encouraged the council to realise some men had to go to Jamaica as there simply were not enough provisions to sustain the large numbers of Scots in the bay. Rations were ordered to be cut and the *Duke of Hamilton* and the *Hope of Bo'ness*, under captains Duncan and Dalling, were detailed to take some 500 Caledonians to Jamaica and provided with three weeks of rations.

Working in a parallel to their predecessors, the colonists began to clear the ground and construct huts and the fort, but there was little enthusiasm for this work, and sickness, weakness and idleness all played their part in ensuring little progress was made. Two warehouses were built for storing the provisions and Fort St Andrew was repaired. Borland commented on the abundance of fine timber for building and the suitability of 'wild plan-tane leaves' which were broad, long and suitable for covering the dwelling huts. No church was built, much to the ministers' consternation, and few attended public worship; the Caledonians, wrote Borland, were 'the meaner sort, none of the best of men'. And some clearly did not want to be there: in mid December, only a couple of weeks after the fleet's arrival, nine men deserted in the *Rising Sun*'s long boat and made for Portobello, where they betrayed their countrymen and told the Spanish about the second fleet and its strength. The majority of these men were not Scots: records in Panama show them to have been Greek, Venetian and English. They had arrived in late December, claiming to have been tricked into joining the Scots, and all readily admitted being good Catholics who had nothing against Spain. One of them, Simon Modesto, claims he was posted to Holland from where the Scots tricked him into joining their ship, telling him he would go to Cadiz in the navy and from there to Persia, but he found himself on the high seas bound for the Americas against his will. An unlikely tale, but Portobello was no place to languish in a dungeon. He claimed the Scots had been violent towards him and the other deserters and they were forced to work hard all day before sleeping on the ships at night. He added there were few people keeping watch and that they were placed high up on the surrounding hills, which facilitated their escape. He dropped one of the few clues as to the Scots' intentions, as to how they aimed to create their entrepôt port serving Europe and Asia. They planned, he said, to establish a population at Real de Santa Maria on the Pacific coast. One can assume they would have then tried to find a way to send the goods across the isthmus between these termini. The lieutenant general of Portobello, Sergeant Major Don Marco de Motaya, would have realised how important it was to send this intelligence to his superiors. Such a position on both sides of the isthmus would have been a real affront to the integrity of the Spanish colonial system. The Spaniards already operated a sophisticated trading route between Europe, America and Asia, through what they called the *Nao De China*, which went between Acapulco and the Philippines. The Caledonians' plans were a major affront to their established monopoly on such trade. Paterson may have wanted to put Panama at the 'heart of the universe' to trade both east and west, but the Spaniards already operated these routes and would not give them up without a fight.

Caledonia was, however, far from becoming a major port. It was awash with rumours and the colonists were jumpy. Nobody had expected to arrive in a deserted bay, or to have to build a trading colony from scratch, and all of this while in fear of imminent attack from the Spaniards: the stress was taking its toll. The second expedition was much less eager to engage with the Indians and Byres appears to have harboured a considerable dislike towards them. The men were scared and the Indians, correctly, had informed them the Spaniards were making preparations to attack them. Thomas Drummond, with his soldierly disposition, was not keen on hanging around the bay while morale and discipline began to fray: he sent Robert Turnbull, a soldier, to the council with a proposal to let him take 150 men and suitable provisions, promising he would lead them into the jungle with the Indians and not return until the colony was safe from Spanish attack. He considered attacks against either Portobello or Cartagena and talked of freeing the men who had been captured aboard the *Dolphin* many months previously. James Byres, who was increasingly trying to control the council, was infuriated and probably also scared, but wanted to hang on to his position of authority even though he was aware of the inadequacy of his own merchant's background and lack of courage, and knew men would follow a natural leader like Drummond. He argued that with only six weeks of provisions left the proposal would not be feasible; so cowed was the council by his bullying that nobody contradicted this assertion, although only some days earlier the figure had been put at six months. Drummond's offer was refused and, apart from Campbell of Fonab's heroics, the Scots would largely wait in the bay, suffering from a defeatist mentality until all would be too late.

Shortly after the announcement of the diminished provisions a plot was uncovered to take some of the councillors hostage with threats to hang them should they not turn over leadership of Caledonia and control of the ships. Apparently co-conspirators confessed and one man's name kept coming up: Alexander Campbell – not Campbell of Fonab, but a carpenter – and he was imprisoned aboard the *Duke of Hamilton* with his wrists and ankles in irons. Apparently he was emboldened after hearing of the councillors' rejection of Drummond's offer and there were possible links between some of the conspirators and Drummond, although it is hard to be sure. Campbell was subjected to a court martial on 18 December 1699 aboard the *Rising Sun*, presided over by Major John Lindsay and several other officers. Campbell confessed to complaining about the poor level of provisioning but denied he was involved in a plot to replace the colony's leadership. However, his evidence was overwhelmed by a number of depositions made against him and it was not difficult for the officers to decide upon his guilt. He was sentenced to death and taken back to his makeshift cell on the *Duke* to await the construction of a scaffold and his death by hanging, scheduled for 20 December 1699. In between time Francis Borland visited him and took pity on the man: he spoke freely to the minister, confessing he had lately failed to pray to God and therefore was not surprised by his 'doleful end'. Borland and some of his colleagues tried to intervene with the council to have his sentence commuted from death to banishment, but the council would have none of it: they wanted to make an example of someone and thought a swinging corpse by Fort St Andrew would cool any other seditious plots.

Campbell was rowed ashore on 20 December and, with drums beating, stepped up to the scaffold built by his colleagues and was duly punished for his involvement. The council knew others were involved but found it easier to take a humble carpenter's life rather than risk a greater uprising by beginning proceedings against other officers. Despite that, the next day Drummond and four other officers were arrested and locked in their cabins: no charges were brought against them, no court martial arranged to test their guilt. No heed was paid to the laws set up by the first expedition (granted, these may not have been known to the second batch of Caledonians), and James Byres, who now dominated the council and ordered the arrests, would have ignored them. Drummond had delivered the journal of the first colony to the council, and they had carefully gone through it, finding, according to Borland, conduct by Drummond which displeased them. Byres was jealous of the man and was glad to be rid of a man who challenged and scared him and brought the reality and necessity of conflict with the Spaniards too close. Byres was a merchant who, arriving to find no hint of a trading colony, was anxious to leave and return to his comfortable merchant's life. Drummond would remain imprisoned until the arrival of Campbell of Fonab.

There is little comment on how Christmas and Hogmanay were spent in New Edinburgh that year. We can assume little celebrating was done, given both the dejected nature of their stay on the Panamanian coast and the failure to write much about it. Not even Borland mentions an act of Christmas worship, as he was focusing instead on the Day of Thanksgiving, Humiliation and Prayer, which took place on 3 January 1700. The three ministers had met aboard the *Hope of Bo'ness* on 5 December 1699, shortly after their arrival, and not only did they complain of the almost non-existent state of Caledonia, but they were also deeply concerned by the scandalous and blasphemous behaviour of their fellow colonists. They agreed to approach the council and ask that 3 January be set aside to thank God for their safe arrival and to confess their sins, particularly as many involved in the colony were motivated 'by their own selfish and worldly interests' to help curb the brutish abominations committed, 'such as Atheistical swearing and cursing, brutish drunkenness, detestable lying and prevaricating, obscene and filthy talking, mocking of godliness, yea, and among too many of the meaner sort, base thieving and pilfering, besides Sabbath-breaking and contempt of all Gospel-ordinances ...' Even those who did not commit such abominations were ignorant about the Lord, thought Borland, and did not appreciate God's work and forgot that 'when his hand was heavy upon us in our late sickness at sea, which many of us have already forgotten, and returned with the dog to the vomit'. Borland took a dim view of the behaviour of his fellow Caledonians and, when things did not work out, was not shy in pointing the finger of blame at the God-angering behaviour of his companions.

On the first Wednesday in 1700, the three remaining ministers duly went about their day of prayer, but it seems the Caledonians largely shunned the opportunity to hear Borland on thanksgiving, Shields on humiliation and Stobo on prayer and supplication, as their instructions were 'little regarded by most of them'. It is both surprising and to be expected that religious guidance was treated with such indifference and perhaps contempt by the Caledonians. The awesome power of nature must surely have made the men feel insignificant and weak before greater powers, as they lay in the bay pondering their fate. Their predecessors, the Spanish, had carried out all sorts of feverish rituals and dedications to God. One need only think of Latin American cities with religious names: Santa Fe de Bogotá, Asunción, Santa Maria, San José, San Juan, Santiago. The list goes on. Presbyterianism proved to be considerably less comforting, which may also have been down to the character of the ministers, who did not miss an opportunity to speak badly of their fellow Caledonians, castigating them without understanding them. But fear also drove the worst excesses of the clergy, and they were woefully unprepared for their adventure. Borland expected special treatment and was dismayed not to have his own hut. He was hurt and confused and complained that when the ministers did meet it was normally 'in the shady, dark and silent woods'.

The ministers were soon given an opportunity to leave the seventeenth-century Sodom and Gomorrah that was New Edinburgh and they departed on an expedition with Robert Turnbull to visit some of the Indian encampments close to the Scottish colony. The ministers had pretty much given up on any form of missionary work because the language barrier was too difficult for them and because 'alas we have reason to fear we shall do them more hurt than good; for the first of our language that they learn, is cursing and swearing... ' Nevertheless out of 'curiosity' the ministers embarked upon their visit to the Indian settlements on 16 January 1700, crossing the great harbour towards the south-west coast and from there they hacked their way through the steamy jungle, up several steep hills and across many small rivers and streams. They followed the banks of the River Acla the

Greater until they reached Pedro's village, where they were well treated and provided for, fed as they were with dried meat, plantains, corn and potatoes. It was a strange meeting in the smoky clearing of the wet jungle: the Indians amused by the arrival of three large, red-faced, black-frock-coated men, puffing and panting, eager to be given their hammocks to lie down, dry off by their fire and recover from their arduous journey. The ministers were similarly struck by what they saw: ' a poor naked people, living as we use to say, from hand to mouth, being very idle and lazy, and not industrious, peaceable and friendly to those that use them kindly, but very revengeful and covetous.' When they had recovered from their journey they embarked on a short service, which the Indians gravely listened to in silence. Despite the ministers' suspicions that the Indians' priests consulted the devil, they showed little enthusiasm for conversion or the nitty gritty hard work of showing them the path to the Lord, despite the fact that Pedro was able to communicate with them.

The next day the Scottish party left and headed back down the river until they came upon Acla the Lesser, which they followed down to Prandies Bay where they saw more Indian houses, with their open sides and palm-fronded roofs to protect against the sun and rain. They marvelled at the fields of orange trees and surely helped themselves to a couple of sweet mandarin-style little oranges, deliciously fresh after the mouldy fare brought up from the ships' holds. They followed the coast along in a western direction until they came to another Indian settlement and lodged in the house of an Indian named John. They carried out more worship, met again by polite but stony silence, and the next day left, returning to the coast to make for New Edinburgh. Despite the pleasant surroundings they found the journey hard going, being unused to wielding a machete and walking in the oppressive heat, so they cut down to the coast, expecting to find an easier route by the seashore. But they soon started to struggle as the journey began to take its toll: the path by the sea required them to cut back up into the jungle continually because of the jagged, uneven nature of the Caribbean coast, and it was not long before 'we quite lost ourselves, and were bewildered, that we knew not what way to move, nor how to extricate ourselves. Standing still therefore in our bewildered and melancholy condition, we heard the noise of the sea, and judged it to be our surest guide at present'. They cut back down to the coast with some difficulty, as they had to pass through thorny thickets and dense growth, but were glad to get to the sea and resolved not to go back and forward into the jungle again. Their route by the sea was not, however, much easier, made difficult by numerous oddly-shaped and sharp, slippery rocks which fatigued the little party. The Reverend Shields in particular was struggling, fainting and fitting on the journey and if it had not been for the fortunate ('like Hagar in the wilderness') discovery of a freshwater stream, from which they could drink deeply, Shields may not have survived. In the event, as the sun was dropping low in the bay, the missionaries made it back to Caledonia and offered up prayers to God as they clambered aboard their ships. It was an experience that would not tempt the ministers to return to their missionary duties.

Shortly after their return the rate of deaths from fevers and fluxes picked up and many more men were dying every day. Rumours also began to spread of Spanish attack, but in the colony there was mainly lethargy amongst the men and suspicions and jealousies harboured between their leaders. A Spanish cruiser had been pacing up and down the coast, watching the Scots and gathering some intelligence on their strength and movement. Four guns were taken from the *Rising Sun* and pulled up to Fort St Andrew to fortify it hurriedly in face of what seemed like an inevitable Spanish attack. On 7 February 1699, James Byres decided he would take a sloop to Jamaica to procure supplies – an odd choice on two counts: the second expedition was well aware of the English proclamation prohibiting help to the Scots, so it is hard to understand how he hoped to be well received in Port Royal; furthermore, given that he had assumed leadership of the council, his place was surely to lead from within Caledonia and he should rather have sent a lieutenant or other junior officer to Jamaica to seek supplies.

Byres no doubt wanted out and he would never return to Caledonia, despite some fairly feeble efforts to get back there later, when the Spanish had blockaded the entrance to Caledonia Bay. The provisions he was supposed to bring from Jamaica were certainly needed, for, as the Reverend Shields pointed out in the letter sent with James Byres to the moderator, no tradesmen or other European colonists had come to trade with the Scots in their first two months. Therefore no bonnets or plaid had been traded for fresh meat or flour. Despite Paterson's insistence that Darien was placed in a strategic location for trade, the Scots were completely unsuccessful in actually trading.

On 11 February 1700 Campbell of Fonab arrived by way of a sloop from Barbados. It had managed to sneak past the Spanish cruiser and came hurtling into the bay. The colony was full of fear, as the Spanish were reported to be only few miles away, advancing through the jungle. Campbell's splendid presence and soldier's manner calmed the Caledonians' nerves, and they crammed on shore and from the desks to catch a sight of the straight-backed, red-coat-wearing captain being rowed across to meet the remaining council-lors aboard the *Rising Sun*. He also brought some provisions with him which were welcomed, the Caledonians being in 'great straits at this time' according to Borland. The men were heartily sick of their poor rations of codfish and biscuit. The council had been in a state of inertia for the last few days since Byres' departure, and it was as well he had left, because Campbell was very much one of those 'for the taking of towns'. The council had no trouble agreeing to allow him to take over the defence of the colony, they had little idea what to do themselves and they gave him licence to do as he wished. The two ships destined to take the 500 or so Caledonians to Jamaica were ordered to remain, partly because the Scots had to maintain their numbers to defend the colony and partly because the dry season winds once again made the departure of ships from the bay very difficult. Campbell also decreed that the men under lock and key should be released and he was delighted to meet his old comrade in arms, Thomas Drummond. But Drummond was not the man he used to be and had been sick for some weeks, stuck in the stuffy air of his cabin. He was infuriated that Byres had left the colony and no doubt was on his way back to Edinburgh to bad-mouth him. Campbell asked him to help in the defence of the colony, but Drummond wanted no more to do with Caledonia and asked permission to leave. Campbell reluctantly granted this, confused at his friend's actions and unable to understand the effects of months spent in the unhealthy atmosphere of Caledonia. Drummond would take advantage of a ship bound for Jamaica and left Caledonia, which he had so struggled to nurture and protect. The Scots could ill afford to lose such a capable man.

Being a valiant and honourable soldier, Campbell viewed attack as the best form of defence. He learned from Robert Turnbull's Indian friends that a landward force of Spaniards was congregating at Tubuganti, and decided within less than two days of his arrival that he would lead an expeditionary force up into the mountainous jungle to attack the Spaniards before they attacked New Edinburgh. This resolve and dynamic leadership had been lacking in the colony and all were cheered by Campbell's decisive action. Morale lifted as the Scots prepared themselves for battle. On Tuesday, 13 February 1700, Campbell led a detachment of 200 men across the bay accompanied by Lieutenant Robert Turnbull, who brought with him under his command a small militia of around thirty Indian fighters whom he had been training and at the same time learning more of their language. The men had not eaten properly for months, having been poorly sustained on the Company's inadequate rations, but the fittest and healthiest men were chosen for what the Scots thought would be a decisive engagement. They marched four miles up the hills, struggling through the deep undergrowth and slipping on the soggy, rotten ground until they reached Pedro's village, where they spent the night, the officers staying with him in his house. The next day they left early in the morning to take advantage of the cooler morning air, as the jungle became a stifling, humid furnace by midday, and continued their trek across a high mountain ridge and down to a river that ran into the Pacific.

Turnbull marched out front with Pedro, some volunteers and thirty Indians, and before long the Indian scouts came running back to inform him that the Spanish were digging in on top of the next mountain ridge and fortifying their encampment at Tubuganti by cutting down trees and using the timbers to build a palisade. Campbell brought the main party up to where Turnbull was waiting and they discussed how to proceed. It was only midday but the Indians were keen to wait in their position and ambush the Spaniards as they passed, making for New Edinburgh. Campbell viewed this proposal dimly: he was a soldier and an officer and did not propose to lie in wait in a cowardly and dishonourable fashion. The Scots led the party on for another two miles until they came upon a freshwater stream and at this point the Indians refused to march any further: there was no further water until Tubuganti and they made camp for the night in the firm knowledge that tomorrow they would confront the enemy. The Scots were anxious. They cleared some damp leaves and earth from the sodden jungle floor to make space to lie down, fearing biting ants, snakes and other unfamiliar insects that scuttled around the jungle floor. They tried to go to sleep but inevitably their minds kept drifting to the next day's engagement and a natural fear of pain and death. Some of the brave soldiers trying to sleep on the mountainside would be dead by the next sunset.

The detachment woke early with the sun's rise and the strange, disorientating call of tropical birds and the pulsating metallic calls of wonderfully odd jungle insects. They ate what they had and forced some water into their nervous stomachs before checking their equipment and readying themselves for battle. Turnbull picks up the story in a letter written to his cousin, the governor of Stirling Castle:

> The next morning Capt. Campbell was very willing to march but the Indians would not upon any account, telling us that if we marched up the hill we would be all killed from an ambush: Capt. Campbell would have two men to go and see where the Spaniards were. The Indians told us they had sent forward spies but would not send any more. I used all the persuasions I could, promising them great rewards and telling them I would go with them myself. They told me I would be killed. I told them it was no matter though I was killed so that the Commander could have perfect Intelligence.[7]

The Indians laughed at this but Turnbull turned the situation to his advantage by telling the Indian chief in his own language that the Indians were terrible cowards, and this they could not stand. They were appalled by the insult and immediately began charging up the hill to confront the Spanish alone. But nor was this part of the Scottish plan of attack and Turnbull had to race up the hill after them, shouting to stop them and tell them not to lose the attacker's advantage of surprise. They calmed down and fell into an orderly column.

> Two of the Indians [were ordered] to go with me so I marched up the hill with twelve of our own Gentlemen. I marched in two hours to the top of the hill until I came within a bow shot of the Spaniards and I heard them cutting down trees and speaking very fast for there out sentries had run in and told them of my march and I retreated about two pair of buttos [sic] and lodged myself in a convenient post and wrote to Captain Campbell that if he pleased he might march ...

Campbell was indeed ready to attack the Spaniards and he led the main column of men up the hill to where Lieutenant Turnbull and his advance party were waiting. There Turnbull explained that they could attack the fortification because they would have the advantage of attacking downhill, because the fort was not on the hill's crest, but a little further down the hill. We do not know the reason for this Spanish strategic blunder; perhaps it was to provide the fortification with fresh water. Campbell wished to see the layout before deciding upon a plan of action, so he crawled forward through the undergrowth with Turnbull until they reached the edge of the clearing, and through the bush they peered into the smoky clearing to have a better look at the fort. We know from sketches given to Lem de Hooges, a Dutch engraver who produced a gold medal which would be presented to Campbell by the Company, that the fort was a large, star-shaped fortified palisade with eight points to the star, and contained within it were barracks, kitchens and fires. Campbell was impressed by the fortifications, as the star shaped construction provided them with plenty of cover to protect the palisade walls. Campbell decided no time should be wasted and that the fort should be attacked at once. Turnbull was keen to see a bit of action and asked Campbell where he should position himself for the attack. Generously Campbell responded Turnbull could take whatever position might please him and at once he offered to take the vanguard and advance with his troops of volunteers.

I marched immediately down upon them, who had only one sentry advanced running in without firing. I marched until I came within 20 feet of their breastwork where the Spaniards lay over with their arms presented, making signs for me to advance [mocking him by waving him on] I fired upon them and had only time to prime again until I was shot from a volley from the left hand, and the ball is lodged in the right shoulder. The company had no loss by falling gentlemen, making no stop, but went on bravely, neither did the Spaniards show themselves to be cowards, standing till our gentlemen did grip their firelocks [rifles] by the muzzle, but then Captain Campbell came down on them so furiously with the rest of the officers and soldiers, that the Spaniards were forced to give way with considerable loss for we were the masters of the fort.

They had realised the game was up; as soon as the Scots plunged over the wooden walls most had fled out the back of the fort through gates into the jungle. It had been a brief but heroic battle. Campbell's fast and furious charge had proved itself to be decisive, overwhelming the Spaniards from their superior defensive position and greater numbers. The Scots showed themselves to be courageous, charging into a heavily guarded, properly constructed fort, whilst the Spaniards responded with volleys of musket fire. Turnbull showed himself to be as brave as Campbell and they both left the battlefield injured: Campbell also sustained a wound to the shoulder. When the musket smoke cleared up into the damp forest, the Scots had sustained seven dead and seven more injured. The Scots say many more Spanish died as they succumbed to Scottish musket shot, bayonets and swords, attempting to protect the defences, but contemporary Spanish accounts describe only the deaths of a mulatto, Don Miguel de Oquendo, and three others, with several injured. The Spanish certainly had many men, over 200 under Don Miguel Cordones from the Panamanian militia companies and 200 Indians under the command of Camp Master Carrizoli.

The Scots gathered their Spanish prisoners together and put them under guard. They helped themselves to the Spanish provisions and looked about the fort, gathering provision, munitions, information and trinkets, including the personal effects and fine coat of the Spanish commander, Don Balthasar, a knight of the Order of St James, no less. The Scots buried their dead and said prayers over the bodies. Sadly, nobody saw fit to keep a record of the brave Indian dead. They settled down for a more comfortable and well-deserved night's sleep in the fortification, but Campbell was anxious to return. Not only was his wound making him slightly feverish, but he had read Spanish despatches that talked of a great fleet being sent to Punta Escocés to meet up with the landward army he had just defeated. At sunrise the Scots burnt down the remains of the fort and began their march back to New Edinburgh, a much easier undertaking, given they were going mostly down hill and were buoyed by their victory. They returned to New Edinburgh on Sunday, 18 February 1700, and were welcomed as heroes; the Caledonians celebrated in a noisy and boisterous fashion, which dismayed the Reverend Borland, who wrote gravely:

> Instead of glorifying the God of our salvation, there was little to be seen amongst most of our men, but excessive drunkeness, profane swearing ranting, boasting and singing: and so came of it, for shortly after, our present smiles were turned into frowns, our clear sunshine was overcast with dark

and threatening clouds, Providence had a quite contrary aspect upon us, and we were soon as much dejected and cast down, as we had been vain, proud and lifted up. About this time we were betrayed by several strangers coming in among us, under the pretence of friendship and necessity. An English sloop came into our harbour, pretending to be from Jamaica, but was really a spy from the Spaniards, as afterwards we understood, they had gone from us to the Spaniards, and were in their company, when some days after this, the Spaniards arrived upon our coast with their Fleet.

The Scots immediately regretted their wasted months of idleness and their failure to make strenuous efforts to properly prepare for this moment, which they should have realised was inevitable. Almost overnight the celebration of Tubuganti was to become a distant memory, in New Edinburgh at least. More concerning for the Scots was the fact the 400-man expeditionary force they had encountered at Tubuganti did not of course simply disappear, but regrouped, formed again in the centre of the province and made without delay for Don Juan Pimienta's camp on the coast. In fact, Spanish documents claim this expeditionary force was to have exchanged signals with Pimienta and the Spanish fleet in the bay. It is not clear if communication from the cordillera (top of the mountain range) to the coast was actually carried out, but a system was in place to allow the various Spanish commanders to communicate. Indeed, the Spanish reports claim, although for obvious reasons they would, that they were not forced to surrender at Tubuganti, but retreated because they did not want the Scots to become aware of how many men they had, with what arms they were possessed and in which direction they were going.

Back in Scotland, however, the news of the victory at Tubuganti was to be greeted with yet more exuberant partying that would soon get out of hand. For the Company's supporters, most of the news received from Darien had been discouraging, which had had both a morale-lowering effect and, even worse for a Scot, raised real financial concerns. As the Lord Chancellor, Lord Marchmont, wrote:

It is not easy to imagine what changes the humours of our people take all of a sudden. But I do observe, that the minds of this nation are so bent upon that undertaking, in which their colony is employed, that whenever, by any accounts they get, they are brought to hope that these lately sent have repossessed the settlements they are easy and good-natured; but upon occasions that seems to cross that hope, they turn ill-natured, and fall again to blame the proclamations.

This had led the Scots to petition King William to call Parliament to allow a debate and criticise the proclamation which had so harmed Caldeonia, but this address to His Majesty was coolly received and the Scots were informed Parliament would not be meeting. Further angered, a second address was sent to the king, which truly infuriated him, but he had little choice but to agree to convening Parliament in May, given how long it had been since the previous Parliament. When the Parliament did open it debated the state of morality in the kingdom before adjourning until October. The Scots were furious: not only was their investment falling apart, but their attempts to seek the help of their sovereign had been rebuffed and he was being downright unhelpful in listening and responding to his Scottish subjects' concerns. In the last years of his life, William was focusing on the bigger picture and the need to keep Spain on side against the French to protect his Dutch homeland. He was very aware that any sign of support for Caledonia would have been viewed very dimly in Madrid.

This brief Parliament did little to cool rising Scottish passions, and a further address was sent to the king, which he again rejected. His irritation and anger were reaching boiling point and this tinder of resentment needed only the smallest of flames to set it alight. The flame was the arrival on 20 June 1700 of dispatches from New Edinburgh informing the Company of the Scots' victory at Tubuganti. A Jamaican sloop had left New Edinburgh in late February and it carried various letters and reports from the council and others. The Jacobites, who for a week or two previously had been fomenting trouble in Edinburgh, were delighted by this news and saw an opportunity to cause problems for William. Crowds converged on Edinburgh's central streets to toast the victory, as up and down the High Street glasses were raised and the sweet name Tubuganti was cried to the heavens. As the alcohol took its effect, the celebrants soon took the form of a mob and decided that every household should place candles in their windows to celebrate the Scots' magnificent victory. As people scrambled around to find candles to light to place in their windows to ensure they would not have their windows pelted with stones, the mob began to construct large bonfires on the main thoroughfares and quickly Edinburgh was given over to the smells of acrid smoke and alcohol, and the noise of smashing glass and cheers. The night soon turned uglier, as more and more windows were smashed and the mob decided to take the tolbooth and liberate its captives. The tolbooth guards quickly surrendered as the mob began to burn down the door and they fled into the wild night. It was an ugly, noisy and drunken affair and by dawn the crowd had dispersed as the alcohol turned the anarchy of the night into the thick hangover of a grey Edinburgh morning. All around lay streets littered with smashed glass, and soon the fusiliers marched into the city at the orders of the Privy Council and took control, reinforcing and rearming the city authorities to ensure their could be no repeat of the lawlessness. The emotions of the citizens of Edinburgh were tied to the fate of the lives of their fellow citizens in New Edinburgh and, unfortunately for both, the outlook was not good.

ELEVEN

THE CARIBBEAN

JAMAICA

It took the Caledonians weeks to sail the relatively short distance from Punta Escocés to the south-western part of Jamaica where Bluefields Bay is situated. The Copa jet made it in less than three hours, direct from Panama to Kingston. The plane was filled with noisy blue-tracksuited students, cheering loudly as they returned to their island. The plane banked steeply to the right and swooped low over what remained of Port Royal, stuck out at the end of a long cay, which housed the noisy runway of Norman Manley International Airport. I had come to Jamaica for three main reasons: to find the graves of any Scots or others involved in Caledonia; to find out more about the life of John Campbell, the most successful Caledonian, who fled to Jamaica; and to visit Bluefields Bay, the site of tragedy of the Caledonians, where several wretched ships of both expeditions limped, fleeing the torment of New Edinburgh. The Caledonians had fled to Jamaica, hopeful of a warm welcome, provision and medicines, but little was on offer.

Modern-day Kingston has a reputation for danger and the statistics do not encourage the first-time visitor: the third-highest murder rate in the world and in 2005 over 1,700 people were murdered out of a total population of around 2.5 million. Most of this violence is drug- and gang-related and takes place in Kingston's notoriously impoverished neighbourhoods. An enormous van-like taxi took me down the long cay onto the island, passing turquoise waters and waves crashing onto either side of the narrow road which took us into the heart of the city. The driver asked after the purpose of my trip: he had never heard of the Scots from Darien nor was he sure whether there was significant Scottish heritage on the island. He asked me about cricket, and there the conversation came to an end.

The taxi thundered quickly through dishevelled streets on the outskirts of Kingston. The city was chaotic and disorganised, the road meandered around, covered in dust in parts, hemmed in by a mixture of poor concrete buildings and scrappily painted wooden buildings. The streets were a cauldron of people and noise, energetically flowing by as we pushed on through to the city centre. Loud blasts of reggae emanated from homes and parked cars as we drove by. The van was flagged down by a young lady dressed like a 1950s school teacher in an impeccable twin-set and matching hat. She jumped into the front passenger seat and after a few minutes realised she was not alone, she seemed apologetic and unnecessarily gesticulated as if to leave. Foreign taxi conventions are always different.

The hotel was a nondescript, suburban-looking building located in New Kingston. The 'new' connoted it was part of Kingston a little further up the hill from the original centre around the daunting 'palisades'. It was hard to find any sense of a city centre, or a focal point in the city. New Kingston is a sprawl of suburbia drifting down from the hills to the choked-up original city. The hotel reception had a picture of the Queen of Jamaica (Elizabeth II) and a run-down reception desk with extensive security. It was run by a friendly family of Indians, known as East Indians on the island to differentiate them from the West Indians (colonialism weaves a tangled web). Many Indians were brought as indentured labourers to the island when the British outlawed slavery in the early nineteenth century, and whilst they make up only around 1.5 per cent of the population, they are dominant in many aspects of commerce, creating some tensions on the island.

The hotel was ideal because it was near Halfway Tree, a former village on the outskirts of Kingston, which would have led colonists down to the south-west of the island, now engulfed in the noise and chaos of Kingston. Halfway Tree is the home of the St Andrew Parish Church, founded in 666. It was in all likelihood visited by the wretched Caledonians. It was an obvious starting point in the search to find the graves of dead Caledonians or English officials involved in the history of the Company of Scotland.

Leaving the hotel in the middle of the afternoon, the heat and the traffic were suffocating. Kingston thrives on chaos. Looking north I could see the foothills of the distant Blue Mountains and the urban sprawl creeping its way north. The most expensive homes, with their considerable security, are located in the hazy distance, far from the heat and noise. Walking for less than half an hour, regularly asking for Halfway Tree, I was always being provided directions from very formal Jamaicans. There was something of a 1950s quality to the interactions. Halfway Tree used to be populated by cotton trees and travellers would rest there on their way in and out of Kingston. Today the cotton trees had been replaced by cheap shops and the travellers were Kingstonian shoppers thronging the streets with brightly coloured bags. A tall red-brick clock tower stood in memorial to a long-dead British king.

The church was set back from a busy main road, surrounded by a considerable graveyard and a screen of green trees. A large sign with the name and date announced the church and its founding date. Contemporary accounts of the Darien Scots do not mention the church by name, but given its name, age and position, it is almost certain those Scots coming from Bluefields Bay and other places in the south-west would have rested here on their way to visit the English governor. It appears to have been the only church in existence to bear the name of Scotland's patron saint. It is and was, however, an Anglican church (the colonial authorities' church would have been the Church of England); not all Caledonians were Scottish and it cannot be assumed all were Presbyterian. Even those Presbyterians must have felt the need pray in a church named after St Andrew, even in an Anglican church, after the devastation of Darien.

Walking under the elegant gate entrance, a low wall on either side, the church bore a remarkable similarity to a rural English church. Large trees provided shade along the path to the entrance and continued down the side to the graveyard, where a large community of homeless people had congregated, laid out on the larger graves, hanging their clothes from lines and chatting quietly amongst the gravestones. The church was dark and cool inside and large, with impressive dark wooden pews and a large amount of stained glass. Around the walls were memorials to people who had died and served their community far from home. Jamaicans were also remembered. had a list of names of Caledonians known to have perished on the island and some had been provided with sufficient charity to have received a decent burial in a place like this. The task was simple: to find their names etched through time on a grave, or memorial or even just in writing in the parish records.

The walls contained many mounted engravings and the floor was home to a number of large tombstones and engraved memorials. But, despite an extensive search, I could find no Caledonians, nor anyone who died around 1699 or 1700. One name rang out of the wall, Lieutenant-Colonel James Haldane, of the 4th troop (Scots) Life Guards, 1715–1741. Was this the son of John Haldane of Gleneagles, who helped organise the Company and travelled to Europe with Paterson to seek additional investors? John Haldane had a son called James, but he was born in 1692 and died in 1742, so the dates did not match, but there was surely some form of family connection. The Life Guards was a pre-Union regiment formed in Scotland to protect the king, and it is possible they would have been deployed after Union, as the Scots Life Guards were marched to London after the Act of Union. I noted the times of the services and resolved to return the next day for both the Eucharist and a detailed search of the graves. Before I left I called into the shabby church office, where a large number of sprightly but elderly Jamaican women were excitedly discussing something. My arrival caused a hush and raised eyes looked at me inquisitively, as I stood sweaty and dishevelled before them. I explained I was looking for the graves of certain long-dead Scots and asked if they had records. Wrists rose to their eyes and they peered disapprovingly over their watches. It was nearly 5 p.m. They returned to their discussion. I was not sure what to do, so sat down meekly on the stairs which was the necessary apologetic response and a buxom older lady soon appeared, anxious to help, and asked me to return after the following day's service and she would have the parish records ready for me.

By the time I left, the Kingston rush-hour was well and truly in swing and the streets were choked with traffic and heat. Port Royal, if not Kingston itself, was once known as the wickedest city in the world for the number and variety of entertainment available to the wealthy pirates and merchants. It was said property prices were as expensive as in central London before the 1692 earthquake. So with that in mind, I headed out in a fresh shirt in search of some evening entertainment. I had with me a guidebook that was twelve years out of date but had been kindly lent to me by the ambassador in Panama, who previously had been the Deputy High-Commissioner in Jamaica. Devon House was mentioned and I wandered up to its rather shabby grounds and wondered where were the bars and restaurants in this former grand Georgian home, which looked almost derelict, but as I wondered into the courtyard behind there indeed was a restaurant, ice cream parlour and a comfortable bar.

Red Stripe is the local beer. Delicious cold. Would the Caledonians have had the money for a beer? The bar was slowly filling up and beside me sat a large family of Haitians speaking beautiful French, engrossed in conversation. They were obviously wealthy, as the bar was not cheap, and when the waiter came to take their order, the father made a great show of ordering wine, only French wine would do, he said. Colonial ties run deep.

The next day after a breakfast of yams and *callaloo*, a kind of spinach and okra mix, I returned to St Andrews for the morning service. It was short and brief and disconcertingly the congregation was split into two: all Jamaican and black, but one half were properly involved in the service and given communion, whilst the other half languished at the side and seemed to just have come in out of the heat. I was directed down to the respectable side and sat, disappointed to discover there was no sermon. Given that many Caledonians, and certainly the leaders, were Presbyterians, they may well have been uncomfortable in this Episcopalian setting. After the service I returned to the church office in search of the records and after a lengthy wait, the parish secretary bade me enter and asked me what I was looking for. I gave her a potted history of Caledonia, but there was no recognition, although she was clear there were several graves dating back to the seventeenth century, so a discovery was possible. She handed me over a thick file which contained all the parish records the church had, but it soon became apparent to me this was simply a list of the inscriptions found on the tombstones and plaques in the church, not proper parish records, of members, deaths, births, etc. Jamaica was proving disappointing.

The list before me contained no reference to any Caledonians and although it was a long shot, my disappointment was great. I took some time clambering amongst the gravestones and enlisted the help of two of the poorly clothed inhabitants of the graveyard to help me find anyone who had died between 1699 and 1710. It was still early, but the sun was strong and it was uncomfortable walking over and around tombstones. Back in the church and I sat silently in the cool, gloomy air and wondered if Caledonians, too, had taken refuge in this same place of worship. It would be hard to be sure, but I said a prayer for them and their terrible suffering on this island.

From there a taxi sped me downhill to downtown Kingston. Kingston Parish Church is in the centre of the city and has graves dating back to 1699. The original structure no longer stands, but in its place is a simple white church with a tower in small grounds off the main William Grant Park, surrounded by the Parades, which were described in my old travel guide as 'clamorous and daunting'. They were strewn with street vendors and people going about their daily business, but were no more intimidating than many other developing cities. A heavy police presence attested to the crime problem, and the police looked fine in their navy uniforms with smart blue stripes down the trousers and bulky Kevlar vests on top. I looked around the church's graveyard outside first, and there were many graves of English people dating back to the early eighteenth century, but no Caledonians and few Scots. I entered the church by a small door at the side, embraced by the cool air. The church was brighter than St Andrew, but simpler and laid out in a standard cross shape, with many tombs on the uneven stone floor. I got to work winding my way through the pews looking for dates around 1700 or one of the names on my list of Caledonians who perished. Despite an exhaustive search none were apparent, but importantly the tomb of Admiral Benbow was there, set out at the front of the church. I mused on the important role he had played in the Caledonians' tale, helping the Scots protect themselves from the Spanish Barlovento Fleet. Although he had been unable to assist them when the first expedition arrived in Bluefields Bay, he plainly felt moved to protect his Scottish brothers when out at sea, when he could. His tomb read:

> Here lyeth interred the body of John Benbow Esq. Admiral of the White, a true pattern of English courage who lost his life in defence of his Queene and country November 4 1702. In the 52nd year of his age by a wound in his leg received in an engagement with Monsieur Du Casse, being much lamented.

Despite the earlier help he had given to the Caledonians, he may not have been much lamented by them by the time they arrived in Jamaica. Benbow refused to provide assistance to Colin Campbell when he rode to meet him from Bluefields Bay in 1700 and refused to help crew his ship, the *Saint Andrew,* down to safer anchorage in Port Royal, where Benbow was stationed. He had other things on his mind and knew he had to go out to face a strengthened French fleet and had little time to help the Scots any more, especially as they were making his job of policing the Caribbean more difficult. He now lies before a simple slab of black stone in front of the altar in the modern church.

From there I walked around noisy downtown Kingston to St Andrew's Scots Kirk, which did not exist at the time the Caledonians visited Kingston, but it is a curious and rather beautiful building amid the squalor of the neighbourhood. It is unadorned, but not plain, and speaks of Presbyterian wooden bareness, reminiscent of the Old South Meeting House in Boston. I wandered around taking in the names of the many Scots buried there, Scots who might never have come to Jamaica in such numbers if it had not been for the failure of Darien and the creation of the Union and their prominent role in the British Empire. The church recorded the lives of James Watson from Johnston, Major J.K. Fingzies from Elgin, Alexander Goldie from Mid Lothian and Andrew Scot from Penicuik. These Scots had done well for themselves and most were recorded to have been merchants.

Most Caledonians who remained on the island sold themselves to planters as indentured labourers and were no doubt buried in simple graves with no plaques on the wall to bear testament to their lives. Kingston is a long way from Elgin in every respect. An old man wandered into the church, a lay member, and asked me if I needed any help, I told him about my research and asked him if he knew anything about the Caledonians, but he looked bemused and shook his old head. He knew nothing about Panama and not very much about the Scots or Presbyterianism, but he did tell me to try a visit to Port Royal.

Leaving the cool of the church I wandered back out to the Parades to try to find a bus or taxi to the long cay where Port Royal sits. After a brief and remarkably generous discussion about fares, a driver agreed to take me and we sped through the lunch-hour traffic with terrible gospel music playing on the radio. Old wooden homes lined the streets and colourful shops, advertising their wares; *Bling Paradise* said one, whilst another uninvitingly advertised *Computers for Sale* in crayon on a damp square of cardboard. We passed the airport and drove to the end of the cay where the driver left me, unsure, he said, where anything of historical value may be. In fact, there are few historical buildings there and most of the town is given over to rather attractive single-storey wooden homes and a pack of three-legged dogs. It was once the wealthy and wicked city that lured buccaneers to its taverns where expeditions and plans were hatched, none more audacious than Sir Henry Morgan's attack on Panama City in 1671. Today it is sleepy and visited by Kingstonians in search of an afternoon out and some cold beer and fresh fish. I strolled over to Gloria's Rendezvous, an apparently famous restaurant with great fish. The menu simply read, in chalk on the wall, 'Fried, Stewed or Brown'. The fried fish was delicious with ice cold Red Stripe. After that I headed in search of St Peter's Church and Fort Charles. The Fort dates back to 1655 and was not badly damaged during the earthquake. We can be fairly sure the Caledonians came here when they called upon their English hosts.

As with all historical tourist destinations on Jamaica it was quiet and I wandered around on my own, tailed by various custodians. I sneaked a quick photograph and then was rapidly admonished. A large plaque on the wall reminded me Horatio Nelson had been based there for a while, and thought back to the raucous celebration of the two hundredth anniversary of Trafalgar at the ambassador's residence in Panama City. Nelson himself had been sick whilst in Jamaica and history might have been very different if he had not recuperated so well in Port Royal. Benbow was also quartered here, and it was probably here that Councillor Colin Campbell met him to ask for help in salvaging the *Saint Andrew* and bringing it down the coast to the harbour from Bluefields. Campbell would have envied the cooler, drier climate of Port Royal over New Edinburgh, the riches and the entertainment on offer. New Edinburgh at its best was always a long way from being comparable with this settlement.

St Peter's Church was built in 1725, but it was closed and nobody was around to help. I scouted around the graves, but the combination of beer and hot sun was taking its toll, so abandoning my search I found a bus that smelled strongly of marijuana, and headed back into Kingston. Early the next morning, I took a taxi down to the public market and bus station to find a bus to take me out to Black River. The bus was inevitably the cheapest way to get around the island and hire-cars the most expensive. The visit through the market to the bus station was an alarming, dangerous and foul-smelling one. Rarely on the American continent have I seen such poverty or felt quite so fearful. With relief, and as quickly as I could, I got into the minibus for Black River, and steadfastly refused the stream of products pushed into my face through the window by aggressive vendors. Water and crisps were tempting, but boxes of soggy doughnuts or shiny machetes seemed less necessary. When the bus was full we still did not depart, instead plastic buckets and wooden slats appeared to provide makeshift seats where there were none and once more large bottoms were deposited we were ready, at last, to go.

The bus veered around potholes through the streets of Kingston whilst most people fell asleep in the hot bus, heavy with the smell of orangeade and cheap plastic. I had taken much longer bus journeys, one even of thirty-five hours to Managua in Nicaragua from Panama, but this mere three-hour journey surpassed all in terms of discomfort. As my tolerance ran close to running out, mercifully we stopped in the mountains, and I staggered out of the bus with buckling legs. I made for a kiosk to buy water and admire the cool surroundings and the striking, flower-laden countryside. Hibiscus and clematis grew untended and wild on the roadside. It was beautiful and as the feeling came back to my calves, I remembered to enjoy myself again. The Scots would have taken this route from Bluefields to Kingston. By foot it would have been a long way, and even on horseback it would have taken at least a long day's ride to get there. Weakened from their terrible crossing from Caledonia, it would have been a demanding journey. Back in the bus I paid my fare and received no change until my lycra-clad neighbour shouted out and 100 Jamaica dollars were returned to me.

I had come to Back River to track down the most successful of all the Caledonians who decided to stay on the island. He was an officer in the second expedition and was called John Campbell. He was from Inveraray in Argyllshire, but was soon to become known as Campbell of Black River and became the *custos* (a sort of lieutenant governor) of the parish, and a privy councillor. I knew he was buried in or around Black River and I wanted to find his grave. Both Scottish expeditions arrived at Bluefields Bay when they fled the Panamanian coast, and the Scots fanned out from Bluefields Bay, populating this lush corner of south-west Jamaica. It was the beginning of a long Scottish association with the area, and my map showed me a Culloden, an Auchindown and a Craigie all in or around the area.

Black River itself was founded some time around 1670, and became the capital of St Elizabeth Parish, growing by taking advantage of its position at the mouth of the large Black River. It became an important port for the slave, pimiento, sugar and logwood trades and a series of small wharfs were built along the sea front to facilitate this. Behind on the main street, with great views over the bay, large wooden homes were built in the Caribbean style, made from wood with intricate fret work, balconies, decorative gables and window coolers.

Many have survived and as I walked through the small town in search of an inexpensive hotel, the once grand but now faded Invercauld Great House Hotel looked tempting. The house was built at the end of the nineteenth century for a wealthy Scots family, the Farquharsons, who named it after their family seat back in Scotland. It is said John Campbell encouraged many Scots to follow him and he helped them to come to Jamaica to settle. The Farquharsons may be disappointed to see their once gracious home has been spoiled by ugly new villas and a cheap swimming pool. After some rapid bargaining over the price I was promised a room in the old house, left my bag and went off in search of the Caledonians.

I headed for the town hall and court to ask about the Caledonians and the Campbell family. The enquiries were greeted with a look of bewilderment, whilst a group of Jamaican girls looked on uninterested. At the local library the staff had little idea what I was asking for me but let me wander around to look for some books. Beyond copies of *The Da Vinci Code* and third grade biology books there was very little and I was about to leave when someone showed me a copy of an encyclopaedia of Jamaican heritage. Thankfully it included an entry about the Campbell family in Jamaica and in particular about John Campbell, who was described as an officer who had served in Darien and died in Black River in 1741. Even better, it stated he was buried at the Old Works, Hodge's Pen, near Black River. Hurriedly I photocopied the entry and went in search of lunch before tracking down Campbell's grave.

On the main street of Black River a modest restaurant served goat curry and beer. Absentmindedly I watched part of the World Cup semi-final and thought excitedly about tracking down the grave of one of the prominent Caledonians. After lunch, in search of Campbell of Black River, I flagged down a taxi driver and explained where I wanted to go. He gave me no indication he did or did not know where it was, but we headed out of the town to the pretty fields at the far side and only once we were there did he ask me again where I wanted to go. He had a vague idea that Hodge's Pen was the land around the crossroads we had stopped at, but had never heard of the rest of the directions. I suggested we ask some people. We flagged down another taxi, who told us there were graves a little up the road, in the fields on the right-hand side. We stopped, and I climbed over a gate and strode through the fields, making for a ruined building several hundred metres away. By the ruined building sat three neat graves, covered over with brush, but they dated to the late nineteenth century by their design. As I pulled the greenery from the light coloured stone, I could see only nineteenth-century dates and left them to their peace. There were none that I was looking for so I headed back to the taxi driver, and we proceeded to visit a number of farms in the area, but everyone looked blank and shook their heads.

The driver was getting fed up, but I insisted on stopping once more and we drove up to a house under construction, carefully pulling our hands in at the windows as two dogs barked and bit at the air as the taxi trundled by over the dirt road. The younger of the two workers knew nothing, but he called over an old man, who stuck his dark head in through the window. He was nearly seventy, with short grey hair, three or four teeth and a large, sweaty forehead. He looked at me seriously and then said, yes he knew where it was. It was on the other side of the main road, down towards the sea. 'Pen', he said, meant place near water and he reckoned it was not Old Works, but Old Wharf. That made sense.

Before me were a series of fields of good agricultural land, lush and fertile, but with few cattle. I could make out the sea quite a distance away and headed towards it on foot, as the old man had suggested. The sun was hot, the grass long and the many barbed-wire fences were challenging. After twenty minutes, a pretty, sandy beach appeared and I supposed this was where the Old Wharf once stood. It was the perfect site, but there was no sign of buildings or wharfs, nor of a graveyard. Campbell would not have been buried on or too close to the beach, but he may have lived nearby and would have been buried in a small family plot. Large black vultures flew overhead. The area behind the beach contained many mounds and trees, but nothing that looked like a grave. Heading round the coast, passing through the mangroves, it was eerie and quiet and damp underfoot. All over the floor of the mangroves were crabs with one claw much larger than the other. Mutant-like with their one big claw, they scuttled across the sandy ground making a sound like rain falling on dry leaves. The whole ground seemed to move as they fled before me. As I became deeper and deeper entangled in the mangroves, caution took over. Black River is renowned for its alligators and here was I, alone, and wandering around mangroves. The grove continued for a considerable distance and I fought my way back to firmer land, more appropriate for graves and from there began to comb the land around, but I felt dispirited and lost. Far from where the old man had told me to go and no graves anywhere. It was getting late and there were too many fields to cover, so I decided it would be better to go back to town, look for some maps, ask around and try again tomorrow. Exhausted, I headed back up to the road and flagged down a car to take me back into Black River.

The Invercauld had prepared a room: musty and run-down at the back of the house on the ground floor, the view obscured by curtains stapled around the window. There was a fire exit door opening into the gardens that did not close. Refreshed by hot water, soap and sleep, I headed down the sea front to a bar called the Waterloo, in the ground floor of another great house, full of local, bling-clad fisherman drinking Red Stripe. Curiously, Campari was also a popular choice. I asked around about Hodge's Pen and nobody seemed to know where it was, but one man, Leslie, a fisherman, suggested I take a boat up the coast to try to find the Old Wharf from the sea instead of by land. It seemed like a good idea and would avoid another day crawling around mangroves. He had seen me standing by the road earlier and wondered what I was doing. I explained to him about the Caledonians and Campbell. A cool breeze came off the sea as I wandered the empty streets, and most places appeared closed, giving the place an eerie feel reminiscent of an English seaside resort out of season, so I returned to the hotel to eat. As I passed the Waterloo, a young man came out and asked where I was going now. Dinner, I said, giving him a quizzical look, as he watched me expectantly.

The only guest at the Invercauld, I sat at a table for four in the empty restaurant. Four great fans circulated the air and mosquitoes bit at my ankles.

A young girl appeared and told me there was goat curry and nothing else and so I reluctantly ordered that and sat patiently waiting looking out at the faux classical columns by the pool. I was tired and a little drunk and ate mechanically, exasperated at my failure to find the grave of Caledonia's most successful Jamaican immigrant. The Jamaicans were, however, charming, exuding politeness and friendliness and, when they relaxed, a rough sense of humour.

Breakfast, thankfully, was curry-free. Striking out for the little wharf where the fishermen kept their boats at the mouth of the river, I walked through the town, turning down to the left before I reached the bridge over the river and walked through a small neighbourhood of poor wooden homes with women sitting outside selling fresh fish. By the side of the river a series of long wooden boats, a collection of shacks and a group of men were sitting around talking. They looked up at me, surprised, when I approached them, explaining I wanted to hire a boat to take me up the coast to find an old wharf. I sat down on a little wooden box and after their suspicion had dissipated they perked up and asked me why. I regurgitated my well-versed one-minute summary of Caledonia and its Jamaican connection to a series of smiling Jamaican faces. A young-looking local wanted to know more about John Campbell. Where was his grave? What did he do? Where did I find out the information? And, enticingly, he asked me was he a pirate? Was there treasure? The fishermen were still seated smoking marijuana. One of them asked me if I was Scottish. He was an older Rastafarian and when I nodded, he said how much he liked the place and that his son had attended Strathallan School. Sitting by the wharf, encircled in blue smoke, it felt a long way from the rugby fields of Perth, but was a pleasing and unexpected Scottish connection.

The owner of the boat eventually appeared and, from the little I could understand of his heavy accent, he agreed to take me for $10. He pulled the outboard out of the wooden shack and dragged it down to his boat, whilst I hovered uneasily at his side, unsure whether to help or not. But before we got any further, and after a quick look up to the mouth of the river where it met the sea in a cloudy cauldron, he called it off. The weather was too rough, although nobody had supposed that was a problem before.

As I crossed by the bridge, returning to town, I flagged down a car to take me back out to what I assumed to be Hodge's Pen, and of course asked the driver. He used to be a fisherman and knew what I was talking about. Yes, he knew Hodge's Pen, yes, he knew there used to be an old wharf for exporting logwood and yes, he had heard of some old graves around that area. I beamed optimistically, as we headed back through town and out the other side. His name was Roy and he was a weatherbeaten fifty-year-old Jamaican wearing only a pair of baggy shorts and no shoes. He wanted to hear the story of the Caledonians and was sure he had heard of John Campbell, he was sure the graves were on farmland near the little beach I had visited the day before, and he thought the area had been used, years ago, for logwood exportation. It soon became apparent, as we wound our way around the fields, that Roy had no clear idea of the whereabouts of the graves. What he lacked in knowledge, he certainly made up for with enthusiasm, as he bounded from mound to tree looking for any potential grave sites. Unless someone maintained the graves, they would quickly become grown over in this climate, and may already be lost. Given that knowledge of all things Scottish and the Campbell family was non-existent in Black River, I had few hopes that anyone came out here regularly to clean the graves.

Eventually, ever-smiling Roy and I made it back to where I had begun the day before. 'This,' he exclaimed, 'was where the old wharf used to be, and from where logwood was exported.' It would seem reasonable to conclude that this was the spot where John Campbell had once stood and from where he had sent off previous cargos of logwood that would have made him a rich man. He had certainly picked an enchanting spot surrounded by rich land, clear waters and a yellow, if muddy beach. Roy was becoming anxious to leave and he took my number, keen to call me should anything else come up and I thanked him.

I sat down against a tree to cool off after the heat and exhaustion of running over the fields. There were no eerie, deformed crabs, just silence, in fact there was nobody around at all, so I stripped off my clothes and hung them on the tree to dry, and like sweaty Scots before, jumped into the cooling Caribbean. The seabed was muddy and my feet sank down into it, so I wriggled out quickly and swam deeper to clearer water, where, suspended and relaxed in the colder water, I could see white lumps below me. Taking a deep breath I dived down to discover empty conch shells. Coming back up for air I went down again and grabbed two and made for the surface, eyes stinging from the salty water, and as best I could I cleaned them in the water, and choosing the better of the two, swam back to the shore. The sun did not take long to dry me and with a feeling of disappointment I pulled my clothes on and crawled back to the path from the beach. Campbell may well have been here, and he had picked a far better spot than Caledonia, but his grave had eluded me.

Back on the road, it took some time for a car to stop and give me a lift back to the Invercauld. It was time to move on up the coast to Bluefields Bay, to see where the Caledonians had arrived when they first fled Darien. It was also where many of the Scots settled in Jamaica, given its proximity to Bluefields. I took a collective taxi from Black River to Whitehaven and from there changed cars for Auchindown, near to Bluefields. We sat waiting for a while until an impossible eight people were squashed into the car and headed along the road, past Culloden. As we neared Auchindown, the driver pulled over into the entrance of a Sandals resort. We drove through gates down a long drive until we stopped and waited near the entrance. Nobody made a move, until I realised all eyes were on me. I had not mentioned Sandals but plainly the taxi driver assumed that since I was a foreigner, this must be my destination. I stayed put. When we reached the main road, again the door was opened and I was told to get out. Indignantly I refused, but the driver explained there was a roadblock ahead, and there were too many people in the car.

Abandoned, I tried to flag down another car, but standing in front of the gate to Sandals this elicited a very different response from passing Jamaicans. For the first time in the Jamaican south-west, people appeared resentful and even unfriendly, gleefully waving from half-empty cars. Since I'd left Kingston the Jamaicans in the countryside had always been friendly. The reaction by the gate at Sandals did not speak well of relations between the holidaymakers and the local community. It was best to walk, and no sooner had I rounded a few curves than the sign for Auchindown appeared. I turned off the main road and walked up to what looked much like an English country lane in late August. The sun did not take long to remind me, however, that I was in the tropics, walking uphill in the afternoon with a small pack on my back. By the time I had climbed for an hour, without water, I realised there was little reason to visit Auchindown beyond its name. The only connection with the Caledonians was the weakness of white Scottish bodies in the tropical sun. Auchindown was pretty, small and not in the least Scottish.

The taxi from Auchindown did not take long to sweep into Bluefields Bay and from the open window of the back seat I was given a glimpse of a stunning, perfectly rounded, turquoise bay and asked the taxi driver to stop. If I could not sail into the bay, at least I wanted to walk around it. The view was beautiful, and standing by the side of the road, taking in the calmness of the sea, it was hard to imagine how much more traumatic the arrival of two sets of Caledonians from the first and then the second expeditions would have been. Further from the side of the road I wandered down to a large home or guest house, which had a beautiful jetty leading out into the bay with a pagoda at the end, but the area was closed off and I was left by the fence straining at the view.

It is not clear what sort of a settlement would have existed in Bluefields Bay when the Scots arrived in 1699 and 1700. It was a recognised bay for buccaneers and there would have been a safe harbour, taverns, houses and probably a wharf of some sort. Today the town is sparsely populated along the length of the bay. Small wooden homes lie on either side of the road and are dotted further up the hill. Small, perfectly crafted colourful wooden shops line the roads. Inside, on neatly arranged shelves rows and rows of enticing bottles of Red Stripe, Guinness and coconut water tempt passers-by. Nearby the vendors relaxed in the shade, shirtless, smiling and waving. The whole bay had a powerfully relaxing feel, and the combination of the wide bay, with its contrast of the narrow yellow beach and strip of turquoise water before the vastness of the royal blue sea, was incredibly inviting. From the other side of the road, steep mountains rose up into the sky, laden with heavy green growth. Lower down, the trees were full of mangos, bell peppers, pimiento and large numbers of clematis and hibiscus flowers; it was easily the most attractive place in Jamaica.

Venturing into one of the wooden stores I tried to buy some water, but there were only alcoholic or fizzy sweet drinks. I asked the friendly owner about the Scots, local history or old churches, but correctly anticipated his response: a cheerful shake of the head. In reality the bay is little changed from 1700, when the Scots arrived, and now. Bluefields Bay must have really looked spectacular with large ships anchored in the water. Further around the bay I came to a particularly attractive spot of beach and swam in the sea. The Caledonians barely had the energy to swim when they flopped over into these waters to reach the shore: they were malnourished and weakened from fevers. Sadly they had little energy to think about the beauty of the place they had arrived at; hundreds of their compatriots had died in the crossing from Darien and their priority was to find food and shelter. Despite Jamaica's beauty, given its location in the tropics those who were ill would have been better sailing further north to the English colonies in North America, to a dryer, cooler climate.

Arranging shelter for the evening was easy, I had planned to stay at one of the 'great houses' which used to belong to a Scottish family who harvested sugar and pimiento from the surrounding hills and fields. Making for the local police station I was to call the owner to come down the hill to collect me. The station was shut, so I wandered into a little shack beside it, and asked to make a call. A short Jamaican called Chubby was happy to help and I made the call. I bought an ice-cold Red Stripe and sat down on the side of the road and talked to Chubby about poverty, politics and the quiet life. One beer became two, and I could have stayed for longer but the owner of the hotel arrived and so we parted, smiling. I was a little drunk and I headed up the steep hill to the great home. The owner, let's call him Fred, was northern European and perhaps a little eccentric. He knew little of the history of the Scots, but did know his home was once owned by Scots and he stopped his rickety van halfway up the hill to let me take a look at the graveyard. I crossed the path and turned into a perfectly walled, overgrown, small graveyard. There were few graves, but those that remained were well preserved and made of light marble, laid out beside each other. The tombstones told of a Scottish family, the Sinclairs, who had lived, worked and died in Jamaica in the nineteenth century. They had been the owners of the great house. Who knows what brought them to Jamaica, but they would have been likely to know of their earlier compatriots and their fight for survival in this very same bay.

The great house was dilapidated and the neatly arranged Sinclairs would have been horrified to see it painted yellow and purple. Between the old cook house, still standing in its original stone, and the wooden-built main home, which had been modernised (after a fashion), a dirty pool and an empty and filthy Jacuzzi sat in what had once been a beautiful front garden. The main part of the house, a one-storey building built entirely of wood, had several bedrooms and bathrooms off the main corridor leading down to a 'reception' consisting of a desk on which lay strewn an open bag of marijuana. Several large Rottweiler dogs paced around, growling. Like Fred, the house could best be described as eccentric, but not necessarily charming. The visit, however, was made worthwhile by the view. From a large wooden terrace, which spanned the length of the building, an incredible view of the entire bay, the beach, the small town and the surrounding mountains panned out, softening in the late afternoon sun. Before me was a mesmerising vision of undulating green jungle and soothing blue sea. There was no better place to behold Bluefields and the scene of the Scots' terrible arrivals and departures as they fled via Jamaica from Darien. It was hard to place their tragedy alongside such peace and beauty.

After the hot, sweaty day in the sun, I showered and reappeared on the terrace. There were no other guests, and I helped myself to a large Campari over decidedly unpleasant-looking ice. Fred appeared at my side and we chatted as the sun fell in the sky, the shadows lengthened and sea slowly changed its colours. He said he had decided to turn the Great House from a cheap hostel into what he called an 'all-inclusive resort'. It still seemed pretty much a cheap hostel, but with drinks and food thrown in. Everything was rendered pretty much irrelevant however, given the majesty of the view. He spoke Jamaican patois, was married to a local woman and clearly loved the island. He was not sure how much longer he could carry on given that there were so few independent visitors to the island. Dinner was good but served by the pool whilst skinny cats mewed and pawed around under the table.

The next morning I walked down the hill to Bluefields Bay. There were no remnants of the Caledonian time here; I could only hope to begin to try to understand better their sacrifice by standing where they had stood over 300 years earlier. There was no comparison and it was difficult understand the suffering and hardship of the Caledonians of the first and second expeditions, who fled Darien for Bluefields Bay. They came to an incredibly pretty bay, but that would have been largely lost on them, given their malnourishment and disease. Standing for the last time before the bay where hundred of Scots had suffered I hoped their sacrifice would not be forgotten and that perhaps one day in Jamaica, some form of recognition of their contribution to history could be made.

CUBA

Jamaica was not the only Caribbean island the Caledonians encountered. As the first expedition left Darien and made for home, the crew of the *Unicorn*, desperate for water, landed on the northern Cuban coast east of Havana at Matanzas Bay. When the Spanish fort opened fire on them they fled, leaving behind their interpreter, Benjamin Spense. The Spaniards founded a city here, originally named San Severino y San Carlos de Matanzas. Today it is simply known as Matanzas, which means 'massacres' in Spanish. The city is located 80 miles east of Havana and very close to the start of the long, thin peninsula known as Varadero: home to dozens of large international hotel chains.

When the USSR collapsed in 1990, Fidel Castro's regime was plunged into crisis, denied the huge subsidies and oil which had maintained his regime for decades. The economy went into freefall in the early 1990s and the Cubans were engulfed in poverty and hunger. The United States took the opportunity to tighten its embargo in the hope that the Cubans would opt for internal 'regime change', but Castro had seen off many other crises, and as quickly as he could he opened up his country to international tourism, primarily from Canadians and western Europeans. Today, many years later, Cuba is a sophisticated sponge to soak up visitors' money from the moment they arrive until they leave. Tourist cards must be bought, airport taxes must be paid and everywhere the exchange rates to buy the newly introduced Cuban Convertible Peso are designed to take somewhere between 10 per cent and 20 per cent of the value of the foreign currency.

I arrived late at night from Panama. Because of the US embargo, the Helms-Burton Act and other measures, passports of visitors to Cuba were not stamped, and the vast army of immigration officials was designed to keep the queues down. Most tourists landing in Cuba head for Varadero, and indeed the beach resort town now has its own international airport. Most others go to Havana, which dominates political, artistic and cultural life on the island. Arriving at night did not disguise the ramshackle, run-down poverty of the outskirts. I passed through the ageing port facilities and from nowhere burst on to Havana's famous *Malecon* and the impressive view of the bay and fortifications on the hill overlooking the city. I had decided to stay in Old Havana for a night or two before heading to the fortifications in Matanzas, where Benjamin Spense had been imprisoned. Spense provided his captors with a detailed account of his time in Darien. I wanted to visit Matanzas and try to find the fort where the Spanish had sighted and bombarded the *Unicorn* and where they had then taken the unfortunate Spense.

When the Scots sailed into Matanzas Bay in 1698 they would have found a relatively small settlement, as the town was only five years old and would have been dwarfed by Havana, located some distance to the west. However, the bay itself is a fine size and must be several miles across at its widest point. I arrived by car from the east and immediately noticed a small tower on the waterfront towards the mouth of the bay which must have been used as a battery to protect the bay and bombard ships from the eastern side. It gave me the first clue that the fort must be located on the far side of the bay. Finding a little track leading up to the tower I drove up past several ageing cars that had not been fortunate enough to emulate the success of the impressive antiques still on the road in Havana. Parking by a small factory, I headed down a path between head-high grass that wound down to the rocky coastline, getting closer to some of the tangible footprints of the Caledonian story.

The tower was closed and there was no clear sign or anything remotely touristic suggesting it might be opened. It was in a state of good repair and had clearly been renovated quite recently. It would have served as a battery by the Spaniards and would have been used to mount canon and house some soldiers with muskets to protect the eastern entrance to the bay. I fell into conversation with one of the factory workers and asked him about the oldest fortification in Matanzas. He told me there was a castle on the far side of the bay, built at the same time as the city was founded, which was used as a prison by the Cubans and had recently been reopened and was in the process of being restored to convert it into a tourist attraction. With this useful information I set off to enter the town properly and find the former prison where the Caledonian interpreter had been imprisoned and interrogated by the Spanish.

Matanzas was scruffy in places but contained some grand public buildings. There was a fine cathedral and a number of impressive bridges. Logically, and from what I had been told, the first Spanish fort in Matanzas, the location of Spense's incarceration, must have been away from the town centre and up the western side of the bay, towards the mouth, for the cannons to be well positioned to counter a pirate attack and so it was in that direction that I headed, stopping every so often to find out if pedestrians knew where the 'castle that used to be a prison' was. The answer was inevitably 'no' but as we neared the more industrial side of the city there were glimpses of what looked like a low, squat fortification close to the coastline.

The lack of road signs fuelled by Fidel Castro's fear of invasion made it difficult. After stopping countless people and asking, I eventually came close to the castle-like structure I had seen from afar, but with bitter disappointment. The 'castle' turned out to be an early twentieth-century large red-brick fortified entry gate to the ports and not a 300-year-old Spanish fort, but as I turned to leave the security guard called after me 'la cárcel, la cárcel?'. He gave me further directions to continue just a little further up the coast, and when we arrived there the low-sitting stone castle appeared. It was a classic Spanish design, with a thick outer wall, a large ditch, thick, steeply sloping walls up to turrets, with a large plaza and fortified buildings inside. I felt pretty sure this had to be it, and as soon as I could I was across the wooden entry bridge and inside.

There was no ticket desk, but four or five middle-aged woman lounging in armchairs asked me what I wanted and soon had me handing over some dollars to be allowed inside. A guide was even produced. He confirmed what I wanted to know, that the fort dated back to 1693, and given its size and position and the relative smallness of Matanzas at this time, there was little doubt that this was the fort that opened fire on the men from the *Unicorn* and where Benjamin Spense was taken prisoner. Spense would have been dragged in where I had just entered, surrounded by delighted Spaniards, whilst they trained their muskets on him and he feared for his life.

I climbed up the impressive fort's wall and the vast sweeping bay of Matanzas lay before the walls: undulating blues of the Caribbean sea. The Scots would have found little cover as they tried to row across the bay in search of fresh water. The Spaniards would almost certainly have assumed at first the Scots were pirates and must have been delighted to have realised they had captured someone who could provide them with real intelligence about Fort St Andrew and the plans of the Caledonians. The Spanish intelligence-gathering system was cumbersome but it did function and intelligence was shared between the Caribbean island, New Spain (Mexico) and Panama and on up to Andean heartlands. The Spanish officials had been informed of the Scots' arrival in the region from sailors in Saint Thomas, which had been passed on to colonial officials in Havana, who passed it on to the viceroy in Mexico. Either way, when the musket and cannon shot cleared from the air and they realised they had a prisoner, they must have been delighted to realise he was a Scot from Caledonia: confirming both the rumours of their departure and also providing them with a source of information about the colony and its plans – so much the better, he even spoke Spanish.

Matanzas was a new town in the late seventeenth century and the officers in charge of the fort would have feared a raid and their new town being burnt down by pirates. In all likelihood the Scots landing party in search of water was only lightly armed in their rowing boat, led by Captain Anderson himself. The Spaniards would not have been interested to learn they were not in fact pirates, but starving and thirsty traders seeking a route home.

Inside the Spanish fort, Spense would have found himself within a square, thick-walled structure with a lowered central plaza and large walkways around the walls above the buildings off the plaza below. From these thick walkways there was a powerful view across to the battery on the far side and down into the town, and most importantly far out across the Caribbean Sea. The stone of the fort was little changed from Spense's day, but the building on top was not original and housed a rather lurid display of Indian costumes, and papier-mâché exhibits. The rest of the rooms contained offices, a kitchen and a communal area for the large numbers of staff who were sitting around. There were no historical displays, nor any form of museum. My guide, Luis, had a hazy view of the role and uses of the fort over the years, but spent far more time discussing the fort's role as a prison and disappearing off to take phone calls. His agitated state would be explained some 30 minutes later when a group of over 100 Venezuelan tourists arrived wearing identical T-shirts of Hugo Chavez – Fidel's once great friend and the now dead president of Venezuela.

When Luis finally disappeared and did not come back I made my way downstairs to the inner courtyard, buildings and the prison cells below. The day was hot and windy, but down in the darkened rooms there was a strong smell of damp. I was resigned to the fact I would never know in which cell Spense was held, but by wandering in and out of all of them I felt sure our paths would cross. It is not clear how long Spense spent in Matanzas before his value as a source of information on Darien was realised and he was transported along the road to Havana, where Spanish spies worked on him to find out exactly what the Scots had been doing and what their future plans were. Spense certainly had little chance of escaping: the walls were high and thick, and the only way down to the submerged plaza and cells was a small staircase that would have been well guarded. Certainly life on the *Unicorn* was hellish and many more Caledonians died between Cuba and New York: Spense was at least removed from that ordeal. I walked up to the walls and looked out over the blue bay of Matanzas. The Scots had come here, desperate, thirsty and hungry. Aboard their ship men had been dying for want of clean water and decent nutrition, and despite the fort they knew they had to get hold of fresh water if they were to survive the journey up to New York. They must have marvelled at the healthier climate on the northern Cuban coast, and rued the day they set sail with William Paterson for the other side of the Caribbean.

Spense would have set off on the same journey I took: the 70 miles or so from the San Severino Fort to Havana. These days the road is a smooth two-lane highway, and because of the Tourist Convertible Peso a toll road exists which ploughs up and down little hills, whilst the sea shimmers down to the right and rolling hills dotted with palm trees set off the view to the left. Spense must have known he faced an unpleasant reception in Havana, when they realised who he was and what information he might be able to offer them. Arriving in Havana by road from the east is impressive: the city and its fortifications appear to sit up on high on both sides of the mouth of Havana Bay. The impressive Castillo de los Tres Reyes del Morro was finished in 1630, and it is almost certainly where Spense was held. It sticks out on the eastern peninsula of the mouth of the harbour: a menacing lump of rocky fortifications. Today, further up the hill from El Morro is La Cabaña, a more recent fort overlooking the bay. It was built in response to the British invasion of Havana in 1761, when they managed to take El Morro, and bombard the walled city across the bay into submission. The British swapped their Cuban gains for Florida some months later. This sequence of events may have provided Spense with some cheer if he had known about it, and it certainly helps make Havana an interesting place to explore today, as historians credit the British period of administration with turning the city around from sleepy garrison city to major trading post. Spanish mercantilist policies had limited the natural inclination and great location for trade, but the British opened up the island, buying and selling slaves, sugar, fruits, etc. and after they left the *criollo* population were keen not to lose their new-found wealth.

It was here in Havana that Spense was reunited with his fellow Caledonians, Robert Pinkerton, James Graham, John Malloch and David Wilson, the crew members of the *Dolphin* taken captive in Cartagena when the Dolphin was forced into the Spanish port. Given that the English resident who visited the Caledonians in Cadiz was said to have been appalled by their suffering and pitiful appearance, I wondered how poorly they were during their time in Havana. The modern-day visitor to Havana can expect a much warmer welcome.

TWELVE

THE FALL OF CALEDONIA

The Conde de Canillas was directing the Spanish war against the Scots from Portobello, where he was more concerned about getting funds from other officials throughout the Spanish lands, who, despite orders from their king, were slow in providing the much-needed pesos to maintain the campaign. As ever in the Spanish Empire, accounting practices were more important than military tactics. Whilst Pimienta was fighting and bringing his siege engines (*peltrones*) and other war machines closer to Fort St Andrew, Canillas was huddled in conference with the official accountant of the presidency of Panama, Don Pedro Prieto, and worried over the destination of 2,000 *platanos* (plantains) for the soldiers. He was well aware of the complex chess game that was Caribbean politics and warfare and dreaded more incursions, and more limb-aching campaigns in the jungle. As he wrote to the Spanish king in early 1700, he was concerned:

> I greatly fear what developments Time may bring forth, and lest, having received no chastisement, these Scots remain, and imitating them, other nations display similar boldness, relying upon the weakness of your majesty's arms here in America.[1]

Canillas, like Paterson, was aware of Panama's strategic location and that its defence was an imperative. He was making efforts to ensure the Scots were removed and he was delighted when two Scottish prisoners fell into his lap. He personally oversaw the taking of their depositions, with the help of an Irish soldier, Michael Burke, acting as translator. John Jardin was a 25-year-old illiterate labourer and his friend William Strachan was a 34-year-old tailor: both had sailed with Drummond in the *Caledonian* from Leith, endured the hardships of the first settlement, the hunger of the journey to New York, the perilous journey back from New York via Saint Thomas and found themselves again in Caledonia in late 1699. However, only a few weeks after returning, fed up with a diet of 'two small biscuits and a little codfish once a day', both men had decided to desert the colony. They contracted Indian guides, paying them with linen (no doubt stolen by Strachan from the ship's stores) and crossed the cordillera in search of gold. But the Indians had other ideas and betrayed them to Don Luis Carrizoli, the camp master and Spanish agent in Darien. He shipped them to Panama City from Santa Maria where they freely betrayed their countrymen and divulged much useful information.

Jardin may have been illiterate, but he could count, and told his Spanish inquisitors that there were 1,270 people in Caledonia, of whom 1,000 were ashore in the fortification, under the command of twelve infantry captains. He told them only six to eight women had arrived. The ships were armed, the largest with sixty pieces of artillery, of twenty-four and fifteen calibre, and the other ships carried thirty guns. This artillery had not been landed, he reported, and nor had the fort been strengthened, engaged as they were in settling the land after the arrival. But the most important information was provided by Strachan, who commented that he did not know 'the precise total [of Caledonians] at the present moment, for every day many desert. Nine men fled in the boat. The reason for these desertions is that the work is heavy and the food scanty'. He confirmed what Jardin had said: the fortification had not been repaired nor had artillery been mounted ashore. Canillas listened to this intently and the very next day sent the depositions to his king.

From Portobello on 13 January 1700 Canillas sent out another dispatch urging fast action against the Scots. He was aware squadrons of English and Danish fleets had converged at St Thomas, and although the Spanish had discovered they were considering an attack on Puerto Rico, Canillas worried they might come to the Scots' aid and put more obstacles in his way to prevent his removing the Scots from *Rancho Viejo*, as he called Caledonia.

Despite the morale-boosting victory at Tubuganti, the endgame was fast approaching for the Scots on the Panamanian coast. The Scots who had ventured beyond the bay in their little sloops had reported there were many Spanish warships along the coast and it was not difficult to ascertain the fleet's intentions. Borland took up his pen again to bemoan the terrible situation in which they found themselves:

> And now sadder times and heavier disasters and calamities befell the poor Caledonians, than they had hitherto met with. On the 23rd and 25th February, there arrived in our view about eleven sail of Spanish vessels great and small: They came to anchor within Golden Island, over against Prandies Bay. We daily expected their coming into our shore to attack our Fort and ships. Our people were now filled with fears and sad thoughts of heart about our condition and the event of what might befall us. So all hands, Sea-men and Land-men were put to work, to fortify the place as well they could …

The Scots were gripped by hunger and exhaustion and, worse, by a feeling of impending doom as they looked out on a forlorn horizon of menacing Spanish ships. Amongst the several vessels anchored off the bay was the fine Spanish warship the *San Juan Bautista* (John the Baptist), and gathered alongside were support vessels, sloops, etc. This was not the entire Spanish fleet, however, and more ships were expected from Portobello. Commanding this fleet was Don Juan Pimienta, aboard the *San Juan Bautista*, the flagship of Don Diego Peredo's fleet. Happily for historians, he kept a diary of his campaign against the Scots in those violent months of February and March 1700. The fleet had sailed from Cartagena on 12 February 1700, making for *Boca Chica*, which was a Spanish military base off the coast, where artillery and carriages were loaded in preparation for the offensive against the Scots. This time the Spanish were serious.

The *San Juan Bautista* grounded itself on a shoal during the loading process and the departure of the fleet was delayed until the ship was warped off the shoal, which took some time because of strong winds. It took the Spanish fleet ten days to arrive at *Rancho Viejo,* during which time the fleet cruised up the coast via Baru Islands and Palma Island, encountering other Spanish vessels and exchanging fire and giving chase to two foreign, probably French, traders. Which no doubt underlined to the Spanish, and echoed Canillas' concerns, that the Scots had to be punished to make an example of foreigners disrespecting Spanish sovereignty in this vital part of the empire. Despite the difficult journey, made somewhat awkward by strong currents and the need to tack the ships into head winds, Pimienta was determined to have his fleet meet as soon as possible off the Isle of Pines and once there be joined with further ships from Portobello, sent to aid the forces from Cartagena.

Just before sun down on the 23 February 1700 Pimienta reports arriving and was immediately concerned by the currents and the dangerous reef off the shore, but at the same time was keen to carry out reconnaissance of the Scots' position and strength. He reasoned it better to stay away from the perilous shore and instead dispatched Captain Jorge Corezat and a local pilot, Andres Bernal, to go ashore with a small boat of troops and supplies to find out what they could of the Scottish port. The Spaniards were not having an easy time of it on account of the rough seas. Pimienta's ship was forced to carry out short tacks and found it difficult to maintain its position, but with heavy seas and little wind the *San Jaun Bautista*'s topmast gave way and the ship had to stand to stern out to sea whilst repairs were carried out, which caused the ships to drift considerably from Caledonia. Captain Corezat's expedition had no success either: they had been dispatched too far from Punta Escocés. The flagship then made back for the Scottish port and passed near it on 28 February, but again was buffeted off course and on 1 March 1700 the mainsail tack and the main topmast back-stay gave way, resulting in more pointless drifting, which brought the fleet back alongside the Isle of Pines, where they were unable to anchor. Pimienta asked Captain Corezat to head out to round up the fleet, which had been scattered because of the rough seas and to bring the 'convoy' to his command.

Finally anchored one league off the Isle of Pines, on 2 March 1700, Pimienta received some useful information from a captured Indian making his way from New Edinburgh back to El Coco. He told Pimienta the Scots had sent a column of 200 soldiers and 50 Indians into the jungle to confront around 1,000 Spanish soldiers. But to Pimienta this would not sound like the famous victory of Tubuganti, informed as he was that three Spaniards died and ten Scots. Far more importantly, the terrified Indian told him the Scots' flagship was called *The Sun* (*The Rising Sun*) and she had fifty guns, and there was a second, smaller, armed vessel in the bay. The Scots, he said, had built fortifications of palisades and fascines with batteries of guns and that the Caledonians had 700 men, but only around 400 were able to fight as so many were ill and every day more became sick, because of hard labour and poor provisions. Pimienta was cheered to hear this news, but also alarmed as the Indian also told him the Scots were expecting relief to arrive. He would also know, from his own tumultuous days at sea, that keeping a fleet or an army together, motivated and healthy in this part of the world was no mean feat.

The Caledonians looked out to sea with fear: alarmed at what the appearance of the Spanish fleet might mean for their personal survival. The council was unsurprisingly immediately dismayed by this development and was keen to sue for terms, but Fonab stood firm against this move and cowed the weak council into agreeing to defend the colony. Fonab had been injured at Tubuganti and his festering wound prevented him providing the forceful leadership the Scots needed to overcome their present difficulties, but he remained a charismatic figure and shamed the weaker men into agreeing not to cut and run. From his sickbed he ordered that Fort St Andrew be properly provisioned for a siege. Containers were filled with water and brought inside the fort's walls, and those trading goods that could be melted down to make shot for the muskets were duly put to the smelt to better arm the colony's defenders. The ship's surgeons trawled through the ranks of the hundreds of sick men, trying to find those who were able enough to carry out defensive or supporting duties in the forthcoming battle. More imaginatively, one of the smaller boats was packed full of tinder, paper, wood, tar and oil and readied to be a fire ship, with the intention that it would creep out at night, grapple itself to a Spanish warship, then set itself alight and burn down the enemy ship. James Spence volunteered to captain the vessel and was told his family would receive £500 for his bravery, given the unlikely chances of his own survival. But the only fire that would break out would be within the Scots' own ranks, as Borland sorely recounted:

> Many were the awful rebukes of God upon us at this time. Besides a threatening enemy without, and fore and wasting sickness and mortality within among ourselves, it pleased the Lord also to afflict us with a dreadful fire that broke out among our Huts, and burned down to the ground several rows of them, which was on February 28, by the casual firing of some gunpowder. Hereby many of our men lost all their good and clothes, and several of the

sick people being hastily pulled out of their Huts, to save them from the devouring flames and exposed to the open air, it increased their sickness and hastened their death. Thus the anger of the Lord burnt against us round about, yet few of us duly laid it to heart.

On 3 March 1700 the Scots sent two sloops and the longboat from the *Rising Sun* out of their protected bay to take a closer look at the fleet ranged against them and to gather an idea of what artillery and how many men the ships might contain. The Spanish fleet at this stage was two leagues off Golden Island and saw the Scots attempt to return to their port. Pimienta ordered his sailors to give chase with their launch and harried the fleeing Scottish ships. The sloops safely made the entry into the bay, but the longboat, heavy and clumsy as it was, had to make for the coastline, and wrecked itself on a reef, whilst the terrified Scots tumbled overboard and swam, ran and dragged themselves to the beach and fled into the jungle. The Spanish, sensibly, did not give chase – they were still encountering problems of their own in the heavy seas. On 4 March 1700 the *San Juan Bautista*'s main topsail gave way again, and this was repeated on the 5th and 6th when the flagships spotted five other vessels and attempted to give chase. Luckily for Pimienta, the approaching vessels were the Spanish cruisers the *Florziant* and the *San Francisco Xavier* accompanied by other smaller vessels.

On 7 March 1700, with the Spanish fleet at last complete and having found some calmer waters off Golden Island, Pimienta held a council of war aboard his ship. He was informed by two Frenchmen who had entered the Scottish harbour that what the captured Indian had told him was true. Pimienta resolved, now his forces were together, to find an appropriate landing place and begin placing artillery ashore, whilst at the same time finding out more accurately where the Scots had placed their batteries. Pimienta enjoyed warfare, viewed it like a game of chess and was content to play each move carefully and in a measured way.

By 9 March 1700 Pimienta's men had discovered that it would be impossible to land near New Edinburgh, so they placed two vessels to blockade the harbour mouth and scouted further along the coast. They soon found Carreto Bay, where the landing of artillery would be possible and by luck also captured three bedraggled Scottish deserters, who informed them the Scots had 500 regulars, not including the seamen. Pimienta ordered another council of war and they resolved to send 200 men on foot in three companies to Carreto Bay, to establish a base camp and to attempt to discover the Scots' positions. At the dark of midnight on 10 March 1700, the Spanish slipped ashore under the command of Don Juan de Herrera and during the next few days, once their beachhead had been established, they began to bring ashore artillery and supplies. Pimienta remained on board, out at sea, where his problems with his fleet failed to stop: fire broke out on one of the smaller ships, burning down its mast and tackle, but prompt action aboard managed to halt the spread of the flames. Pimienta was anxious for news of de Herrera and sent another eighty infantrymen ashore some days later.

Juan de Herrera had landed without incident and had not encountered any resistance from the Scots, but the next day his men were unable to land the artillery pieces because of the difficult nature of the jungle terrain. The Indians told them to move to a small bay around one and a half leagues from Caledonia. This the Spaniards resolved to do, and rations for eight days were handed out to the men, who marched through the jungle along the coast to this new landing site. It was an unpleasant march, up hills and through thickets; the route even involved wading across a powerful river, with powder and rifles precariously held aloft, the tired soldiers trying not to lose their footing on the slippery stones. Shortly thereafter as they climbed up a steep hill close to Caledonia, they surprised four Scottish sentinels who were clearly terrified and fled without firing a shot. The Spaniards cautiously pursued them until they met another Indian, who informed them the Scots had taken up a position at the base of the hill. The Spanish began to prepare for an assault, and began to clear space in the jungle to make some sort of defensive position, clearing branches and trees for a better, more unrestricted view of any advance. The Spaniards assumed the Scots would regroup and seek to drive them off the hill. They waited for the assault, and waited. With unease settling in, the Spanish ensign ordered an advance party of fifteen men to go ahead whilst the rest followed on behind, and when they reached the bottom of the hill, marched a further half league and coming out upon an open area suddenly stumbled across the nervous Scots. Frightened men in red uniforms grabbed their muskets and shot at the equally frightened men in yellow and blue uniforms, who fired off an impressive number of rounds before disappearing into the jungle to seek the support of the main Spanish party.

Captain McIntosh was the Scottish officer positioned at the narrow neck of land which joined the Scots' peninsula to the mainland. The first expedition had dug a large ditch to attempt to cut the peninsula off from the mainland and turn it into a reinforced island. McIntosh was a brave man, determined not to let the Spaniards pass, and immediately led his soldiers up the hill, chasing after the retreating Spanish soldiers. The Spaniards had greater numbers and rained down a considerable amount of musket shot on the Scots, who were soon forced to take cover where they could behind tree trunks. McIntosh rallied his men and reinforcements arrived: together the weary men charged up the hill a second time to repel the Spanish advance, but with the slippery jungle floor and the Spanish advantage of height on the hill, the Scots were repelled and the Spanish held their line. McIntosh urged his men on for a third assault but this time he was injured badly and the Scottish line collapsed, they fled, leaving behind ammunitions, arms and worst of all at least seventeen dead comrades. The Spanish had only thirteen injured. It was not an encouraging sign of things to come for the Scots.

Back in New Edinburgh, this dismal start to the armed campaign to defend New Edinburgh frightened the Caledonians. McIntosh died several days later and yet more men died from the diseases that still raged in the muddy streets of New Edinburgh. The Scots felt encircled: with Spanish troops and artillery at the end of the peninsula and a blockade of the mouth of the harbour the Scots' position was a dire one, and who better to describe it than gloomy Borland:

> The hand of the Lord was very heavy upon us at this time; our sickness and mortality much increasing, and many daily dying. Most of our able officers were taken away by death: Major Lindsay [at some stage after sixteenth March] ... died about this time. This sad visitation did much dispirit and discourage the surviving, that hitherto were in any health: for men were speedily taken away by this sickness. Some in tolerable health today, and cut off by sudden and violent fevers and fluxes in a very few days.

Borland's recipe for this condition was a day of prayer ('a spiritual weapon') to beseech the Lord for help against both the Spaniard and the flux, but the council were scared and fed up with the meddlesome ministers. They declined to set a day aside, claiming the colony was too busy. The ministers prayed together and separately, desperate for deliverance from their hellish predicament.

On the other end of the peninsula, the Spanish had not in fact taken the vital narrow bit of land which linked the Scots' peninsula to the mainland, but, sensibly, citing wet stores, a lack of ammunition and the necessity to treat their wounded men, the Spanish officers decided to return to the Matanzas river, where they set up camp, fortified their position and sent their wounded to be treated by the ships' surgeons. Pimienta came ashore to direct operations, after dispatching letters to the Conde de Canillas advising him of their situation and asking for reinforcements. The Spanish commander was well aware that 700 men were insufficient to take a forti- fied position against 500 men. In the view of Pimienta, the fort was not all it could have been and clearly he felt less than secure, lodging there. He may well have pondered the fact that his colleague had fled a similar construction at Tubuganti. When the Scots did approach, a mere two scouts, Pimienta had the entire camp put into battle array and was dismayed to learn the Scots had managed to crawl close enough to see the layout of the trenches and fortifications. The jungle at night with its eerie noises unnerved him and the very next day, 15 March, he sent a drummer with the following letter to the Caledonians:

Having arrived with the naval fleet which I anchored at Rancho [Viejo] and with the land forces of infantry having come to camp at Matanzas River, the generosity with which my king, my master, wages war, constrains me to say to the gentlemen commanding the Scots who are settled in the vicinity called Zamora, that it is time they made their representations, now, before I am obliged to order the naval fleet to force that port, and these land forces to storm their trenches. I shall regret having to do this because, under the circumstances, it would not be possible to give quarter, and also because, on account of the winds which prevail on this coast, my ships would be unable to emerge from that port after the engagement to go about their business in which I may need them.[2]

The threat to the Scots was clear, but more intriguing is Pimienta's admis- sion regarding the coastal winds. What did this hope to achieve? After days being tossed around the coast, he clearly felt exasperated by the uncomfortable experience. The Scots responded that the want of a good interpreter hindered their understanding of the letter: they may not have enjoyed, in any event, learning that Matanzas translated as slaughter. They declared they were honourable men and were unconcerned by the threats and that they had a right to the land. Pimienta was content with this response and happy to wait, he knew the Scots were in a tough position and this was confirmed by the appearance of yet another deserter in the Spanish camp the day after the letter was received. The deserter, a twenty-two-year-old man from Aberdeen called John Frasier, betrayed his kin, telling Pimienta the positions of advance posts and numbers and strengths of the remaining men. He also reported on the illness and weakness caused by dysentery. We do not know his reward. Pimienta, tellingly, recounts in correspondence to the Conde de Canillas that, 'although the stores are, in quantity, as he has said, in quality they are of the worst sort; as is borne out by what I have seen and a biscuit he carries'.

The Scots' position was weakened by yet more deserters and in a detailed letter from another of the Spanish commanders out at sea to the President of Panama, we are provided with a detailed account of the Caledonians' position provided by Frasier, as follows:

> Questioned concerning their fortifications, he says they have ashore thirty pieces of artillery, 24, 18 and 12, most of them trained towards the sea, including among them two bound in raw hide. All are mounted, most on trucks. Given their skill, he has no doubt they have put these pieces into working order. He further says that the large ship carries thirty pieces on one side, and, on the other, stone to ballast the ship, and midway hawsers, which we see from here. The enemy has also fireships – a pink and two schooners. This deserter charges us earnestly to observe every precaution at night, because the enemy intends to fire our vessels.

The Scots officers were clearly concerned by desertions to the Spanish and spread the rumour the enemy would provide no quarter if the men crossed sides. They also mounted a vigorous watch to ensure men did not slip out into the jungle to trade information for decent provisions. Frasier said the provisions consisted of half a pound of flour, a quarter pound of salted meat and what fish they could catch themselves and what fruits the Indians brought them. He said it would last for six months, but this was contra-dicted, more accurately, by a later deserter who told the Spanish there was only two months' worth of supplies and that hunger would 'compel them to surrender'.

The Spaniards were careful not to do nothing rash and were prepared to wait. On 18 March 1700 they sent a frigate back to Cartagena with strict instructions to stop only for forty-eight hours to reprovision and come directly back. Pimienta did not want to fail for lack of supplies. On 22 March he was encouraged by the arrival of Captain Juan Antonio Cortés, direct from Tubuganti, with a column of Indian militia from the Pacific coast. The arrival of more men emboldened Pimienta, who had shown little stomach for leaving the fort at Matanzas, and instead spent his time supervising the construction and strengthening of the fortification. On 25 March, however, he sent Cortés out with the Indians and Captain Don Manuel de Puga with a force of sixty men. Cortés reached a high hill from which he had a clear view of the great bay of Caledonia and the grubby patch of huts that made up New Edinburgh. He took in the attempts to fortify Fort St Andrew, the smoke rising from the fort and the desperate scurry of ragged-clothed and shabby, red-jacketed men. He feared he had overextended his men in getting so close and sent word back to camp for reinforcements. A further 150 men arrived to hold the position.

Pimienta enjoyed viewing the campaign as a grand chess game and with forces in position closer to the Scottish settlement, the mouth of the harbour blockaded, he began to arrange his pieces on the board to increase the pressure on the Scots. He sent Captain Don Juan Felix Moreno along the coast by boat to attempt to land closer to the Scots and when they were fired on, he then ordered men to march from inland behind this outpost which had its desired effect, as the Scots, fearing being cut off with no means of retreat, promptly retreated from their position, allowing Moreno to land and take the closer bay, which could be used for landings. With the news that Carrizoli would soon be joining him, Pimienta was buoyed by the thought of greater forces and was determined to push his men closer to the Scots. On 28 March the Spaniards, landing at the closer inlet, marched up through the jungle, dislodging a Scottish outpost and sending the men fleeing. They climbed to the top of a steep hill and again engaged the Scots, who this time put up significant resistance and both sides sniped a each other for some time across a jungle clearing at the top of the hill. The Scots were desperate to hold onto their damp hut atop the hill and their advantageous mountain position which overlooked New Edinburgh. But the Spaniards were better armed, better fed and in general better spirits and they carried the day. The Scots fled, leaving behind several dead comrades, arms, ammunitions and one terrified prisoner for the Spanish to interrogate. As the Spaniards looked around the hut, they were shot at: the Scots were charging up the hill in a vain attempt to wrest it back from the enemy. They made several advances but were unable to dislodge the Spanish, who soon brought up further men, and dug trenches to fortify their position and the supply route to the small bay.

The military reverses and allied pressure were taking their toll on the Scots. By the Spanish advance around New Edinburgh and the mounting of artillery pieces, the Scots were unable to reach their water hole. This, in effect, spelt the beginning of the end for Caledonia. Their morale had been sapped by the steady stream of soldiers retreating from the hills around the fort, the number of dead and injured returned, the incessant sickness and the discouraging crack of gunshot that slowly began to drift closer and closer to the fort. The council were keen to sue for terms and were pleased to see Campbell of Fonab, suffering from his wound, was no longer in a position to embarrass them into fighting. The council and some leading officers met to discuss their pitiful situation: defeat was everywhere and more deaths inevitable. The men wanted out. With no fresh water, they had been reduced to digging a hole within Fort St Andrew, and this weakened the ill and made more men sick. Borland paints a dreadful picture:

So our poor distressed people were necessitated to dig for water within the Fort, which is brackish, puddle unwholesome water: this was most hurtful and pernicious to our men, especially so sick and low, as the most of us at this time were. Such water would have made whole men sick, and must needs then be more dangerous and hurtful to the sick and dying; especially considering how bad and unwholesome our old salt and spoiled provision now was, and as for other liquors at this time, to give the sick and dying, we had little or none, or any other sustenance that was suitable or comfortable, and moreover our surgeons' drugs were almost all exhausted and our fort was like a hospital of sick and dying men.

What had happened to the land of plenty Lionel Wafer had described?

They could not hope to hold out for long. They agreed to seek terms, although Campbell of Fonab would have no truck with any sort of surrender and refused to sign the letter sent to Pimienta. It was brief and to the point. The Scots were concerned about relations between their king and His Catholic Majesty and would like to know what conditions would be offered them. No mention of capitulation or surrender was mentioned. Pimienta received the letter and the accompanying drummer at vespers on 29 March 1700. He was pleased: his tactics of carefully applying pressure bit by bit had succeeded and he need not commit his men to a bloody and messy assault on the fort. He was wary of this, as whilst the Scots were in a poor condition, they still had two large armed ships capable of opening fire on the advancing Spanish columns from the sea as they crept along the coast to the fort.

From the comfort of the *San Antonio*, Pimienta responded to the Scots:

What I wrote your honours by my drummer some days ago was that the generosity with which the king, my master, makes war, obliged me to say to your honours that it was time to speak, before my ships should enter that port, and my land forces those trenches, because, otherwise it would be difficult for me to grant quarter.[3]

Pimienta further threatened and encouraged the Scots into surrender by promising them 'the consideration and treatment due to vassals of an allied monarch', but also reminding them they were not soldiers but members of a trading company and as such he need not comply with the formalities that war and honour would normally demand. To ensure these points would be reinforced in the minds of the Scots, the very same day Don Pimienta oversaw the landing of two pieces of field artillery which were taken to the Spanish advance camp. Pimienta himself, with some difficulty ('It was almost inaccessible by foot') climbed the hill to inspect his troops' position and found everything satisfactory. Upon his return a letter had arrived from the hapless Scots:

In our two preceding letters we have confessed our misfortune not to be able to understand fully the meaning of your first communication, for lack of an interpreter who can translate it; and we are today in the same difficulty, but we gather that you wish to know what we demand and also by what right we have taken possession and established ourselves in this place.[4]

Included with this letter, to the irritation of the Spanish commander, was the much-vaunted Act of Parliament establishing the Company, which no doubt Pimienta did not bother to read. He impatiently responded that he did not inquire as to why the Scots were there, 'much less do I desire to know on what conditions you are willing to leave', before reiterating that the Scots ought to surrender soon and take advantage of the fact that they would be treated as vassals of a friendly king and not simply members of a trading company. He warned them that further delay and confusion could lead to 'misunderstandings, misfortunes and rupture between the two crowns'. Pimienta carefully prepared for such a rupture and ratcheted up the pressure on the Scots by ordering forward another 150 men to within half a league of Fort St Andrew, and sending with them artillery pieces. At the same time he also tasked another officer to take 100 men to fortify and build trenches to improve the defences of the forward Spanish position in case of an attack by the Scots. Pimienta was a wary and careful man and probably also of a rather nervous disposition. He records in his diary the same night an alarm sounded in the camp and he kept his men under arms to be prepared for the advance of dangerous Scots from the dark jungle for most of the night, but none appeared and to his irritation the reason for the alarm was not discovered. The hot jungle was not a welcoming environment.

On April Fool's Day, after his disturbed night's sleep, Pimienta was in no mood to be woken early, but he was informed a Scottish officer and drummer had arrived bedecked in white handkerchiefs. It was Thomas Kerr, one of the engineers sent with the second expedition, and he had come to ask for a truce until the afternoon of the next day. Pimienta, anxious for progress, was annoyed nobody from the Scots' side with authority had come to parley, but such persons were promised for the next day. Kerr suggested prisoner exchanges for the duration of the cessation of hostilities and this was duly arranged. Two lucky Scots captains were granted 'all pleasant treatment and entertainment possible, to be afforded them': Pimienta was proud to be a gentleman and enjoyed observing the courtesies of civilised warfare. The next morning, even earlier, at 7 a.m., William Vetch and James Main approached the Spanish camp trailing behind a drummer beating out a parley. Main came as he spoke some French and hoped to be able to translate. Pimienta was hopeful of a decent proposal and an end to his campaign. He disliked the jungle, the disturbances in the night and the nagging fear of contracting a deadly flux or fever, so when the Scottish proposal was made by Vetch he was deeply disappointed, it was, he wrote, 'not a proposal worthy my consideration'. The Scots had asked to be allowed to leave Caledonia with their artillery, ships, stores and personal property. This did not correspond with Pimienta's view of warfare and he was not prepared to permit the Scots to leave under such terms. He dismissed Vetch and then upon learning the Scots had continued to fortify their fort during the ceasefire, he ordered the attack to continue. The Scots were surprised by this and inquired why hostilities had resumed before the end of the armistice. Pimienta pleaded ignorance, but his men, under Don Martin de Zevallos, fought on and successfully took another enemy post with 150 men, causing the death of two or three desperately retreating Scots.

Pimienta's hand was further strengthened the following day when Luis de Carrizoli, the camp master who helped the Spanish to administer Darien, arrived with 120 Indians, who according to Pimienta 'did nothing but devour our stores'. These were the troops the Scots had fought at Tubuganti, but other Spanish sources claim the number was more like 200. Was the Spanish commander recording a lower number of men to justify less rapid action? Pimienta, aware of the difficulties of maintaining an army together in such conditions, pushed his men forward to apply further pressure to the Scots, to bring forward the eventual capitulation. On 4 April he led his men up the hill overlooking New Edinburgh, 'the height and roughness of which seemed insurmountable, for it was all dense wilderness, without road or trails and nearly perpendicular'. Don Martin de Zevallos was entrenched at the top in a secure position, and Pimienta decided to make camp there, but not before taking the precaution of sending twenty-five men further down the slope on the Scots' side to better defend the fortified campment on the summit. For several days thereafter the Spanish daily crept closer and closer to Fort St Andrew, coming within musket shot of the wooden palisaded walls. After days of rancid water from the hole in the fort and inadequate sanitary conditions, the Scots' death rate had increased, while the rains had turned the centre of the fort into a boggy, stinking hell. The wood was rotting in the fort and men slipped around, getting hopelessly bogged down when trying to move from one side of it to the other. Weary, wet men trained their eyes on the misty horizon waiting for the emergence of charging Spanish troops, but apart from dangerous musket shots, the final assault had yet to happen. Everyone waited nervously. New Edinburgh rotted alongside the fort: the jungle was already demonstrating its power over mankind, slowly retaking the land, as shoots of green started to pop up between the sagging huts and muddy roads.

On 7 April 1700 Don Miguel de Cordones also arrived down off the cordillera from Tubuganti with his militia soldiers. They arrived several days after the Indians, possibly because they were less used to travelling in the terrain than Carrizoli's Indians. With several hundred men more ranged against them, the Scots would have been better advised not to have permitted this force to flee after their skirmish in the mountains at Tubuganti. Pimienta had his own problems: there were more men to feed and more arguments over scarce resources, he was tiring and unsurprisingly records in his diary that many of his own men were sick. The correspondence between the various Spanish officials in Cartagena, Portobello and Panama and the officers in the field paints a clear picture of tensions. There were great arguments over how 2,000 pesos were to be spent and much discussion of the fact that some men ate, while others only looked on. Spanish officers complained they were eating nothing more than biscuit, like a common cabin boy, and mistrust was sown between the men from Panama and those from the richer town of Cartagena. Spanish morale was plummeting, as petty arguments began to break out over each commander's jurisdiction. With this pressure bearing down on him, on 10 April Pimienta sent a drummer to the Scots with a letter:

> With continued consideration to the amity and alliance which the king, my master, maintains with his Britannic majesty, I send this drummer to ask your honours whether, finally, in the situation in which I see that you are, and that in which your honours see that I am, you desire to surrender on the honourable conditions which I have proposed, or whether you stubbornly purpose to stand to the last assault by sea and by land, which I think your honours are not able to withstand, nor I prevent your total destruction.[5]

It was not a welcome letter and the last lines were far from easy for the Scots to swallow, but they still retained some courage and immediately replied:

> We reply that those [conditions] you offer are unworthy [of] acceptance by men of honour, so shameful that to comply with them would so stigmatize us that we could never return to Scotland nor show ourselves in any of her ports. Wherefore we consider it better to die honourably than to live without honour.[6]

The soldier in Pimienta was pleased by this brave stand and the general in him understood. For the sake of his own men, honour required a little compromise. He sent a drummer to the doors of the fort requesting the Scots send an officer, with authority, to parley with him. It was not a moment too soon for the Scots, as Borland described:

> While the poor Caledonians in a melancholy wilderness were brought thus very low, environed with enemies by sea and land and plagued with contagious sickness daily wasting them ... and filled with everything that can make a lot bitter and uncomfortable as gall and wormwood; and had no external, visible probability of hopes of any ... relief from abroad, refuge on all hands seeming to fail them. Divine providence (that is never at a loss, and in the mount useth to be seen) so ordered that the Spanish general Don Pimienta himself, offered to capitulate ...

It is most unlikely Pimienta would have chosen the word 'capitulate', but he decided he would permit the Scots to evacuate with all military honours, with all their chattels and vessels and artillery, except the *Rising Sun*. The Scots were not able to agree to such terms, as generous as they were, and requested an extension of the ceasefire to return to discuss the more generous proposal with their colleagues. They duly did so and returned, insisting on taking the flagship with them. Pimienta was uncertain, but his desire to be gone from the sultry place and return triumphant led him to agree. It was a convenient solution for all and achieved what by then everyone, Spanish or Scottish, desired, which was to be gone from the unhealthy peninsula. Articles were drawn up in Latin, as Pimienta refused to have them in French, and were duly signed. Despite the weariness of the campaign, the wet weather and illness, a fairly well-drafted and legal document was constructed by both sides. In short the Spanish agreed to allow all the colonists to return to their ships, with the colours flying and drums beating, together with their arms and ammunition. Pimienta granted them two weeks within which to have their ships ready to sail and their possessions on board. This may sound generous, but with only around 300 Scots in some sort of reasonable state to work, the process of wooding and watering their ships was no small effort. The Scots also tried to ensure their Indian friends would not be harmed after their departure, but whilst Pimienta signed the articles of capitulation, agreeing not to *molest* them, he soon imprisoned Andreas in chains. The Reverend Shields was particularly aggrieved by this and presented a petition demanding better treatment. Pimienta told the Scots the manner in which his Catholic Majesty treated his subjects was no concern of the Scots and shot back at Shields, 'Cura tua negotia' (mind your own business), to which, somewhat weakly, Shields responded, 'Curabo' (I will).

More importantly for some of the other unfortunate Caledonians, Article VI of the agreement, stated that:

All persons taken prisoner by either party since his majesty of Great Britain and his subjects did first bring a colony to this place, shall be forthwith restored and delivered up.

This was the 'get out of jail' card for the hapless Caledonians captured in Cartagena and for the likes of poor Benjamin Spense imprisoned in Matanzas in Cuba. It was, at least, thoughtful, that the Scots in their miserable condition in New Edinburgh remembered to plead for their colleagues; however, Pimienta's signature as Governor of Cartagena would mean little to the Spanish officials in Seville and Madrid who would determine the fate of pirates in Spanish jails, and it is likely they never saw the articles of capitulation.

Pimienta was keen to secure the rotting Fort St Andrew and one hour after the articles were signed and some hostages were exchanged his men took control of one gate and one rampart of the fort, which was entitled to be taken by some thirty soldiers. Pimienta successfully secured that the Scots were to leave behind their artillery, the mostly unused cannons mounted in the fort and other 'warlike ammunition'. Both parties further agreed that upon the long journey home, they would not interfere or harm either nations' shipping or subjects, unless provoked. Gibson and Vetch signed on behalf of the sorry Scots. As the colony wheezed its last gasps of life, it suddenly transformed itself for the first and last time into what it was really there for: a place of trade. The Scots anxiously welcomed their Spanish customers and traded what goods they owned with the intrigued soldiers. There can be little doubt plaid and periwigs were not sold, but the Spanish found uses for armaments, cloths and other utensils the Scots sold off for cash 'and by this means some of our people came to be provided with money to bear their charges, when they arrived at another port, which proved a favourable providence to many of them' recounted Borland. Money may have been insufficient recompense for as many as up to sixteen men were dying each day.

Borland describes Pimienta at this time as a 'little thin man in stature, but mighty proud, passionate, stiff'. Pimienta was deeply unhappy after the capitulation that a small frigate had entered the bay by New Edinburgh and anchored. It was the return, no less, of Thomas Drummond from Jamaica. In Port Royal he had found a sulking James Byres and two of the Company's ships: *The Speedy Return,* which had been used to bring Daniel Mackay back from Scotland, and *The Content.* Despite the fact that the proclamation still appeared to be in force, he filled both with provisions and sailed them back to reinforce his fellow Caledonians – evidence that the proclamation was more for diplomatic show, to appease the Spanish, than to have any real effect. It would appear that after the abandonment of the first colony the proclamation had fallen into disuse as greedy merchants sought to make profits.

The Spanish had already chased the ships away on 10 April 1700, but persistent Drummond had retuned under cover of darkness the next day, but when the crew of *The Content* saw the lights of the Spanish frigates, they took fright and swept out to sea, making a speedy retreat for Jamaica. Pimienta was furious over this lapse of security. He wanted guards put aboard to ensure there was no communication between the recently arrived Caledonians and their capitulated brethren. He did not trust the Scots and nor did they trust him: Borland tells us the Scots feared the Spaniards to be 'false' and 'treacherous', however, it was the Spanish who really feared the

Scots would not keep to the articles, as they had seen letters from Byres to the Caledonians by way of Indian guides, telling them to stay put and firm, as additional men and provisions would soon be sent. Oddly, it seems this was no more than a ruse written by Byres to worry the Spanish, and was designed to fall into their hands.

Drummond was glad to be back in Caledonia, but horrified by the results of his late arrival. He was struck by the feebleness of the Scots and as a military man, like Campbell of Fonab, he was shamed by the surrender. There was little he could do. 'Thus divine Providence brought it to an issue, that the Spaniards were glad of, and many of the poor distressed Caledonians, were sensible of God's wonderful, seasonable and preventing mercy, that had thus delivered them from falling a prey to the teeth of their bloody Poppish Enemies, with whom they expected to find no mercy, though withal they lamented the sad loss and disaster that had now as formerly befallen their native country,' explained Borland in his lament.

The 'Poppish enemies' delivered a final insult to Borland particularly, and to the Presbyterian sentiments of the Scots, when they entered Fort St Andrew in ceremonial dress on 22 April 1700, after the Scots had finally boarded their ships but while they were still waiting for the wind to allow them to leave. Taking a large warehouse, Pimienta knelt with his fellow officers, whilst a priest said mass and consecrated the place to San Carlos. The Scots looked on in disgust from aboard ship, but they could ill afford to be rude, as they required Spanish help to warp their vessels out of the bay. For the patriotic Scots it must have been hard to have required the help of Spanish sailors to leave from the bay they once boasted could contain 1,000 ships, to sail out and watch the Spanish royal standard flutter in the breeze above the rotting walls of Fort St Andrew, as soldiers in blue and yellow uniforms carefully watched to ensure the Scots departed and Indians feared for their future once the Scots had gone. By 25 April 1700 all the Scottish ships had cleared the bay, some leaving anchors they had been unable to haul up for the lack of strength in thin, weak arms. They stood on deck together, mournful, glancing for the last time over at the mass grave of hundreds of their compatriots and watching the dream of Scottish colonial trade and wealth dissolve on the watery horizon.

Don Pimienta was not sorry to see them leave; he was anxious to return to the comforts of Cartagena. He left Don Miguel Cordones and a handful of men at 'Rancho Viejo' to govern there until the Conde de Canillas appointed a proper successor from Panama. Fort San Carlos (as it was renamed) was spruced up a little and Pimienta made sure his men were equipped with fresh supplies recently arrived from Cartagena. He also had the good sense to leave them with a canoe, a tortoise net and a small drag net. Their physical needs would be taken care of, and, of course, their spiritual: all necessary sacraments were left behind for the saying of mass, in which prayers were offered up, ensuring the place did not fall into the blasphemous hands of Protestant Scots again.

Aboard their poorly careened ships, the Scots were also praying to God. The journey from Caledonia was arduous, exhausting and deadly. The seven ships of the fleet set off together with the intention of making for Bluefields Bay in Jamaica, but very quickly the difficult currents and unpredictable winds ensured the tired arms of the sailors were unable to keep their ships together. Borland's sharp pen provides a harrowing account of life on board:

As they had been exercised with sore sickness and mortality while in Caledonia, so now when we were at sea it much increased upon us, and no wonder it was; for the Poor sick men were sadly crowded together, especially aboard the *Rising Sun*, like so many hogs in a sty or sheep in a fold, so that their breath and noisome smell infected and poisoned one another: neither was there any thing suitable or comfortable to give to the sick and dying; the best was a little spoiled oatmeal and water; and poorly were they attended in their sickness; and it was a most uncomfortable and dangerous work, for the poor ministers to go down among them, and visit them in their sad and dying condition, their noisome stench being ready to choke and suffocate any; malignant fevers and fluxes were the most common disease, which swept away great numbers from amongst us; from aboard of one ship, the *Rising Sun*, they would sometimes bury in the sea eight or nine in one morning, besides what died out of the other ships; and when men were taken with their diseases, they would sometimes die, like men distracted in a very sad and fearful manner. But this was yet more lamentable to be seen among these poor afflicted and plagued people, that for all God so afflicted them, yet they sinned all the more, were so hard and impenitent as before; would still curse and swear, when God's hand was heavy on them, and their neighbours dead and dying about them. I remember it was the observation of the reverend Mr. Shields concerning this people, that he had conversed with many sorts of people, in several parts of the world, and he had served as minister for several years in the army in Flanders, but he had never seen or been concerned with such a company as this was, for the greatest part of them.

It is very likely the bulk of the Scots shared a reciprocal attitude to these uncharitable, judgemental ministers, who had not enough sympathy in their hearts to forgive men brought far from their homes and family, to endure suffering and embrace unpleasant deaths. If they swore in their suffering, it was the least that could be expected.

Not far from their abandoned Caledonia, the *Hope of Bo'ness* began to take onboard too much water. Captain Dalling thought it unlikely the boat would make it to Jamaica, so he brought her alongside the *Rising Sun* and slowly the sick passengers were transferred from one ship to another across choppy, unsteady waters. Dalling knew his vessel was in trouble and bravely took the decision to sail for Cartagena, where he hoped to sell his ship and buy the freedom of his men. It was a daring step, Pimienta may well have signed articles of capitulation, but there was little to stop him seizing the ship and flinging her men into rotten cells. These men, after all, had cost the Spanish royal purse dear. However, Dalling managed to get the creaking and badly leaking ship into the impressive harbour at Cartagena, where, with some luck, he sold her for 'a low rate' but secured his freedom and, according to Borland, after many dangers made it himself successfully to Jamaica.

One of the sloops fell behind after developing leaks and in the heavy seas and strong winds managed to miss Jamaica completely; it ended up shipwrecked off the coast of the Cayman Islands. Miraculously, most of the men were rescued by the inhabitants of the Cayman Islands only to then die there, weakened by their time in the tropics. Others were fortunate enough to make it to Jamaica, where they were reunited with their fellow displaced Caledonians. The *Ann of Caledonia* carried the injured and feverish Campbell of Fonab. He had no desire to see his dishonourable compatriots in Jamaica and sensibly made straight for New York, where the cooler climate and better medical treatment ensured he survived.

The Rising Sun itself made for Bluefields Bay in Jamaica and after the hellish passage described by Borland pulled into the bay on 7 May 1700. The *Hope* and the *Duke of Hamilton* arrived at roughly the same time. The journey had been a devastating one: around 250 people died and were heaved overboard to be met by a watery grave after months of hardship. Perhaps they were the lucky ones, as the three months or so the Scots spent on Jamaica were far from happy ones. They were deemed to be poor for credit and nobody wanted to purchase their rotten, damaged or just plain useless goods. Many deserted and welcomed a life of hard labour on a sugar plantation; after months of poor provisions on board the ship and in Darien, the idea of debt peonage was an attractive one if it meant eating properly again. Discipline and order had also broken down and the men refused to follow the orders of the few remaining officers. The inhabitants of the island were wary of the yellow, skeletal Scots who, consumed with hunger and despair, were not above stealing to survive. Some charitable souls provided them with medical help and food, and paid for proper funerals for some of those of higher birth who died whilst there. The sickness and dying did not stop after reaching Jamaica: around 100 men died, 'the intemperance of many of them here where they had the opportunity to get strong liquors in plenty, did hasten their death', commented Borland.

One death not caused by alcohol which Borland lamented much was that of his friend, the Reverend Alexander Shields, who died from 'violent and malignant fever' on 14 June 1700 in Port Royal. He had made surprisingly little use of his time on the island, preaching only one Sabbath ('The ways of the Lord are right', Hosiah, 14:9) largely because he had become so sick and tired of his blasphemous flock, with whom he had laboured so hard and received so little success. He was buried by a kind English family in the graveyard of the new town of Kingstown. Borland was yet more alone when around the same time, two of his divinity students also died: Mr Greg and Mr Potter. His reflections that God took away the callous sinners, of course did not apply to these good men of the cloth: they were blessed to be removed by divine providence from their troubled circumstances, 'for the righteous are taken away from the evil to come'.

If it was any small compensation, the Scots learned that the Spanish, holed up in Fuerte San Carlos, were also sick and dying in Punta Escocés, but they remained in place, determined to hold on to the bay until they were sure the Scots would not return. Relief was on its way and the *Margaret* sailed from Dundee, arriving at what used to be Caledonia to find the fort possessed by sickly Spaniards. They did not try to retake the fort, but left shortly afterwards and sailed for Jamaica. They, too, were caught in a storm and their mast was damaged, resulting in the relief ship limping into Bluefields Bay, where they found their countrymen in dire straits. The few provisions that remained were distributed amongst the hungry survivors and letters of credit were established, with some local merchants allowing the men to find some means to feed themselves whilst they half-heartedly prepared their ships for the journey back to Scotland and to shame.

Towards the end of July 1700, the Scots set sail in their flagship vessel. One hundred and forty persons were on board and few people gathered on the hills of Bluefields to wave them on their way. Borland was happy his fellow minister, Alexander Stobo, was aboard with his wife, but he himself had decided to return to Scotland via England with an English ship via the port of Boston. Students of history should be grateful for his decision: the *Rising Sun* made it to the Gulf of Florida, where her masts and sails were destroyed in a storm. Another thirty Caledonians had died on board since leaving Jamaica, but in this desperate situation, the captain, James Gibson, showed his skill as a seaman and had the crew run up a jury mast and in such desperate condition, the once mighty oak hull limped into Charleston. There she met the *Duke of Hamilton*, which had arrived only a few days earlier, but was safely at anchor several miles down-river.

The *Rising Sun* had taken on board so much water she was unable to cross the tidal bar at the mouth of the river. The water below decks was six feet above the keel and so the weakened men got to work, throwing overboard cannons, useless trading goods and the like. The aching men worked the pumps and spent day and night trying to lighten the ship. As they worked a small ship passed by but refused to help, though it did stop to allow James Byres, Alexander Stobo, his wife and several others off. They were the lucky ones: three nights later a storm descended upon the river mouth and pulled the *Rising Sun* up like a toy, spinning her out to sea and drowning around 100 Scots, including Captain James Gibson. The *Duke of Hamilton* also sank but with less loss of life, owing to her anchorage. Mrs St Julien Ravenel, who was on shore, recounts how Archibald Stobo came to be ashore:

While the epidemic was still raging, in September of the same year, a tremendous hurricane hit the town ... outside of the bar the ship the *Rising Sun* which had on board the survivors of the unhappy Scotch Colony of Darien, was lying at anchor. She was on her way from the isthmus to Scotland and had stopped for water and provisions. The congregation of the 'White Meeting House' hearing that the Reverend Archibald Stobo was among the passengers sent down to invite him to come up to preach for them on Sunday. He came bringing his wife with him. They and the boat's crew which had brought them were therefore in Charles Town when the storm arose and were the sole survivors of the wreck. The bodies of their companions strewed the beach of James Island. It need hardly be said that the congregation of the White Meeting House were obedient to the finger of providence. Mr Stobo was 'called' to the church and proved himself an excellent and influential minister, leaving many descendants in the province.

Stobo had watched, terrified, from the shore. He viewed the loss of life as God's punishment and duly wrote to Borland:

> They were such a rude company that I believe Sodom never declared such impudence in sinning as they ... You saw them bad, but I saw them worse, their cup was full, they could hold no more. They were ripe, they must be cut down by the sickle of His wrath.

This must have been what he was taught at Edinburgh University before he left Scotland. He, himself, had been lucky: recently married, he and his young wife, Mrs Elizabeth Park, were fortunate to have survived the deprivations of New Edinburgh together and were in reasonably good health on arriving in the English colony. He agreed to preach to a congregation, thus saving his life. Stobo saw the hand of God in his survival and settled in South Carolina.

Life was hard for these impoverished Scottish refugees, but they had God on their side and strength in the knowledge that they had survived the hell that was Caledonia. As the harsh memories of Darien began to fade, life amongst the émigré population became more settled and predictable and the Stobos rejoiced over good news: the birth of their daughter in 1710. They named her Jean and she matured into an attractive young woman who accepted the request of one James Bulloch for her hand in marriage. They had a son in 1730 and named him Archibald after his energetic grandfather. He would go on to be come Georgia's first chief executive and commander-in-chief and was a Revolutionary soldier. After some time, the Bulloch family moved on from the Carolinas to Georgia, where they were prominent amongst those involved in the American Revolution; surely not hard for descendants of an embittered Scot whose Darien dream was felt to have been dashed by the English. The family progressed and expanded and left the Southern states and several generations later, on 28 October 1858, the Reverend Stobo's great-great-great-granddaughter, Martha 'Mittie' Bulloch, gave birth to a boy in a large apartment on 28th East and Twentieth Street, New York City. His name was Theodore Roosevelt, and at the height of his political powers he kicked open the door to the universe and aggressively snatched the key to the world from the Colombian government when he engineered the secession of Panama from Colombia to obtain the land to begin building the mighty Panama Canal in 1903. The popular American president would later boast: 'I took the isthmus, started the Canal and left Congress not to debate the Canal but to debate me.' When the Panama Canal opened it locks in 1914 there would be no better manifestation of William Paterson's dream than this great trading shortcut between two oceans. Paterson could not have imagined how his vision would be realised, albeit later than he had hoped.

THIRTEEN

SOUTH CAROLINA
AND GEORGIA

The cool air seeped imperceptibly across the polished wooden floor. My room was immaculate, furnished in a grand Edwardian style, with enormous pieces of wooden furniture. The smell of floor polish and heavy cinnamon potpourri was circulating in the air. Two vast dormer windows looked out on to the main street to reveal a series of immaculately kept lawns, white picket fences and two-storey homes in a mostly postbellum style with large wraparound verandahs. Further down the road a large sign announced 'Darien Florists'. I had just arrived in Darien, a small town of around 2,000 people in rural Georgia.

The Southern sun was still strong in mid October and I had immediately relaxed in my room after the long drive from Atlanta and the stress and confusion of the complication of the ring roads and exits along the freeway. I had checked into a beautiful bed and breakfast and rested before heading out to explore the town. My hosts were an upright, Southern-to-their-roots couple who took great care in welcoming me in a thick Southern drawl. They were thrilled to have a Scottish guest with my 'proper' British accent. The bed and breakfast was called the Open Gates and I was shown to the Magnolia room, which true to its name, overlooked several large magnolia trees. It was the room preferred by writers, my host trilled.

From the window and the air-conditioned cool I could see Darien was not much bigger than perhaps New Edinburgh had been at is peak; there was one long main road and off that a few shady green squares populated with small but attractive, mostly white-painted homes. At the end of the main road there was a large bridge crossing the mouth of the Altamaha River; the very reason for this Darien's existence. Taking the similarities further there was also a large fort standing discreetly at the coast to protect the settlement. It was mid-afternoon and the town looked quiet from the window. I had barely seen any cars around and there were few shops or restaurants.

After having read about the original Darien for so long it was curious and not a little bit disconcerting to see the name on street signs, on little electricity company flags in the ground, above shops and in hotel names. To my mind 'Darien' meant jungle and failure, sweat and illness; not this vision of Southern prosperity – a tidy vision of well-cut lawns and immaculate, gleamng homes. A large, well-maintained water tank on high stilts overlooked the town and announced DARIEN in bright colours with a pretty flag alongside. An up-market florist's with manicured roses lit up the main street and colourful green signs welcomed and bade goodbye to this prosperous town in the heart of McIntosh County, Georgia.

Darien was settled in January 1736 by a group of hardy Highlanders led by John McIntosh Mohr, who sailed with his men from Inverness on 18 October 1735 aboard the *Prince of Wales*. Highland names are abundant in the group who left Scotland for the frontierland of the southern American colonies: McDonalds, Macleans, McKays, Munros, McBains and Morrisons. Like the Caledonians, they sailed with their minister, the Reverend John McLeod, who established a kirk and ran the first school. The Scots were hardy; they were there to do battle with the Spaniards who did not accept British claims to this land. Florida, which borders Georgia, remained formally Spanish until the Treaty of Paris in 1763. McIntosh Mohr alive both to his task – the establishment of a British colony in the New World against Spanish aggression – and mindful of his own people's history, named the colony in memory of his comrades who fell in defence of Caledonia. Some thought was given to naming the fledgling settlement New Inverness, but ties of history proved to be too strong.

Darien, Georgia, is the physical manifestation of the results of Darien, Panama – a consequence of the failure of Caledonia. Where the Scots failed the British succeeded. The Highland journal, the *Caledonian Mercury*, made clear Highlanders were to be 'a gallant barrier', there to protect British interests and land from Spanish and possibly French aggression. This was to be a common role for the Scots within the British Empire, but, as Tom Devine has illustrated in his book *Scotland's Empire*, this went far beyond being mere cannon fodder. 'The Scots thoroughly, systematically colonised all areas of the British Empire from commerce to administration, soldiering to medicine, colonial education to the expansion of emigrant settlements … [there was a] relentless penetration of Empire by Scottish educators, doctors, plantation overseers, army officers and government officials, merchants and clerics … Penetration of the English Empire by stealth after 1707 turned out to be much more effective and profitable.' James Oglethorpe, the English general and founder of the colony of Georgia, recruited the Scots during tense times. The War of Jenkins' Ear begin in 1739 and it was largely thanks to the brave Highlanders that Georgia managed to repel the attack from Spanish Florida at the battle of Bloody Marsh in 1742, which led a colonial official to record 'Mr Oglethorpe is extremely well pleased with the behaviour of the Scotch Highlanders on Allatomacha [*sic*] river'. The Scots relished their victory over the Spaniards, small comfort following their ancestors' humiliation forty years earlier.

The Scots at Darien, like the Caledonians and like General Oglethorpe, were opposed to slavery, and drew up a petition explaining their opposition to a practice widely relied upon in the colonies around Georgia, which said:

> It is shocking to human nature, that any race of mankind and their Posterity, should be sentenced to perpetual slavery, nor in justice can we think ourselves of it, than that they are thrown amongst us to be our Scourge one day or other for our sins: and as freedome to them be as dear to us, what a scene of horror must it bring about! And the longer it is un-executed, the bloody scene must be the greater.

Race was a problem in Darien and the town faced its worst months during the American Civil War, when in June 1863 the town was burned down. Like most of Georgia, whatever the views of the early settlers were, slavery was widely practised and accepted. A legacy of racism remains, as I would discover on the evening of my arrival there. Darien is a sleepy town around 60 miles from Savannah and 20 miles from Brunswick: both have eclipsed their coastal neighbour. There was little passing traffic, no obvious means of employment, and almost no tourists, although on the banks of the river, a little beyond the town, there stood the re-created wooden fort, originally occupied between 1721 and 1736 by His Majesty's Independent Company garrison and known as Fort King George. It was the major tourist attraction for many miles around, a lonely outpost of wooden huts surrounded by a wooden palisade alongside the coast. As this was constructed only twenty years after Fort St Andrew it is easy to imagine something similar was constructed in the other Darien. As uncomfortable as life would have been by the River Altamaha in these draughty, roughly hewn huts, the climate alone would have made the settlement more durable: the surrounds were less humid and hot and the position was much healthier than New Edinburgh. Dusk began to fall and I sat on a small outcrop by the reconstructed palisade wall. Would the McIntoshes and others from Inverness have lost fathers and elder brothers at Darien? Did they sit here and wonder if Darien was similar to the swampy, hot coastal plains of Georgia? Clearly the Highlanders did think of their forefathers, and this pretty town stands as another reminder, another memorial to the courage of Scots in far-flung lands.

Back at Open Gates I showered and descended the creaking wooden stairs to a dark parlour off the spacious hall. There were crackers and decanters of wine, and I ate and drank and asked the owner, Kelly, if she knew of the Caledonians. She did, but not by that name, she knew the outline history of the colony. It was reassuring, I had travelled following the Caledonians in their desperate journey across the Americas and Scotland and so few people knew of their story, but here in a sleepy town in rural Georgia, the story of Darien was alive and well and local residents were proud of the fact they knew this history, knew of the role of the Caledonians in shaping their town.

Kelly advised me to have supper at Skippers and I was soon to find something distasteful that would have made the egalitarian Caledonians less proud of modern-day Darien. The restaurant was a homely, wooden affair on the banks of the river, with great views and a series of attractive, bright rooms. I sat at the bar and ordered a cool beer and, buoyed up by the need to write, spoke to some of the locals, and they *were* locals, fishermen mostly, and people who worked in the tourist industry around the area. There was not much more to do, I was told. As gloom descended on the riverside bar, something suddenly hit me as I finished my beer: there were no black people in the bar, everyone was white. I asked the barman why there appeared to be a racial divide. 'They have their bar – Jakes – and we have us bar,' he said, not a little aggressively. I nodded and sipped the fresh glass of beer carefully put down before me. 'That's a shame,' I said and he shook his head, 'Better all round, for everyone.'

The idea was both shocking and depressing and it was an affront not only to modern ideas of decency but also, I hoped, even to the ideal of the Caledonians – their parliament and laws aimed for equality and they certainly drank with the Indians. The tough men from Inverness who came to Georgia and settled in this town took their stand against slavery, led by Oglethorpe, but these noble ideas seemed to have been eroded or forgotten in modern-day Darien and I no longer felt comfortable at Skippers. I asked the barman where Jakes was. Somewhere over the back towards the freeway and he gestured over his head away from the dark and shining river. He turned away, irritated by my evident unease. People turned away from me as I made to say goodnight. Anger boiled over as I fumbled with my car keys in the car park. The South is a complex place with a terrible history, but the atmosphere of the bar was sickening. As someone approached the bar I asked him where Jakes was and he shook his head, laughing as he passed me.

I headed away from the river and drove slowly down the main street looking for someone to give me directions. By a gas station I could see a young black guy and I asked him where Jakes was. He looked puzzled and told me to head back, turn to the right and head up to the freeway. As I left, he touched my arm and told me to be careful. I headed out, following his directions carefully, but nowhere could I find anything resembling a bar or restaurant or even a little shack selling beer. I returned to the town and at the same gas station pulled in, stopped and asked a group of older, again black, men. 'Jakes,' one of them said, looking at me, and slowly shaking his head, 'never heard of it,' he said. 'Nope, not around here my friend. I suggest you go on home.' It was that last comment, the friendly advice, that made me stand back and look at him again and in the dim light I could see a dog collar: a man of God in the deep South was not aiding me on my way to hell's door. I asked again and drove around for another forty minutes, but I could not find it and nobody appeared able or willing to help. Open Gates, air-conditioning and a little more wine awaited me.

The next morning I walked the full length of the town and realised for the first time what had not been apparent to me the day before: the half of the town nearest the river was exclusively white and the other was exclusively black. I walked back to the hotel and left, disappointed.

The road from Darien to Savannah was busy and fast. Savannah was my next stop tracing the footsteps of the Caledonians. Although it was October the land was steamy, swampy almost and the air was humid and heavy. I drove with the windows down and the hot air tangled my hair into knots. The radio played a selection of lachrymose Country songs. I passed a large church which announced 'A crossless life is a pointless life'. A sentiment the Reverend Archibald Stobo would very much have agreed with. Stobo is perhaps less well-known than his fellow Darien minister Borland, because he did not keep a record of his time in Caledonia. But as we know, he was fit enough to go ashore and preach at Charleston in 1700, and this devotion saved his life. I had come to the Carolinas and Georgia to find out more about Caledonia's most successful survivor and his descendants, who did more to fulfil William Paterson's dream than any other. In Savannah I hoped to see where those descendants had lived, and from there I would go to Charleston to see where the Reverend Stobo founded around five churches, the most famous being the James Island Presbyterian Church. I also planned to return to Atlanta for a meeting of the Theodore Roosevelt Society, where I hoped to meet some of Stobo's descendants and visit Bulloch Hall, the home of Theodore Roosevelt's mother.

Stobo was the most successful of the survivors of Caledonia. First and most importantly his connection with Theodore Roosevelt provides an extraordinary link across 200 years from the vision of Paterson to the achievement of Panama as a vital hinge in the world economy. But Stobo had other great offspring. His grandson, Archibald Bulloch (1730–1777) who was born in South Carolina, was a great Revolutionary leader who fought against the British and was Georgia's representative at the Continental Congress. Whilst the Reverend Stobo was very much a figure of Charleston, his grandson Archibald remains important to the history of Savannah.

As my car neared the centre of town I sensed the change from the countryside and the atmosphere of small-town Darien. Savannah was altogether a much bigger place, there were large squares, well laid-out roads, monumental buildings. The architecture was a curious mix of Gothic and Greek Revivial, Italianate, Georgian and Regency. Heavy green trees covered the streets and filled the squares. The town was established in 1733, only three years after Archibald Bulloch was born, and it had grown quickly, taking advantage of its prominent position on the Savannah River. I parked and found a cheap hotel for the night by Forysth Park and headed down to the river, the source of Savannah's existence and success. I had hoped for charm and style but instead was faced with a dark colonnade promenade filled with cheap bars and tacky tourist shops. I could have been in Orlando. There seemed to be nothing indigenous about the area and nothing which properly or authentically represented the town's rich history and traditions. I left and walked through the heavily ornate streets past large air-conditioned banks in period buildings and headed a little further back from the river.

I was searching for Orleans Square. In the early nineteenth century, Bulloch House had been built by the Reverend Stobo's ancestors and they clearly had in mind his legacy when they built this imposing villa in one of Savannah's finest squares. It was designed by renowned architect William Jay, an Englishman who emigrated to Savannah to build Regency-style villas for prominent Georgians. He moved to Savannah in 1817 and Archibald Stobo Bulloch House was built between 1818 and 1819; it was one of the first houses to be built here by the fêted English architect. It is little wonder, as Rev. Stobo's grandson became one of the most prominent Georgians of his day. His father, James Bulloch, was an immigrant from Glasgow who came to Charleston in the early 1720s. The family was educated in Charleston and Archibald Bulloch became a prominent lawyer and politician. In 1758 the family moved to the neighbouring state and so began their long association with Georgia.

Bulloch made a success of his move to Savannah in 1764 and marred Mary De Veaux, the pretty daughter of a prominent local judge, and renewed his interest in politics in his adopted state. He became a prominent member of the local Liberal Party and campaigned against the increasingly oppressive measures taken by the British Parliament against the American colonies. In 1775 he was elected at the Provincial Congress of Georgia to be its president and formally took over the leadership roles within and beyond the state against Britain. As a member of the Continental Congress he attracted much praise and attention by arriving in homespun clothes; a visual symbol of Georgia's and his own personal resistance to British goods and the embargo.

Bulloch fought during the American Revolution. In March 1776 he served with Colonel Lachlan Macintosh in the Battle of the Rice Boats and was later involved in expeditions to Tybee Island to destroy British positions. By 1776 he became the first president and commander-in-chief of Georgia in the temporary Republican government. On 22 February he was granted dictatorial powers to aid the state's resistance following the British invasion of Florida. Two days later he was dead; some suspected poison, but the cause of his death remains unknown.

Bulloch's onetime commander, Colonel Lachlan Macintosh, was none other than the son of John McIntosh Mohr, who had sailed his men from Inverness to found Darien, Georgia. Lachlan was born in Badenoch, Scotland, and was taken by his father on the journey to America. These two men joined against the British army – the grandson of one of the few surviving Caledonians fighting alongside the son of the man who named his town Darien in honour of his compatriots, must surely have talked about Caledonia, and the irony of their fighting a British Army which included Scottish soldiers in the American Revolution. Lachlan Macintosh was appointed to the Continental Congress but never attended and died in Savannah on 20 February 1806.

En route to Archibald Stobo Bulloch House I headed through the hot streets of the town to Colonial Park to find Lachlan's grave. Colonial Park is a vast green park in the centre of the city, several blocks back from the river; it runs for over four blocks in one direction and almost every white person in the town between 1750 and 1850 was buried here, though most of the graves are unmarked. Lachlan's was marked, however, and I found it in the hot afternoon sun: a simple stone surrounded by a small mental fence, well cared for, well preserved. He was buried alongside a nephew.

From there I headed to Orleans Square and found it off Barnard Street, a short walk from the cemetery. The square was surrounded by unremarkable buildings and in the centre a slightly unkempt park had taken over the square with a large round fountain in the centre. In this once grand address the name of Archibald Stobo had flourished from the swampy soil of New Edinburgh via the suffering on the *Rising Sun*, through his piety in the churches of South Carolina, through his children and offspring. The house named in his honour dominated this grand square until 1916 when it was demolished to make way for a Municipal Auditorium, which itself was consigned to history in 1971 to leave what was before me now: a large, flat, dull car park. No more was there a grand staircase supported by six Corinthian columns, large reception room and impressive grounds. As at Fort St Andrew before it, history had left few visible traces. It was a fine location, however, for the ancestors of a man who arrived in this country with no more than the clothes on his back and his bible, half-drowned and starved from the journey and the deprivations of New Edinburgh.

That evening over a cold beer in a run-down bar in the back streets of Savannah I thought about the roles of these Scots in Revolutionary America. Some fought for the Americans against the British, which by then would have involved fighting against their own kinsmen from Scotland. Did Archibald Bulloch feel a strong sense of vindication for his grandfather fighting the British, in his mind the English, to avenge his grandfather's experiences at New Edinburgh? And how easy was it for John MacIntosh Mohr to fight the Spaniards in the border skirmishes between Georgia and Florida? Was this also vengeance for how the Spaniards had humiliated his people in 1700? A painful history that would have been told and retold through generations of Highlanders. And how did Lachlan McIntosh, a Scot born in Scotland, feel about fighting his own people in a bloody war so far from his former home? These complicated experiences challenged in my head traditional concepts of identity, loyalty and nationalism. Could people be so easily assimilated and moved? What were the motivators? And would any of this have happened had Caledonia succeeded?

I left Savannah early the next day and drove across the border from Georgia to South Carolina. I was headed for Charleston, where some few lucky Caledonians had sought refuge and where scores more ended up dead, drowned by a storm and washed up on the beach. The land between the towns had a salty, coastal feel and the air hung heavy in the sky. The car radio blasted out irreverent Country lyrics: 'Tequila makes her take her clothes off' and 'That pantyhose won't stay on, if the DJ puts Bonjour on' wailed the local bands. Whilst Savannah felt formal and staid, Charleston was much more mixed and organic; the city was also divided – down by the seafront there were some extraordinarily beautiful homes whilst further back there were obvious signs of dilapidation and poverty. Charleston as imagined in the glossy brochures is located on a thin peninsula, jutting out from the mainland into the mouth of Charleston harbour with two large rivers or estuaries on each side. On each side of the harbour and further towards the ocean were two large islands, Sullivan Island and James Island, both of which narrowed to protect the harbour, explaining Charleston's location and importance as a port.

Modern-day Charlestown has expanded considerably from its original location at the tip of the peninsula in the harbour and I drove through blocks and blocks of industrial parks and roads past port facilities, cranes and container terminals. The original centre has been gentrified and is a charming series of winding streets with pastel-coloured buildings, no area more beautiful than the Battery, with its broad seafront promenade and street after street of extraordinary colourful Italian Renaissance and Art Deco homes and beautiful gardens. No less compelling is Broad Street and the surrounding area, with its brick and stucco-fronted coloured Georgian homes and the renovated former slave market.

I had come to Charleston to do two things: see the churches that the Revered Stobo established and take a trip out to the harbour to the sand bank and mouth of the Ashley River to commemorate the loss of the scores of Caledonians who drowned when the *Rising Sun* was sunk. After lunch I took my hire car down Broad Street and followed the signs for the James Island expressway. I was looking for 1632 Fort Johnson Road, the site of the James Island Presbyterian Church which had been founded by Stobo in 1706 on a 2-acre plot of land donated by the planter Jonathan Drake. James Island was a comfortable suburban island with little of the charm of historic Charlestown. For Stobo it would have been a reasonable journey by horse and carriage from his church into the town, and I had crossed over a large flyover from the peninsula across the mouth of the river to the island. Perhaps in Stobo's day he took a boat across.

Driving down a quiet suburban road off the main highway I saw a large white church before me on the left-hand side and in front of it was a sign announcing 'James Island Presbyterian Church, Founded 1706'. It took no more than a glance to confirm the church was not the original structure and in fact had been recently constructed. It was large, white and really quite ugly, like a suburban funeral director's. It was laid out in the shape of a fat cross, all painted white, with a small steeple and a large cross over the colonnaded main front door. I parked in the large car park to the side. Rev. Stobo would be pleased to see such a large car park, which presumably serviced a large congregation. Inside the church the floor was made of polished wood and large exposed wooden beams held up the ceiling. Exposed, highly polished steel organ tubes dominated the wall behind what looked like the pulpit. The overall effect said 'evangelical'. I was surprised to get in, so often churches are locked, but there were a few people about and I asked them about the foundation of the church. Reverend Stobo was uppermost in their mind and their prayers they said, and yes they knew about his journeys from Scotland to Panama. I asked where he was buried but nobody knew that, and there appeared to be little else they were able to tell me. I headed out of the cool air thick with the smell of flowers and polish into the humid afternoon heat. There seemed to be little recognition of the Reverend Stobo in the church itself, but I was reassured this Caledonian was warmly commemorated by the current congregation.

I headed back across the bridge into historical Charleston. I was intent on finding the White Meeting House, the church that the Reverend Stobo was asked to preach at in 1700. It was historically a most important place: if Stobo had not been asked to give a sermon there he too would have perished on the *Rising Sun* and there would have been no Theodore Roosevelt and perhaps no Panama Canal, or certainly not as it is known today. The White Meeting House was central, in my mind at least, to the realisation of William Paterson's dream. A quick search showed that the White Meeting House no longer existed but my research on the internet led to the discovery that Meeting Street – a famous street in downtown Charleston – was named after the White Meeting House and so I checked every church on the street and found that the Circular Congregational Church, founded in 1681 by Scots Presbyterians, had once been known as the White Meeting House.

I pulled up outside and noted at once that the main building of the church was round, which belatedly made the connection in my mind to the name. I had only ever seen a round church before in Scotland, a particularly beautiful one on in Bowmore, Islay. I had visited as a child and had been fascinated by the explanation that a round church left no corners for the devil to hide in. The tradition had been preserved here. The church was set in pretty grounds with large leafy trees set around it. It was not the original church, in fact several churches had come and gone over the last 300 years. The current structure, I was to learn, was built after an earthquake hit Charleston in the late nineteenth century and it was rebuilt using brick from the earlier Georgian buildings, which gave the church a soft yellow-brown colour. It looked a little Byzantine with its roundish part, with various rectangular and circular additions. The Reverend Stobo would be concerned to know the church is no longer Presbyterian, but, I learned from a smart wooden board in the church grounds, is instead a member of something called the United Church of Christ, which does however maintain an ecumenical link with the Presbyterian Church. The solid door was firmly locked shut. On this spot the Reverend Stobo would have enjoyed giving a sermon to more receptive ears; he thought little of the Caledonians who required to be 'cut down by the sickle of His wrath', harsh judgement for the exhausted survivors from New Edinburgh. As important a historical figure as he was, I was far from sure, remembering his letter to the Reverend Borland, that I would have very much enjoyed hearing Stobo's sermons on this site 300 years ago. Perhaps it was best the church door was shut.

As it was by now late in the day and hot and I found myself on Meeting Street, I drove the car a couple of blocks down the road and parked outside the South Carolina Historical Society, housed in the oddly named Fireproof Building at 100 Meeting Street. The building was attractive, in the Palladian style with Doric porticos, but more interestingly it claimed to be the first fireproof building built in the United States for the preservation of public records, the ideal location for a history society. I was not sure what I expected to find in the Society's library but felt sure it was worth asking what records or documents they had which dealt with the Reverend Stobo. Inside the cool reception to the library a pretty young librarian helped me and we chatted for a while over what I was interested in. She asked me to temporarily register and then carried out a search of the records. A few documents appeared on the computer screen on the system and the librarian sought them out for me. When they arrived they were of little help and revealed very little about Stobo's life in Charlestown. One document stated that on 10 November 1733 a tract of land of some 833 acres came into the hands of James Bulloch and that it had once been owned by the Reverend Archibald Bulloch. Clearly the good reverend had not neglected matters temporal whilst he cared for those more spiritual, and had a good piece of land to hand to his son-in-law. He had clearly done well for himself. There seemed to be little more of any interest and after a little over an hour I was about to leave when the librarian asked me if I would like to see the 'Stobo bible'. I asked what it was and she was not very sure but asked me to don a pair of white gloves and she disappeared to the fireproof vaults to find it. I sat with eager anticipation. Could this really be the Reverend Stobo's own bible? Could it have been preserved all this time?

The librarian came back with a large buff-coloured manila folder tied closed with string, which she laid carefully on the table before me then said 'enjoy' and left me to it. I sat for a moment, overcome with excitement and emotion: this truly could be a wonderful find. The bible used by Stobo over 300 years ago; the bible he would have held and touched with his own hands in New Edinburgh, and now I would be able to hold it too. It made me feel closer to the Caledonians, even closer perhaps than visiting the site of the colony. I gingerly pulled back the string, struggling a little with the uncomfortable white gloves on my fingers. The manila paper sprang open to reveal a small brown leather-covered bible, with a leather catch which had become damaged. I carefully turned it over and inspected the leather covering, which was a little spoiled and damaged in places but essentially complete. I opened the bible to reveal page after page of perfectly preserved gospel, printed in tiny print, but clearly legible and well laid out. The whole book was remarkable and I felt thrilled to hold Stobo's bible in my hand, waves of history pouring out from its fragile, dry pages.

A note in the manila envelope made clear this bible had belonged to the Reverend Archibald Stobo who founded several Presbyterian churches in the area. It appeared to lend support to the idea – given the date and place of publication, close to when he would have set sail from Glasgow – that this was the bible he may have used in New Edinburgh. It seems likely it was bought in Scotland before the second expedition sailed. This may even have been the bible he would have held when he gave sermons to the Caledonians, the bible he used when he prayed for salvation when the Spanish attacked, the bible he would have pressed against his hands aboard the *Rising Sun* when he feared the ship would not make it on its voyage from Jamaica to Scotland. It was an amazing and startling discovery and moved me intensely. I opened to the bible gently and read several passages. Flicking through the crackling pages I wondered what sustenance the Reverend Stobo would have taken from some of the passages as he read them: Joshua 1:6–9 'Be strong and courageous, because you will lead these people to inherit the land'; Matthew 11:28–30 'Come to me all you who are weary and burdened, and I will give you rest'; Nehemiah 6:3 'I am carrying on a great project and cannot go down'. What inspiration or solace did the he find in this book as he hoped, feared, repented and rejoiced in his travels from Glasgow to New Edinburgh to Jamaica to Charleston? Holding the bible in my hands made me feel closer to the Caledonians than at any other point in my journey following them. I gently closed the bible, kissed it and taking a last wistful look at it, placed it gently back in the manila folder. Back in the fireproof vaults, the bible was sure to survive for another 300 years.

That evening I feasted on classic Southern food: sweet pork chops, creamy grits and collards at the Peninsula Grill in the historic Planters Inn. The food was fantastic. I felt like celebrating after the excitement of the afternoon's find and after a martini in the parlour I was hungry for the fantastic Southern delicacies. The restaurant was dark and heavy to suit the food and I sat in the corner wondering how well Stobo ate in this prosperous corner of America. Much better than he would have in New Edinburgh! The waiter snapped me out of my musings with the bill and asking if I fancied darts with him later that evening. It was tempting, but I was staying in a pretty run-down part of town and was keen to get back to my digs before it was too late. The streets outside were brightly lit and full of tourists and late-evening shoppers. The pastel colours of the historic buildings glowing under the sodium light. I walked quickly some twenty blocks north of the historic Meeting Street back to my hostel and watched as the streets changed, to house dilapidated run-down buildings and large SUVs with thundering music. I had been warned about walking here at night and there was an air of menace in the dark streets.

The next morning I set out early for the harbour front and bought a ticket for a tour of historic Charleston Harbour in a little passenger boat. A small group of tourists in sun hats and I set off for the one-hour cruise around the harbour as a guide spoke earnestly into a microphone, I sought solace upstairs in the fresh air and silence. Most of the crew and passengers of the *Rising Sun* had died in this harbour. The contemporary accounts told that the ship had anchored near the mouth of the Ashley River, which runs from in-country down into north Charleston and down the side of the peninsula which makes up historic Charleston. I had driven over the river yesterday when I visited James Island. The drowned corpses of the dead Caledonians were washed from the harbour across to the beaches on James Island, just visible in the muggy morning from the boat. As the boat left the side of the Battery and cut up the bank of James Island, turning left by the mouth of the Ashley River, I hazarded a guess that this must be as close as I could say to where the *Rising Sun* was destroyed in the storm. It would have been in this spot that the crew made its desperate attempts to fix the masts and sails – all torn off within three minutes, such was the intensity of the storm – and its ineffectual efforts to pump water out of the ship's hold to stop it from sinking too far below the waterline. The *Rising Sun* was in a bad condition by the time it reached Charleston. It only arrived there to be careened because it would not have made the onward journey back to Scotland without further repairs, after spending so much time rotting in the damp climates of Caledonia and Bluefields Bay, Jamaica. I reflected silently in the grey morning with my eyes closed on the terrible bad luck of those Caledonians. If they had arrived a few days later they would have missed the storm and returned to Scotland, or settled and made happy lives in Charleston, like Stobo and his wife. Luck really was turned against the Scots from start to finish. And if Stobo had remained aboard, Panama may very well have been a very different country today. I could hear the guide talking faintly below about the American Revolution and the founding of the city, but there was no word about the fate of the Caledonians, no word about the significance for all Americans of Stobo's arrival in the colonies. The boat turned away from James Island and the coast where so many unfortunate Scots ended their lives and made for some islands further out in the middle of the harbour. There was no way to record their suffering or remember on this tourist boat, but thinking about them and their sacrifice was a beginning.

The same day I returned to Atlanta, Georgia, driving up the highway in beautiful autumn sunshine. I checked into a cheap hotel near the airport, as I was returning to London the next morning, but I had one last visit to make, a visit that would bring me face to face with actual descendants of the Caledonians. The Theodore Roosevelt Society was holding its annual meeting in the city and that evening there was a drinks party and tour of Bulloch Hall in Roswell, Georgia. Bulloch Hall was a Greek Revival mansion built in 1839. It was the childhood home of Theodore Roosevelt's mother, who of course was the direct descendant of the Reverend Archibald Stobo. When Roosevelt was president, only two years after he had forced Panama to secede from Colombia to allow him to begin building the Panama Canal, he visited Bulloch Hall, becoming the first sitting US president to visit the South since the brutal civil war.

As I walked up the immaculately preserved steps I could hear the chink of expensive glassware and the hum of polite conversation. The rooms were full of late middle-aged, well-dressed ladies chatting to smart grey-haired men in preppy blazers. It all looked very 'east coast'. I grabbed a glass of wine and pressed myself into the throng. I was interested to see the beautiful house, another manifestation of the Caledonians and their success through failure, but I really wanted to meet a descendant of the Caledonians. More than anything, this would create a sense of completing the circle as I followed my journey in their footsteps. The man I wanted to meet was Tweed Roosevelt. His father was Archibald Bulloch Roosevelt, named of course after the great Presbyterian minister from Caledonia, and his grand-father was Theodore Roosevelt's third son, another Archibald. I knew he was scheduled to speak the next day on the subject of his great-grandfather's maternal family. After a few more glasses of good Californian wine, I came across him in the large dining room of Bulloch Hall. Introducing myself, his face lit up at the mention of Caledonia and Darien. He would love to visit Darien, he told me, and recounted stories of his adventures retracing his great-grandfather's journey down the River of Doubt in the Brazilian Amazon. I recounted my story of the difficulty of getting there and the relatively inhospitable climate and reception. It was hard to talk for long, given the demands on his time and the busy crowd in the room. We shook hands and promised to stay in touch.

I left shortly after. Slightly giddy from too many small glasses of white wine and the excitement of reaching the end of my journey, I made my way back to my hotel. After visiting so many different places I had at last met an incarnation of William Paterson's dream. The grandson of the Caledonian-descended American president who truly created 'this door to the seas and the key of the universe'. Meeting Tweed Roosevelt in the rich surroundings of Bulloch Hall helped to place in context the suffering of the Caledonians. Much good had come out of their hardship, and at the end of the day, in a manner the Caledonians might not have envisioned, in a place somewhat further along the coast, and over 200 years later than they had hoped, trade was increasing trade and money was begetting money.

EPILOGUE

I scratched the back of my head: the wig sat uncomfortably on it. I envied the three judges the freedom of neither wigs nor gowns. Daydreaming a little, when I should have been listening to the submissions made by my opponent (a leading Queen's Counsel), I wondered if my wig was anything like the periwigs taken from this same city over 300 years earlier. I was appearing at the Inner House of the Court of Session. Parliament House in Edinburgh, where the court is situated, played its role in the Company of Scotland. Both advocates and senators (as the judges have always been called) of the College of Justice invested heavily in the Company of Scotland. We know from Douglas Jones's research that members of the Faculty of Advocates and Writers to the Signet accounted for forty-two individual subscriptions and £8,600 in capital whilst the Faculty also made a further subscription of £1,000 for common use. Four senators of the College of Justice also subscribed.[1] This was a significant investment from the legal community. Indeed, the Lord Justice Clerk, Adam Cockburn of Ormiston, was one of the first directors of the Company.

Work to construct Parliament House began in 1632, providing a permanent meeting place for the Scottish parliament. The first meeting of the parliament was in 1639, and most meetings of the members of the Scottish parliament took place there until 1707. Today the great hall, with its hammerbeam roof (modelled on Stirling Castle) and stained glass echoes to the chatter of advocates and clients, pacing up and down the polished wooden floor before entering one of the many courts which are located off the hall. The fires were burning and a sooty smell hovered over the bow-tied ranks of advocates as I crossed over the hall back into the Advocates'

Library at lunchtime. In this very same hall the last meeting of the Scottish parliament, which took place on 25 March 1707, passed the Act of Union with England. Article 1 of the statute said:

> That the Two Kingdoms of Scotland and England shall upon the first day of May next ensuing the date hereof and forever after be United into One Kingdom by the Name of Great Britain And that the Ensigns Armorial of the said United Kingdom be such as Her Majesty shall appoint and the Crosses of St Andrew and St George be conjoined in such manner as Her Majesty shall think fit and used in all Flags Banners Standards and Ensigns both at Sea and Land.

Whether or not the Union was something that would remain 'forever' would be hotly debated in Scotland in 2014, but back in Parliament House in the March of 1707, James Ogilvy, Lord Seafield, who had steered the legislation through Parliament, had the last word as he signed the exemplification of the Act, saying: 'Now there's an end of an auld sang'.[2] With these words Scotland's fate was sealed and on 1 May 1707 an independent Scotland ceased to exist. Celebrating this special day, Queen Anne travelled to St Paul's Cathedral and solemnised the unification of her realms with a magnificant procession of hundreds of carriages and a powerful service and sermon by the Bishop of Oxford.

An essential staging post in the passing of this legislation was Article 15 of the Act, which required England to pay to Scotland the sum of £398,085 10s, known as the 'Equivalent'. This was in part because the Union would require Scotland to take on part of the English national debt, but the money was really in large part to be used to compensate the shareholders of the Company of Scotland. Plainly, several factors drove the leaders of Scotland into agreeing to the Union, but a key issue for the more commerically minded was the inadequacy of Scottish trade, emphasised by the ruin of Caledonia. There is no doubt, as Article 15 of the treaty and the importance of the Equivalent demonstrate, that what befell the Scots in Darien played a major part in driving Scotland into the union with England.

It was with considerable irony that I observed, during the referendum debates in 2014, how once again Scottish independence turned, in part, on Panama. In the light of the three unionist parties' declaration that there would be no currency union, the nationalists floundered to set out a coherent economic policy with solid currency proposals. Many who were in favour of independence plumped for the 'Panama Pound' solution; the isthmian republic has used the USA dollar since independence but without any political control over the currency. Some nationalists argued, in the face of public disquiet over the euro, that Scotland could continue to use the pound sterling, but with all control remaining with the Bank of England. Inadvertently, Panama once more played a part in the debate over Scottish independence. My old friend from Panama, former ambassador Jim Malcolm, was widely reported in the press warning against a 'Panama Pound', and having such deep knowledge of Panama (though retired in Scotland by the time of the independence referendum), his views found an audience. It was odd indeed for the hot and sticky isthmus to once more figure in the discussion of the viability of a Scottish independent state.

However, the more profound influence of the Darien expedition on the issue of Scottish independence is the curious links between the Company of Scotland, the Equivalent and the Royal Bank of Scotland (RBS). After Union in 1707, the Equivalent funds had to be paid out to Scots. This was not a straightforward business and two societies were formed, one English-based and one Scots-based, with commissioners to distribute the funds. However, in 1724 the two societies were abolished and by Royal Charter the Equivalent Company was formed. In 1727, by way of a further Royal Charter, the Equivalent Company was authorised to form a bank in Scotland, which it duly created and named the Royal Bank of Scotland. Out of the ashes of the charred remains of New Edinburgh, one of the titans of late twentieth-century Scotland would be born. When the Equivalent Company ceased to operate in 1851, its records were transferred to the Royal Bank, which was by then flourishing as one of Scotland's major banks. It is no surprise that when the Bank commissioned a history to celebrate its bicentenary celebration in 1927, the very first chapter was entitled 'The Darien Adventure'.[3]

RBS was hailed as a major world player in March 2000 when it took over NatWest, pulling off the largest takeover in the history of British banking. By 2007 RBS was the ninth largest bank in the world by market capitalisation. RBS was the jewel of Scotland: headquartered and run from Edinburgh. It was the Company of Scotland of its day: massive and known to everyone. When RBS began its attempt to take over the Dutch bank ABN AMRO there was Scottish patriotic fervour in the media and wider business world. Alex Salmond, shortly after becoming Scotland's First Minister in 2007, wrote to (then Sir) Fred Goodwin, the Bank's chairman, offering 'any assistance my office can provide' in what became a distinctly Scottish battle for banking pre-eminence. Once again, just as in the heady days of Edinburgh during the opening of the subscription books of the Company of Scotland, patriotism would play a seductive but fatal role.

Unfortunately for the Royal Bank of Scotland, the 'credit crunch' hit just as the ABN AMRO takeover completed, and the airy illusion of RBS's wealth was exposed; the bank failed in October 2008. Its shares fell from 700 pence in early 2007 to 20 pence in 2011. The UK Government ploughed in £45.5 billion of UK taxpayers' money to save the bank. The Scottish Government was left to watch from the sidelines.

However hard the nationalists tried to shake-off this background, the feeling of economic dependence marred the campaign for Scottish independence, and led to its resounding defeat in September 2014. The parallels to the Company of Scotland are there: naivety; struggles to compete on the world stage; patriotism rather than clear-headed financial thinking; and money from England.

The legacy of Caledonia was apparent in Scotland in 2014. Packing my wig and papers away in the robing room beneath Parliament Hall, I could hear the bitter disappointment in my colleagues' post-referendum chats. I walked across Parliament Square behind St Giles' Cathedral in warm late September sunshine and headed down Cockburn Street, not far from Milne Square, and marvelled at the 'Yes' and 'No' posters and the leaflets being blown down the street. The city seemed eerily calm in the wake of the momentous vote. The Caledonians would not have been surprised. Their struggle 300 years earlier had revealed valuable lessons. I ran onto Platform 2 at Waverley Station and jumped aboard the train bound for London. For now the Union was complete. Many Scots in 2014 mourned the No vote, no doubt as many mourned the destruction of the Company of Scotland at the hands of the Spanish hundreds of years earlier. But as the train pulled out of the station and rolled past Calton Hill, it seemed clear to me that on these two historical occasions, however much we may disagree, we Scots had held our destiny in our own hands.

HISTORICAL CONTEXT

The Scots made two fatal errors by locating Caledonia in Darien. First, they failed to consider the geopolitical picture in the late seventeenth century and, in particular, the fact that William, their king, relied upon an alliance with Spain to help him overcome his longstanding foe, Louis XIV of France. Secondly, they misunderstood the fundamental importance of Darien to the Spanish Empire in the Americas. By placing Caledonia in Darien they caused a very significant upset in the Spanish Empire. Having offended the Spanish, they in turn undermined their own king's major foreign policy objective of the time: the defeat of the French. Caledonia could not hope to survive having made enemies of both England and Spain, the major players in the late seventeenth-century Caribbean.

Europe changed massively in the seventeenth century, and perhaps it was only later that this became apparent. The Scots disregarded the changing situation. Until the Peace of Westphalia in 1648, European politics had long been a game of attempts by the Habsburg family, particularly its senior Spanish branch, to achieve hegemony and at times even impose a universal monarchy on the other, weaker states of Europe. The Dutch, French, Portuguese, separate German states and English were smaller states who, acting together as best they could, tried to check the dominance of Spain. The Habsburgs achieved their dominant position through astute marriages, large acquisitions of overseas empire and sheer size. Under Charles V (1500–58), the Holy Roman Emperor, the Habsburg territory was vast: the Iberian peninsula (excluding Portugal – later integrated under Philip II); vast swathes of the Americas; the Balearic Islands; Sicily; Sardinia; Milan;

Naples; Netherlands; Franch-Comté; Luxembourg; modern-day Austria; and parts of Alsace. To add further prestige and power to these territories, Charles V was immensely powerful in the Germanic states, given his position as Holy Roman Emperor. With this encircling sweep of territories the French felt threatened by Habsburg power and were relieved when Charles V abdicated and his provinces were split, his brother Ferdinand taking the Austrian lands and title of Holy Roman Emperor, whilst his son took the Italian, lowland and Spanish titles, becoming the world's most powerful man, King Philip II of Spain.

Philip was deeply religious and his energies were spent in defending Christendom from two threats: the Turks and the Protestants, who particularly challenged this most Catholic of Spanish kings by forming the Calvinist Dutch Republic in his Spanish Netherlands. For some time the different branches of the Habsburgs followed largely independent foreign policies, both battling for Christendom, but failing to halt the spread of Protestantism. But in the early seventeenth century a coordinated Habsburg dynastic plan was born under the Holy Roman Emperor, Ferdinand I, with the aim of pursuing the counter-reformation, destroying Dutch power and attempting to properly control the lands which fell within the Holy Roman Empire, the mostly small German states. The other European powers, led by France, saw this as a danger to the balance of power and fought to bring about a loose coalition of the other European power, to attempt to keep a balance on the continent. This battle to control the Habsburgs produced the Thirty Years War, which raged from 1618 until 1648, and thereafter, slowly but surely, the major dynamic of European politics changed and the French began to become Europe's dominant great power, replacing the Spanish, who were ruined by American silver and years of weak leadership.

Westphalia changed the political dynamic of Europe, but it would take some years for this to become apparent. One of the key outcomes was Madrid's acceptance, after an eighty-year struggle, of the existence of the Dutch Republic. With Dutch commercial prowess and its fine navy it was not long, despite its size, before the Netherlands established themselves as a major European power. The Dutch Republic was formed north of the Spanish Netherlands, and despite its small size was almost immediately able to see the advantages to having this buffer zone between them and France. When the French and Spanish continued to fight after 1648, the Dutch quickly withdrew and became neutral when the war concentrated on French attempts to take the Spanish Netherlands. France quickly replaced Dutch help with English: Cromwell had attacked the Spaniards in the Caribbean in 1655 and so in 1658 sent his troops in with the French helping to capture Dunkirk. The Spanish soon capitulated and the Peace of the Pyrenees was signed in 1659. An important term of the treaty was that the young King Louis XIV was to take the hand in marriage of Philip IV's daughter, Maria Theresa, and that way he secured himself a claim to the Spanish throne. This was vitally important and was a constant factor in the last decades of the seventeenth century, as the Spanish king was now the feeble and incapable Charles II, who was often assumed by many to be on the verge of death. The fight between the Austrian Habsburgs and the French Bourbons to take the Spanish throne, and the attempts by the Dutch and the English to mediate this dispute, were fundamental to greater power politics in the late seventeenth century.

In 1661 Cardinal Mazarin, the de facto ruler of France during Louis XIV's minority, died, and immediately Louis, aged 23, assumed absolute power and ran the country, and more particularly its foreign policy, himself. He was not yet the formidable Sun King, but over the next fifty years he would dominate French and European politics with his artful diplomacy, strategic warfare and insatiable desire to improve the standing and honour of himself and France. His foreign policy would develop into a strategy to find for his country 'natural frontiers' that were easily defensible: this would lead him to look for fortresses and towns on France's border with the Spanish Netherlands, the western German states and the Alpine Italian states. These would be the areas of conflict, and Louis XIV was constantly pushing to improve France's border position, to make her more naturally defensible.

However, Anglo–Dutch relations soon soured over issues of trade. It was not only the Scots who bridled at Cromwell's Navigation Acts but also the Dutch, who were unable to accept English attempts to limit their trade, which relied heavily on the principles of free trade. War broke out between the Dutch and the English in 1652 and 1654, and again between 1665 and 1667. In July 1667, a generous peace was granted by the Dutch.

Thereafter the Dutch and English entered into the Triple Alliance with Sweden: a Protestant defensive pact that it was hoped would mitigate yet another Franco–Spanish dispute that Louis XIV had begun, taking advantage of the distraction caused by the war between the Dutch and English. The Alliance was already concerned by French military power and their pact contained a secret clause that the French should be pushed back to their earlier borders, so as not to weaken Spain. In the end, the French kept little of their new territory and Louis, cautious as ever, was keen to make peace, troubled by the Triple Alliance. In fact, he was appalled by what he saw as Dutch treachery. Louis viewed their secret deal as a slight against the honour of France. He was furious, and as a Catholic absolute monarch he loathed this nation of Calvinist shopkeepers, who appeared ungrateful to the French and to Louis, who had protected them from the Spanish. There was also sound economic reason for attacking the Dutch: like the English, the French were jealous of Dutch commercial success and their efforts to stimulate French trade were faltering in the face of superior Dutch efforts. He was determined to stymie this upstart nation. This diplomatic folly by the Dutch was to have a huge bearing on the outcome of the Scots' colony. It would place the young Prince William of Orange, the soon-to-be William III of England, in constant opposition to French expansion, and this required the help of the Spanish.

In 1668 the French began diplomatic and military attacks on the Dutch Republic. This represented a considerable break in French foreign policy. Traditionally the French had aligned themselves with the Dutch to limit Spanish Habsburg power, particularly during the years of Madrid's bloody counter-reformation. By preparing to attack the Dutch, the French sent a signal that they were now the dominant power in Europe. European states soon realised that alliances would no longer have to be formed to limit the Habsburgs, but to hold back the Bourbons. Meanwhile, the Dutch struggled to understand that the French might attack them. Their leader De Witt (the so-called Grand Pensionary), was cautious about expanding and improving the army, as it had always been a bastion of support of the Orange family and their claims to leadership of the Netherlands. The Dutch diplomatic efforts were also feeble, but in a sign of the changed dynamic they signed a defensive treaty with Spain in 1672.

Louis meanwhile had ensured a more impressive series of allies and one of them, the English, declared war first in 1672, the French quickly followed and Louis himself went to the front to oversee the war effort

The French unleashed an early powerful assault against the Dutch and were so successful they controlled much of the southern Netherlands within a matter of months. The shattered Dutch army fell back in retreat. In despair, the Dutch opened the dykes and flooded the countryside to protect Holland and Amsterdam, avoiding total collapse. The Dutch people were appalled and De Witt resigned. He and his brother were dragged through the streets and beaten by a furious mob. William of Orange was named Stadtholder of the northern provinces, and immediately saw and understood the threat of French dominance to Dutch survival. He got to work revamping Dutch diplomacy to appeal for help from abroad. He was pushing at an open door: France's devastating attacks threatened not just to defeat the Dutch. This worried the Germans, who began to understand the scope of French ambitions. A coalition of former French allies soon formed, made up of the Dutch, Spanish, Austrians (including the Holy Roman Emperor) and the exiled Duke of Lorraine. The momentum ebbed away and the French and their troops soon retreated from the Netherlands, but sought to hold on to some border lands which forced the war to rumble on until 1679. The English had already left the war, and some there had begun to see a profound change in Anglo–French relations. No longer would the counter-reformation and Caribbean and other colonial conflicts dictate a hostile approach to Spain, but instead the English would be required to act to halt the growth in French power, a purpose that would last until 1815.

Peace was made between the various countries at Nymegen between 1678 and 1679. It was in reality a surprising victory for the Dutch, as the territorial status quo was returned and the French agreed to significantly reduce their tariffs. The Dutch, however, would always be wary of the French from this moment on. The war had been a shocking experience for them: their territory had been ransacked and flooded, Amsterdam was in uproar and much trade had been lost. Nations like England had used the war to steal a march on their rivals and forged ahead with international trade. The Dutch, and most particularly William of Orange, realised that they could not rely upon trade alone and that they would have to take their security seriously.

The Dutch had strongly opposed the French taking control of more of the Spanish Netherlands at Nymegen, although they could not stop the ceding of Franche-Comté to the French from the Spanish. They began to work on a series of southern fortifications and William realised he would have to work continually to maintain a web of diplomatic contacts that could be converted into an alliance to thwart further French attacks.

Louis viewed the peace as a triumph for France which showed off his power as king and leader of his nation, but also his moderation and fairness. He was pleased to have broken up the Triple Alliance ranged against him. He maintained for years afterwards a standing army of 200,000 troops which usefully served to intimidate his enemies, and began to strengthen his eastern border with the German states. The Holy Roman Empire and the Germanic states were faced with attacks from the Turks, who were coming dangerously close to Vienna and were being encouraged by Louis. Louis was at the height of his powers and took Luxembourg from the Spanish, who feebly declared war then sued for peace soon after.

Two events were to change this. In 1687 Holy Roman Emperor Leopold's army convincingly defeated the Turks near Mohács, sending the Turkish army into revolt, which resulted in the overthrowing of the sultan. This led to paralysis in the Ottoman Empire and Leopold was able to focus his attention and his troops on western Europe to limit further French ambitions in the Rhineland. Furthermore, there was a European-wide tide of gratitude and support for the Holy Roman Emperor and the Germanic powers, which had borne the brunt of the fighting. Louis, on the other hand, was held in contempt for his support for the Turks and his failure to defend Christendom. Louis made a further decision which would seriously alienate him from the Protestant Germans, Dutch and northern Europeans: he revoked the Edict of Nantes of 1598, ending toleration for Protestants. Over 200,000 fled France and the leaders in the Netherlands, Brandenburg-Prussia, and Sweden were taken aback by the decision, which resulted in them acting more closely together against French interests. What lingering sentiment there had been in the Dutch Republic to seek to mend friendship with France was extinguished and William of Orange was able to use whatever means were required to protect the Dutch from the dangerous Louis XIV.

The French king was aware of the weakening of his position and was startled to realise the Dutch and German states had begun to copy his military tactics and equipment. The technological and tactical edge the French had had over their enemies had now disappeared. This weakening made Louis determined to act whilst he still could and when his candidate to succeed as Elector in Cologne was rebuffed, he invaded in September 1688, and so began the Nine Years' War. French troops burnt the Palatinate at the end of the year to provide a defensive barrier by making a wasteland, and the Germanic states – Brandenburg-Prussia, Hanover, Saxony and Hesse-Cassel – lined up against France. Soon Bavaria and the Holy Roman Emperor became involved. More ominously for France, in May 1689, the Emperor and the Dutch signed the Grand Alliance, aimed at driving France back to her original borders. This was the type of alliance William of Orange had been seeking, to control the French. He was determined to keep the alliance together and add to it if possible.

It was at the outbreak of the conflict that William saw an opportunity to really change the balance of power in Europe against the French. His Protestant wife Mary was the eldest daughter and heir of the Catholic James II of England and VII of Scotland. However, in the summer of 1688 James's second wife, also Catholic, gave birth to a boy. William realised his wife would lose her succession rights and more importantly, perhaps, he realised James was steadily moving down an increasingly Catholic and absolutist path that would bring him into alliance with Louis XIV, whom, like his brother, he admired. The Dutch realised an alliance of the English with the French could turn the balance of power dangerously against them once more. William planned his invasion of England. The Dutch gave him freedom to use a large number of Dutch troops to attack and William acted with the support of several of the key German leaders. William landed in Torbay in November and by the end of the year the country was his.

James's regime had collapsed and the offer of French help had been declined. William and Mary became joint sovereigns and parliamentary government was established. The Glorious Revolution was a swift one. By December of 1689, and in control of foreign policy, William signed the Grand Alliance as William III and, significantly, Spain signed up too, in June 1690. William was delighted. He had formed a grand alliance to fight the French, that included his country's former intractable enemy, Spain. Further, to his great credit, he had increased the power of the alliance by taking the English and Scottish thrones. His strategy was, above all else, to contain the French by keeping this alliance together. He would not tolerate incidents which undermined this powerful alliance, the essential bulwark to protect his Dutch homeland from the French. Louis, a wily diplomat, would try and open 'secret' negotiations with one or other member of the alliance at a time, to break it down. In 1696 Louis managed to negotiate a settlement with Victor Amadeus II of Savoy, which granted him some favourable territories, but in doing so opened up Spanish-controlled Milan to French attack. The Spanish were so weak they sought an armistice in northern Italy. Louis happily granted this and was able to transfer 30,000 men to Flanders to better engage with William's infantry.

The French bravely fought the Nine Years' War against this impressive alliance for the duration of the war. Many European states copied the French by harnessing their economies to their war efforts. This was the case in England more than anywhere else, as the consequences of William and Mary's coup became apparent. If the French were victorious on the continent, the English would be attacked and could lose their monarchs, but also their constitutional monarchism, religion and way of life. The country did not want to return to an absolutist, Catholic monarchy, likely run as a vassal state by the French. William and Mary's ministers constructed an impressive navy, modernised the army, and revolutionised England's creaking financial structures to support this long and expensive war effort. The national debt was created in 1693 and, as we know, the Bank of England was created in 1694 to help fund the war effort.

With the coalition in place the war dragged on, mostly around the French borders, where Louis used his forts and defensive tactics to subdue the enemy. The alliance forces had great difficulty breaking through the French lines. Louis, however, was able to invade Spain and took Barcelona in 1697. The Spanish demanded help, but little was on offer, as peace was in sight. Both sides had been fielding huge armies of around 250,000 men, but neither was able to make a decisive break on land. A combined Anglo–Dutch fleet had destroyed the French navy at La Hogue in 1692, but the French had resorted to privateering and had sunk over 4,000 English ships. This hurt trade.

Furthermore the war had spilled over to the colonies and the English and French had fought in the Americas. Both sides realised a negotiated settlement was required. Louis had one eye on the Spanish succession. He rightly guessed the invalid Charles II would not live much longer and was determined to end the war, to break up the mighty coalition ranged against him before he began to meddle in the Spanish succession.

A peace conference opened at Ryswick in May 1697, with the Swedes mediating. William's adviser, Portland, did much of the negotiating. Leopold wanted to continue the war for the very reason Louis wanted it ended: the Spanish succession. William wanted the French to recognise him as the ruler of England and Scotland to enable him to strengthen his position there. The Dutch and the English, along with the Spanish, signed the Treaty in September and the Emperor Leopold did likewise one month later, aware he could not fight the French alone. The peace terms included the recognition of William III as British king, and the return of various Germanic lands (but not Alsace or Strasbourg). Louis also returned Luxembourg and lands in the Spanish Netherlands and Catalonia, which demonstrated the importance of the Spanish as allies, and probably also how important Louis viewed gaining good favour in Madrid before the issue of the succession arose. After the treaty had been signed William continued to worry about French ascendancy. He was well aware her formidable army was still intact. He was determined to maintain good relations with the Spanish, to ensure he could place Dutch troops in the Spanish Netherlands to act as a buffer in case of further war with France, even during peace time. The Spanish agreed to this in 1698. William's foreign policy to protect his Dutch homeland depended therefore on good relations with Spain.

As soon as this war ended another issue, which all parties had anticipated, began to form on the horizon: the Spanish succession. Charles II was ill and had become weaker during the 1690s. He had no children and was the last male Spanish Habsburg. The two possible successors to his throne were Emperor Leopold and King Louis XIV. This created a considerable problem, as both rulers were already powerful and if they were to obtain Spain they would also become master of all her enormous possessions in the Americas, the Philippines, the Balearic Islands, Sardinia, Sicily, Naples, Milan, the Spanish Netherlands and Luxembourg. Such an inheritance would fundamentally affect the balance of power in Europe, and as such all the powers were anxious to ensure neither Leopold nor Louis took everything, whilst they were concerned to grab as much as they could. Spain itself was sufficiently weakened in Europe that it was not able to dictate terms, however, they would at the end of the day pull off some clever diplomacy.

William watched this approaching crisis with concern. He had used up a large part of his political capital with the English parliament obtaining funds to fight off the French to protect his homeland, in a war that many in England were unsure about and which had little direct connection for them with the English national interest. He knew further war would be difficult. However, if Louis claimed the Spanish lands, particularly the Spanish Netherlands, for his children, then the Dutch republic would be faced with a formidable threat. He was determined therefore to act as a broker to ensure Spanish lands were distributed in such a way that his old enemy, Louis, did not gain too much. Swallowing the bitter taste he had for negotiating with the Sun King, William tried to broker a deal with him, which could then be presented as a *fait accompli* to the courts in Madrid and Vienna.

By 1698, after rapid negotiations, the first Partition Treaty was drafted, but immediately became obsolete as the designated heir, the Electoral Prince of Bavaria, Joseph Ferdinand, died. By June 1699, the second Partition Treaty was drawn up: this provided that Leopold's son, Charles, took the Spanish and American lands and (crucially for William) the Spanish Netherlands, whilst the dauphin took the rich Italian lands. It was immediately rejected by both Madrid and Vienna: Leopold was more interested in the Italian lands, as this was a priority for Austrian expansion – after all, distant maritime colonies had little attraction for a landlocked country. The policy emanating from Spain was to prevent partition of the lands at all costs, therefore Madrid was hostile. A little time before Charles II died in November 1700, his advisers had him sign a will that hoped to maintain the integrity of his lands: it granted everything to Philip of Anjou, Louis' grandson, but only if he renounced his right to the throne of France. If he refused, then the lands would be given to Archduke Charles: either way Madrid hoped there would be no partition. In the end their plan worked and Philip took the lands, as Louis knew having a Bourbon in power would provide great advantages to France.

Leopold was horrified and sent his troops over the mountains into the Italian lands he coveted. He assumed the Dutch and English would not countenance such an aggrandisement of French power, and William quickly realised Philip V of Spain was granting huge trading concessions in the Americas to French traders, French troops were in Madrid with the new king and worst of all for William, French troops had occupied the Spanish Netherlands on behalf of their king. After all William's careful negotiations with the Spanish, his Dutch troops were forced to leave their defensive positions in the Spanish Netherlands. The Dutch were once more under serious threat from a powerful France. William had little choice but to join Leopold and go to war against France and this time Spain. In The Hague, on 7 September 1701, William organised the Grand Alliance of England, the Dutch Republic and Austria. Its aims were to take the Italian lands from Spain and (at William's behest) the Spanish Netherlands and grant them to Leopold, permit Philip V to keep Spain and her colonies but in the meanwhile the Dutch and English would be permitted to take any of Spain's overseas colonies. The war began but William was not to see the outcome; he died in 1702.

Much has been written about William's antagonism towards the Scots' actions in Darien. It has been presented as a policy by the English to ruin the Scottish efforts in Darien, and for some elements of the English ruling classes this was no doubt true, particularly those involved in and supporting the East India Company who did not want the competition from the 'Scotch Africa Company'. However, William was a Dutchman who in large part only took the English crown, through his wife, to provide more power to defeat his long-term and bitter enemy Louis. The entire dynamic of European power politics after 1648 was about controlling the collapse of Spanish power and the aggressive rise of French power. No one felt this more powerfully than the Dutch, who were forced to transfer their traditional alliance with the French against the Spanish into reverse, to maintain the buffer state of the Spanish Netherlands.

As a young man William had witnessed the rape and destruction of half his homeland; its leaders beaten to death in the street: he was an implacable enemy of Louis XIV, and his entire policy was to keep a variety of alliances in position during the final decades of the seventeenth century to limit French power. Important amongst these states was Spain, who not only provided fronts on the Pyrenees and in their northern Italian lands to occupy French troops, but also eventually permitted William to station his own troops in the Spanish Netherlands to better protect his homeland. Therefore English foreign policy towards Caledonia and the bitter arguments over the proclamation against support for the Scots had much more to do with this Dutchman's desire to protect his homeland than an Englishman's desire for the Scots to fail.

During the most important periods for William in his relations with Madrid – when he was trying to keep the Spanish in the war against Louis at the end of the Nine Years' War, or negotiating terms, or attempting to obtain Spanish approval to place his troops in forts in the Spanish Netherlands to defend them from the French, and when he was attempting to persuade Madrid to accept a partition treaty – the Scots were creating diplomatic problems for him by infuriating the Spaniards by, as they saw it, attacking a key strategic part of their empire. The Scots' timing was terrible. Their appreciation of European diplomacy was inept and they suffered the consequences of this. If they had delayed and launched their expedition only a couple of years later, in early 1701, William would have been much less concerned, given that Philip V had already sided with Louis and the Dutch troops had already left the Spanish Netherlands. William no longer needed to protect the Dutch Republic by careful diplomacy with Spain.

Spain no longer had the great power of earlier times in the later decades of the seventeenth century; she was, however, determined to hold onto her Spanish possessions in the Americas, and there were few places on the Spanish Main more vital and strategic than Panama. The Spanish placed very considerable reliance on the importance of Panama as the major artery in their American territories. The Scots completely failed to understand that they had placed themselves in the beating heart of the complex Spanish imperial system. Panama was at the heart of their empire and was the vital artery that connected the Caribbean (and therefore Spain) with the Pacific,which granted access to the hugely important resources (gold and silver) in modern-day Colombia, Peru and from there Bolivia.

The Spanish were also most perturbed by the affront to the Catholic Church by the presence of Presbyterian Scots in their possessions. For the royal family in particular the protection of the Church, its advancement and the conversion of the Indians (the saving of souls) was hugely important. This is made clear by the letter[1] from the Spanish king to Don Pedro Fernandez Navarrete Cavallero, Admiral General of the Ocean Fleet in 1699, which was in the following abridged terms:[2]

The King instructs that you, Don Pedro Fernandez Navarrete, Knight of the Order of St James and Admiral General of the Army of the Sea, shall observe the following about the ships readied in Cadiz during the voyage you shall undertake to America:

1. The colony established by the Scots last year at the site Rancho Viejo, twelve leagues Leeward, between that place and that of the Cartagena territory which is commonly named El Playon or Coast of the Darien; and the news that although they left that post, it has been occupied since with new boats dispatched by the company established in Scotland for the purpose, have compelled me to prepare warships readied in the Bay of Cadiz in order to evict them, and this expedition being of the greatest importance to the Monarchy, for it concerns: Our Holy Catholic Church; the preservation of The Kingdom of Peru and Tierra Firma; the stability of the rest of the Indies; the riches and trade within them and not least the reputation and credit of our army and nation.

    Therefore to this end it has been determined that the amount of the forces to be sent must be proportionate and considering that in you all of the worthy circumstances that are desired to such task are met, given your courage, your counsel, your quality, military experience both by sea and by land and the standing of your position, I have decided in favour of assigning to your care and command this armament, in expectation that your handling of this journey will correspond with the trust with which I have chosen you, and that adding this merit to your long service with new glorious actions as I expect from you, I shall have one more reason to honour you and show corresponding appreciation.

2. Although of the quality, the power and size of the ten ships, and two longboats that are readied for this expedition none has better knowledge than you, for the repairs, fitting, manning, tooling, ammunition and victuals all were carried out under your close supervision, we see fit nonetheless to tell you that the ships with which the Scots went to that place, according to the information received, were six of different sizes, the largest not exceeding seventy to eighty pieces [cannons], and seeing as you are taking ten, and so much better and larger, these forces are considered advantageously

superior to the ones they may have or that may have joined them.

In this voyage you shall deserve the trust with which I chose you and add this merit to your many services, with new glorious actions, as I expect of you, I shall have yet this motive to honour you accordingly and show you favour with rewards to it all.

3. For the admiralty of this sizable fleet I have appointed Don Mateo de la Haya, Royal Admiral of the Fleet and he being a commander of such valour, and so credited in the art of sailing I hope his experience shall be very useful to the voyage, and that you shall maintain with him the good communication that is required.

4. I have resolved that for the action that shall be executed on land two thousand men be sent on two-thirds of the fleet with a lieutenant or field master general, and to aid him commanders of a rank of valour and credit the attentions demanded by the quality of their positions I press you to preserve very good relations with them, the best means of maintaining them being to not hinder them in any way.

5. As the boats referred to are manned with the infantry corresponding with their size in the style of the armada it would seem that in case there is no risk of battle at sea with other vessels, these ammunitions can be increased for Tierra Firma along with some crew members, this of course would be left to your judgement so that they would be execute in accordance with the complexity of each case.

6. For the accidents that may occur, it would be necessary for the main pilot to set the route in the traditional fashion, setting the path for the way out and whatever is deemed best for the return, accordingly to the time of the year, and not knowing on which one you would make the return as it all depends on what you would have to do in the Indies it makes it necessary to manage them all so you will not run into such unless it is imperative and in your search. And you shall relay information through the Marquis of the Carpis as it is customary.

7. Once the boats have been provisioned with water, victuals, tools and materials, weapons and ammunitions and other items required for this expedition, along with the people and military personnel you shall set sail on a straight path to the port of Cartagena, trying to arrive there as soon as possible.

8. You shall write a letter to the Governor of those islands requesting news they might have there of the Indies and of the Scots or other nations that have set posts or have established settlements and where they are located and the forces they count with or they may have there …

9. From what you gather from this vessel and the findings along your path, as you request in the posts you deemed convenient, you shall follow your trajectory or change it according to the news delivered to you for the Scots or other enemies are seizing on our post or if they were to be invalidating our post, I trust in this case you will decide for the operation that is necessary and more appropriate and more urgent.

10. Once you arrive in Cartagena and dock your ships by the port, you shall greet the town square with a cannon shot where you will be answered and where they will answer back. You shall make Don Juan Pimento, governor of that post, privy to the forces you carry, and their goal, and press him to inform you whether or not there be Scots at the place called Rancho Viejo, when they arrived there, and with what strength in arms, the ships they have, and their sizes, and how many are left, the fashion after which they have built and fortified and what he deems necessary not only to evict them, but completely extirpate them with punishment.

The letter then goes into great detail about marshalling different forces under different commanders from different parts of the Spanish territories, before closing:

With the above information you would seem to be possessed of sufficient guidance to direct your operations to full success, but as even the best informed speculations cannot foresee every possible incident, least when you travel a subject to those of sea and war, we are persuaded to tell you that in all cases not included in these orders we trust that your own counsel govern your actions in a fashion as to add new credit to your person, and greater cause to rejoice in your choice.

Written at Aranjuez the 14th of May 1700. I the king by order of the king our Lord by Sr. don Domingo Lopez de Cobo Mondragon.
(Signed by the war cabinet.)

ENDNOTES

CHAPTER ONE

1. 'Darien: Disaster in Paradise', BBC2, 2003.
2. The Panamanian National Archives contain records entitled 'Archivos de las Indias' which contain records, letters and other history of the Scottish colony. The archive is found on Avenida Peru, entre Calle 31 y 32 (www. archivonacional.gob.pa).

CHAPTER TWO

1. See *A Pirate of Exquisite Mind: The Life of William Dampier: explorer, naturalist and buccaneer*, Diana and Michael Preston. Doubleday, London, 2004.
2. For the best biography of William Paterson see *The Man Who Saw the Future*, by Andrew Forrester, Thomson/Texere, New York, 2004.
3. See *A History of the Scottish People: 1560–1830*, T.C. Smout.
4. T.C. Smout quoting Sir Robert Sibbald at p. 248 of *Scottish Trade on the Eve of Union 1660–1707*.

CHAPTER THREE

1. T.C. Smout, *Scottish Trade on the Eve of Union 1660–1707*, p. 252.
2. T.C. Smout, *Scottish Trade on the Eve of Union 1660–1707*, p. 251.

3. John Prebble, *The Darien Disaster*, pp. 85–89.
4. Rycaut's correspondence is found in Chapter 1, section C of *Darien Shipping Papers* (ed. George Insh).

CHAPTER FOUR

1. *Darien Shipping Papers* (Insh), Chapter 2, Section A.
2. *Darien Shipping Papers* (Insh), p. 71.
3. *Darien Shipping Papers* (Insh), p. 64.
4. *Disaster of Darien* (Hart), p. 192.
5. *Disaster of Darien* (Hart), Appendix 2.
6. *Darien Shipping Papers* (Insh), p. 72.

CHAPTER FIVE

1. *The Disaster of Darien* (Hart, Appendix 2.
2. *The Darien Shipping Papers* (Insh), pp. 74–75
3. *The Darien Shipping Papers* (Insh), pp. 74–75
4. *The Darien Shipping Papers* (Insh), pp. 66
5. *The Disaster of Darien* (Hart), Houghton, Appendix 2, p. 206.
6. *The Darien Shipping Papers* (Insh) p. 88
7. *The Disaster of Darien* (Hart), Houghton, p. 221.
8. *The Disaster of Darien* (Hart), Houghton, p. 216.
9. Archivo Nacional de Panama, Archivo de las Indias. Documento 308, dated 15 February 1699.

CHAPTER SEVEN

1. Archivo Nacional de Panama, Archivo de las Indias, Tomo XVI, 301–320, Documento 308, dated 15 February 1699.
2. Archivo Nacional de Panama, Archivo de las Indias, Tomo XVI, 301–320, Documento 313.
3. Many of the references to the Conde de Canillas are based in the various

documents found at appendices 13 to 28 of *The Disaster of Darien by* Francis Russell Hart.

CHAPTER NINE

1. The Proclamation is published in full at *The Disaster of Darien*, Francis Russell Hart, pp. 153–154.
2. *The Darien Shipping Papers* (Insh), pp. 114–115.
3. All the excerpts set out here come from the *The Darien Shipping Papers* (Insh), Chapter 2, section G.

CHAPTER TEN

1. *The Darien Shipping Papers* (Insh), Chapter 3.
2. *The Darien Disaster* (Prebble), p. 224.
3. *The Darien Shipping Papers* (Insh), p. 184
4. *The Darien Shipping Papers* (Insh), p. 187
5. *The Darien Shipping Papers* (Insh), p. 188
6. Quote from *The History of Darien*, by Rev. Francis Borland, 1779.
7. Author's own photocopy, source unkown.

CHAPTER TWELVE

1. Much of the correspondence between de Canillas and others is found either in appendices 13 to 28 of *The Disaster of Darien*, by Francis Russell Hart or the Archivo Nacional in Panama City.
2. *The Disaster of Darien* (Hart). p. 374.
3. *The Disaster of Darien* (Hart). p. 380.
4. *The Disaster of Darien* (Hart). p. 381.
5. *The Disaster of Darien* (Hart). p. 388.
6. *The Disaster of Darien* (Hart). p. 389.

EPILOGUE

1. '"The Bold Adventurers": A Quantitative Analysis of the Darien Subscription List (1696)', by W. Douglas Jones, *Journal of Historical Studies*, 2:1 (2001), p. 34.
2. *Scotland and the Union*, by David Daiches, p. 161.
3. *The History of the Royal Bank of Scotland 1727–1927*, Neil Munro, printed privately, Edinburgh 1928.

APPENDIX: HISTORICAL CONTEXT

1. Letter from the King of Spain dated 14 May 1700 to Don Pedro Fernandez Navarrete Cavallero, Admiral of the Fleet, Archivos Nacional de Panama, Archivo de las Indias, Audiencia de Panama, Tomo XVII, documentos 321–323.
2. Translated from a difficult-to-decipher script copy of the letter.

BIBLIOGRAPHY

BOOKS

Barbour, James Samuel, *A History of William Paterson and the Darien Company*, W. Blackwood and Sons, Edinburgh & London, 1907.

Bethell, Leslie (ed.), *The Cambridge History of Latin America*, CUP, Cambridge, 1984.

Bonney, Richard, *The European Dynastic States 1494–1660*, OUP, Oxford, 1991.

Borland, Rev. Francis, *The History of Darien*, John Bryce, Glasgow, 1779.

Burton, J.H. (ed.), *The Darien Papers*, The Bannatyne Club private print held at the Advocates Library, 1849.

Cruz, Francisco Santiago, *La Nao de China*, Editorial Jus, Mexico, 2003.

Daiches, David, *Scotland and the Union*, John Murray, London, 1977.

Devine, T.N., *The Scottish Nation 1700–2000*, Allen Lane Press, Penguin, London, 1999.

Devine, T.N., *Scotland's Empire: The Origins of the Global Diaspora*, Penguin, London, 2012.

Dicey, A.V. and Rait, R.S., *Thoughts on the Scottish Union*, Macmillan, London, 1920.

Forrester, Andrew, *The Man Who Saw the Future*, Thomson Texere, New York, 2003.

Fry, Michael, *The Union*, Birlinn, Edinburgh, 2006.

Hart, Francis Russell, *The Disaster of Darien*, Houghton & Mifflin, London, 1930.

Herman, Arthur, *The Scottish Enlightenment: The Scots' Invention of the Modern World*, Fourth Estate, London, 2002.

Insh, George Pratt, *The Company of Scotland Trading to Africa and the Indies*, Charles Scribner's Sons, London & New York, 1932.

Insh, George Pratt, *Scottish Colonial Schemes, 1620–1686*, Maclehose, Jackson & Co., Glasgow, 1922.

Insh, George Pratt, *Darien Shipping Papers 1696–1707*, Scottish Historical Society.

Insh, George Pratt, *Historian's Odyssey: The romance of the quest for the records of the Darien Company*, Moray Press, Edinburgh, 1938.

Magnusson, Magnus, *Scotland: The Story of a Nation*, HarperCollins, London, 2001.

McCullough, David, *The Path Between the Seas: The Creation of the Panama Canal 1870–1914*, Simon & Schuster, New York, 1977.

McKay, Derek and Scott, H.M., *The Rise of the Great Powers 1648–1815*, Longman, London, 1983.

Munro, Neil, *The History of the Royal Bank of Scotland 1727–1927*, private print, Edinburgh, 1928.

Prebble, John, *The Darien Disaster*, Secker & Warburg, London, 1968.

Preston, Diana and Michael, *A Pirate of Exquisite Mind: The Life of William Dampier*, Doubleday, London, 2004.

Smith, Adam, *An Inquiry Into the Nature and Causes of the Wealth of Nations*, W. Strahan, London, 1776.

Smout, T.C., *Scottish Trade on the Eve of Union, 1660–1707*, Oliver & Boyd, Edinburgh, 1963.

Smout, T.C., *A History of the Scottish People: 1560–1830*, Collins, London, 1969.

Wafer, Lionel, *A New Voyage and Description of the Isthmus of America*, James Knapton, London, 1704 (1st edn. 1699).

Watt, Douglas, *The Price of Scotland*, Luath Press, Edinburgh, 2007.

Whatley, Christopher, *'Bought and Sold for English Gold'?*, Economic and Social History Society of Scotland, Glasgow, 1994.

PUBLISHED ARTICLES AND PAMPHLETS AVAILABLE ON THE INTERNET

Bingham, Hiram, 'The Early History of the Scots Darien Company', Glasgow, 1906.

Jones, W. Douglas, '"The Bold Adventurers": A Quantitative Analysis of the Darien Subscription List (1696)', *Journal of Scottish Historical Studies*, vol. 21, issue 1, pp. 22–42.

Bibliography

Museo Del Canal Interoceanico de Panama, 'La Aventura Del Darien', August 2005.

Paul, Helen Julia, 'Risks and Overseas Trade: The Way in Which Risks Were Perceived and Managed in the Early Modern Period', University of Southampton, 2008.

Paul, Helen Julia, 'The Darien Scheme and Anglophobia in Scotland', paper given at *Money, Power and Prose Colloquium,* Armagh, 2006.

Storrs, Christopher, 'Disaster at Darien (1698–1700): The Persistence of Spanish Imperial Power on the Even of the Demise of the Spanish Habsburgs', *European History Quarterly* 1999, Volume 29 (1) 5–38.

ARCHIVES

Archivos Nacional de Panama (Panamanian National Archives).

Documentos Del Archivo de las Indias, 301–320.

Tomos X–XVII.

INDEX

Index